Palgrave Macmillan Studies in Banking and Financial Institutions

Series Editor: **Professor Philip Molyneux**

The Palgrave Macmillan Studies in Banking and Financial Institutions are international in orientation and include studies of banking within particular countries or regions, and studies of particular themes such as Corporate Banking, Risk Management, Mergers and Acquisitions, etc. The books' focus is on research and practice, and they include up-to-date and innovative studies on contemporary topics in banking that will have global impact and influence.

Titles include:

Steffen E. Andersen
THE EVOLUTION OF NORDIC FINANCE

Seth Apati
THE NIGERIAN BANKING SECTOR REFORMS
Power and Politics

Caner Bakir
BANK BEHAVIOUR AND RESILIENCE
The Effect of Structures, Institutions and Agents

Alessandro Carretta and Gianluca Mattarocci (*editors*)
ASSET PRICING, REAL ESTATE AND PUBLIC FINANCE OVER THE CRISIS

Dimitris N. Chorafas
BASEL III, THE DEVIL AND GLOBAL BANKING

Dimitris N. Chorafas
SOVEREIGN DEBT CRISIS
The New Normal and the Newly Poor

Stefano Cosma and Elisabetta Gualandri (*editors*)
THE ITALIAN BANKING SYSTEM
Impact of the Crisis and Future Perspectives

Violaine Cousin
BANKING IN CHINA

Peter Falush and Robert L. Carter OBE
THE BRITISH INSURANCE INDUSTRY SINCE 1900
The Era of Transformation

José Manuel Pastor Monsálvez and Juan Fernández de Guevara Radoselovics (*editors*)
MODERN BANK BEHAVIOUR

Juan Fernández de Guevara Radoselovics and José Manuel Pastor Monsálvez (*editors*)
CRISIS, RISK AND STABILITY IN FINANCIAL MARKETS

Franco Fiordelisi and Ornella Ricci (*editors*)
BANCASSURANCE IN EUROPE
Past, Present and Future

Franco Fiordelisi, Philip Molyneux and Daniele Previati (*editors*)
NEW ISSUES IN FINANCIAL AND CREDIT MARKETS

Franco Fiordelisi, Philip Molyneux and Daniele Previati (*editors*)
NEW ISSUES IN FINANCIAL INSTITUTIONS MANAGEMENT

Kim Hawtrey
AFFORDABLE HOUSING FINANCE

Jill M. Hendrickson
FINANCIAL CRISIS
The United States in the Early Twenty-First Century

Jill M. Hendrickson
REGULATION AND INSTABILITY IN U.S. COMMERCIAL BANKING
A History of Crises

Paola Leone and Gianfranco A. Vento (*editors*)
CREDIT GUARANTEE INSTITUTIONS AND SME FINANCE

Caterina Lucarelli and Gianni Brighetti (*editors*)
RISK TOLERANCE IN FINANCIAL DECISION MAKING

Roman Matousek (*editor*)
MONEY, BANKING AND FINANCIAL MARKETS IN CENTRAL AND EASTERN EUROPE
20 Years of Transition

Philip Molyneux (*editor*)
BANK PERFORMANCE, RISK AND FIRM FINANCING

Philip Molyneux (*editor*)
BANK STRATEGY, GOVERNANCE AND RATINGS

Imad A. Moosa
THE MYTH OF TOO BIG TO FAIL

Simon Mouatt and Carl Adams (*editors*)
CORPORATE AND SOCIAL TRANSFORMATION OF MONEY AND BANKING
Breaking the Serfdom

Victor Murinde (*editor*)
BANK REGULATORY REFORMS IN AFRICA

Bernardo Nicoletti
CLOUD COMPUTING IN FINANCIAL SERVICES

Anders Ögren (*editor*)
THE SWEDISH FINANCIAL REVOLUTION

Özlem Olgu
EUROPEAN BANKING
Enlargement, Structural Changes and Recent Developments

Fotios Pasiouras
GREEK BANKING
From the Pre-Euro Reforms to the Financial Crisis and Beyond

Daniela Pîrvu
CORPORATE INCOME TAX HARMONIZATION IN THE EUROPEAN UNION

Ramkishen S. Rajan
EMERGING ASIA
Essays on Crises, Capital Flows, FDI and Exchange Rate

Allesandro Roselli
FINANCIAL STRUCTURES AND REGULATION: A COMPARISON OF CRISES IN THE UK, USA AND ITALY

Yasushi Suzuki
JAPAN'S FINANCIAL SLUMP
Collapse of the Monitoring System under Institutional and Transition Failures

Ruth Wandhöfer
EU PAYMENTS INTEGRATION
The Tale of SEPA, PSD and Other Milestones Along the Road

The full list of titles available is on the website:
www.palgrave.com/finance/sbfi.asp

Palgrave Macmillan Studies in Banking and Financial Institutions

Series Standing Order ISBN 978-1-4039-4872-4

You can receive future titles in this series as they are published by placing a standing order. Please contact your bookseller or, in case of difficulty, write to us at the address below with your name and address, the title of the series and the ISBN quoted above.

Customer Services Department, Macmillan Distribution Ltd, Houndmills, Basingstoke, Hampshire RG21 6XS, England

---

Asset Pricing, Real Estate and Public Finance over the Crisis

Edited by

Alessandro Carretta
Full professor of Financial Markets and Institutions and Director, PhD programme in Banking and Finance, University of Rome 'Tor Vergata', Italy

and

Gianluca Mattarocci
Lecturer of Financial Markets and Institutions, University of Rome 'Tor Vergata', Italy

palgrave
macmillan

First published 2013 by
PALGRAVE MACMILLAN

Palgrave Macmillan in the UK is an imprint of Macmillan Publishers Limited, registered in England, company number 785998, of Houndmills, Basingstoke, Hampshire RG21 6XS.

Palgrave Macmillan in the US is a division of St Martin's Press LLC, 175 Fifth Avenue, New York, NY 10010.

Palgrave Macmillan is the global academic imprint of the above companies and has companies and representatives throughout the world.

Palgrave® and Macmillan® are registered trademarks in the United States, the United Kingdom, Europe and other countries

ISBN: 978–1–137–29376–3

This book is printed on paper suitable for recycling and made from fully managed and sustained forest sources. Logging, pulping and manufacturing processes are expected to conform to the environmental regulations of the country of origin.

A catalogue record for this book is available from the British Library.

A catalog record for this book is available from the Library of Congress.

10 9 8 7 6 5 4 3 2 1
22 21 20 19 18 17 16 15 14 13

Printed and bound in Great Britain by
CPI Antony Rowe, Chippenham and Eastbourne

Contents

Figures

Tables

Preface

The recent and continuing economic instability demonstrates how excessive financial innovation can cause a global crisis if investors are not able to correctly evaluate new financial instruments and business models adopted by financial intermediaries.

The real estate industry was the first sector affected by a price bubble driven by excessive demand for housing that pushed the price of real estate units above their fair values. Due to the high relevance of mortgage-backed securities (MBS) and collateralized bond obligations (CBOs) in financial intermediaries' balance sheets, the crisis spread across all the financial markets and the price of almost all assets was biased by the pessimistic views of investors and the lack of liquidity. Even bonds issued by governments with an excessive amount of debt were affected by a loss of investor confidence that caused a significant increase in the cost of capital and the probability of default of the issuer. In this new scenario, investors have been looking for the best criteria to measure the value of their investments independently with respect to any irrational market behaviour.

During the crisis, financial markets have shown the increasing role played by investor sentiment in the price definition mechanism and higher volatility of returns. In order to develop profitable investment strategies, investors have to consider the impact of qualitative data and news on the value of financial instruments.

The increasing risk of default of the Sovereign demonstrates lack of knowledge about their risk drivers and proves the usefulness of a more detailed analysis of issuer characteristics for selecting investment in the fixed income sector.

The trend of the real estate sector during recent years supports the thesis of the lack of transparency and quality in the information available in the direct investment market and demonstrates the usefulness of a more detailed evaluation procedure for selecting the best indirect investment.

This book is intended as a tool for policy makers, practitioners and scholars to understand and discuss the new issues related to value measurement in the financial markets. It looks separately at the asset management industry, Sovereign bonds and the real estate market. It is the result of extensive academic experience and strong theoretical and empirical work conducted by the authors, all engaged in research activities in their universities. Most contributors are participants in the PhD programme in Banking and Finance at the University of Rome 'Tor Vergata'.

Ideas and preliminary drafts of the papers relating to the research programmes from which this book was assembled have been presented and discussed in various academic workshops and international conferences. These include ADEIMF (2009, Palermo); AISRe (2011, Turin); European Real Estate Society (2010, Milan); Global Business Conference of Finance Research (2010, San Jose de Costarica); International Finance and Banking Society (2011, Rome); 5th International Symposium on Economic Theory, Policy and Applications (2010, Athens); 8th International Conference on Applied Financial Economics, (2011, Samos); 20th International 'Tor Vergata' Conference on Money, Banking and Finance (2011, Rome).

Acknowledgements

We would like to first thank the contributors. The book has only been possible because of their specific contributions and expertise. Its content has also benefited substantially from the help and useful suggestions of many readers and anonymous referees. Special thanks are given to the faculty members of the PhD programme in Banking and Finance – Martin Hoesli, Manolis Kavussanos, Phil Molyneux, and Thomas Weyman Jones – for their comments, support and advice covering many areas analysed in the text. Finally, thanks to Assifact, Assofin e Experian, which have provided financial and organizational support for the activities of the PhD programme in Banking and Finance at the University of Rome 'Tor Vergata'.

Alessandro Carretta, Gianluca Mattarocci
University of Rome 'Tor Vergata'

Notes on Contributors

Editors

Alessandro Carretta is Full Professor of Financial Markets and Institutions, Department of Economics and Finance, University of Rome 'Tor Vergata', where he is President of the Italian Academy of Management and Director of the PhD in Management programme. He has been teaching banking and finance for more than 25 years. His main research interests relate to banking management, focusing on banking groups and diversification; regulation and control; and corporate governance, culture and organizational change in banks. He has widely published in these areas, with more than 100 books and articles in academic journals. He is a member of committees and on the boards of several journals, research bodies and financial institutions.

Gianluca Mattarocci is Lecturer in Financial Markets and Institutions, Department of Economics and Finance, University of Rome 'Tor Vergata', where he is responsible for the Masters in Asset Management and PhD in Banking and Finance programmes. He teaches corporate finance at 'Tor Vergata' and at LUISS Guido Carli. His main research topics are credit risk management and real estate finance.

Contributors

Mauro Aliano is a postdoctoral fellow in the Department of Sciences, Technology and Education, University of Rome 'Tor Vergata'. His main research interests include asset management, statistics, mathematics and financial time series analysis.

Maria Cristina Arcuri is a research fellow in Financial Markets and Institutions at the Department of Economics, University of Parma. She received her PhD in banking and finance from the University of Rome 'Tor Vergata'. Her main research interests include financial and insurance intermediation, asset and risk management, and strategy and corporate governance.

Francesca Battaglia is Lecturer in Financial Markets and Institutions at the Department of Management, University of Naples Parthenope. Her main research interests focus on securitization, real estate, governance of financial intermediaries and cooperative bank. She is the author of several publications on financial institutions, including articles in the *Journal of Advanced Studies in Finance and Applied Financial Economics*.

Ekaterina Dorodnykh is a PhD candidate in Banking and Finance at the University of Rome 'Tor Vergata'. Her main research interests include stock exchange markets, international financial markets, real estate finance, and European integration. She graduated in international economics from the Kursk State University and holds a masters in European economics, finance and institutions from the University of Rome 'Tor Vergata'.

Vincenzo Farina is Lecturer in Financial Markets and Institutions at the Department of Economics and Finance, University of Rome 'Tor Vergata', where he is involved in the PhD in Management programme. His main research interests include strategy and governance of financial institutions and behavioural finance.

Giuseppe Galloppo is Lecturer in Financial Markets and Institutions at the Department of Management, University of Tuscia, Viterbo. He has taught statistics in finance for many years, and is currently teaching financial markets and financial institutions with particular attention on financial time series quantitative characteristics. His research focuses on portfolio and risk management models, asset allocation schemes and stock market evaluation.

Claudio Giannotti is Full Professor of Financial Markets and Institutions and Vice Rector at the University LUM Jean Monnet, Casamassima. He is Director of the Laboratory of Research into Real Estate Finance promoted by the PhD in Banking and Finance of the University of Rome 'Tor Vergata'. He is a member of the board of the European Real Estate Society (ERES) and of the scientific committee of Assoimmobiliare. He is coordinator of the real estate finance module in the Master in Economia e Gestione Immobiliare (MEGIM) programme at the University of Rome 'Tor Vergata'. His main research topics are corporate finance and real estate economic and finance.

Elvira Anna Graziano is a PhD candidate in banking and finance at the University of Rome 'Tor Vergata'. She is currently developing a research project on the role of media in disseminating announcements of spin-off deals and her main research fields include behavioural finance, financial education, and performance drivers of financial intermediaries.

Giovanni Liccardo is a PhD candidate in banking and finance at the University of Rome 'Tor Vergata'. His main research interest relates to international financial markets, financial derivatives and risk management as well as corporate governance and market regulation regarding rogue trading.

Pietro Marchetti is Lecturer in Financial Markets and Institutions at the University of Salento, where he teaches Management of Financial Markets and Institutions. Previously a faculty member of the University of Rome 'Tor Vergata', his research interests and publications focus on corporate governance, cooperative banking, project finance and mezzanine finance.

Gianni Nicolini is Lecturer in Financial Markets and Institutions at the Department of Economics and Finance, University of Rome 'Tor Vergata', where he is involved with the PhD in Management programme. He is member of the Consumer Credit Research Center (CCRC) of the University of Rome 'Tor Vergata' and his main research topics are related to financial literacy and financial education.

Ugo Pomante is Full Professor of Financial Markets and Institutions at the Department of Economics and Finance, University of Rome 'Tor Vergata', where he is involved with the PhD in Management programme. He is also a professor in the Banking and Insurance Division of SDA Bocconi School of Management. His main research topics are risk management and portfolio management, with particular attention on optimization models minimizing estimation error and asset and liability management and risk control in pension funds.

Claudio Porzio is Full Professor of Financial Markets and Institutions at the University of Naples Parthenope. He was faculty member of PhD Programme on Banking and Finance at 'Tor Vergata' and is a faculty member of Carefin, the study centre on financial innovation at University Bocconi and of SDA Bocconi Management School. His main research interests focus on the relationship between banks and SME, the structure and performance of credit markets, the securities markets and the evaluation and performance of financial investments (with special attention paid to real estate and private equity).

Fabrizio Quarta is Associate Professor of Financial Markets and Institutions at the University of Salento. His main research interests are the role of financial intermediaries, the relationship between markets and financial instruments, government capital intervention in the management of companies, microcredit and microfinance, and corporate financing.

Marco Reale is Senior Lecturer in Statistics at the Department of Mathematics and Statistics, University of Canterbury, New Zealand. Research interests include time series analysis and forecasting.

Gabriele Sampagnaro is Associate Professor of Financial Markets and Institutions at the Department of Management, University of Naples Parthenope. He was previously involved with the PhD Programme in Banking and Finance at 'Tor Vergata'. His main research interests focus on the relationship between banks and SME, portfolio management, private equity and real estate.

Georgios Siligardos acquired a PhD in Banking and Finance at the University of Rome 'Tor Vergata', where he had previously graduated in Business Economics. He also studied film art management at the University of Rome 'La Sapienza'. His main research interests are related to real estate finance and derivatives.

Pasquale Stefanizzi acquired a PhD in banking and finance at the University of Rome 'Tor Vergata'. He is a research fellow at the University of Salento and his main research interests are microcredit and microfinance, corporate financial innovation and public entities.

Anna Valeria Venneri acquired a PhD in Banking and Finance at the University of Rome 'Tor Vergata'. She is a research fellow at the University of Salento and her research interests and publications are focused on credit ratings, public finance, banking organization and project finance.

Abbreviations

ADF	Augmented Dickey Fuller
AFIN	financial autonomy
AIC	Akaike Information Criterion
AIMP	fiscal autonomy
ANN	artificial neural network
ARIMA	Autoregressive Integrated Moving Average
B–L	Black and Litterman
BPN	back propagation neural network
Burke	Burke ratio
CAIC	Consistent Akaike Information Criterion
Calmar	Calmar ratio
CBO	collateralized bond obligation
CDS	credit default swap
CIG	conditional independence graph
CIU	Collective Investment Undertakings
CO	operating costs
CVAR Ratio	conditional value at risk ratio
DAG	directed acyclic graph
DARaP	Decile Average Risk adjusted Performance
DJIA	Dow Jones Industrial Average index
DW	Durbin Watson
E(RV)	expected recovery value
EAD	exposure at default
ECB	European Central Bank
ECM	Error Correction Mechanism
EGARCH	exponential generalized autoregressive conditional heteroskedasticity
EL	expected loss
ELR	expected loss rate
EMH	efficient market hypothesis
FDI	foreign direct investment
GARCH	generalized autoRegressive conditional heteroskedasticity
GDP	gross domestic product
GLS	generalized least squares
HIC	Hannan and Quinn test
I/B/E/S	Institutional Brokers' Estimate System
ICT	Information and Communication Technology
IDR	Issuer Default Rating
I.I.D.	independent and identically distribute

IMC	Investment Management Company
INDL	local debt per capita
IPO	initial public offering
IRR	internal rate of return
Kappa (n = 3)	Kappa corrected for skewness
Kappa (n = 4)	Kappa corrected for asymmetry
Ke	cost of equity
LAFP	loan arbitrage-free pricing
LGD	loss given default
LRG	local and regional governments
M	maturity
MACD	Moving Average Convergence and Divergence
MBS	mortgage backed securities
MCOR	current balance
MLP	multilayer perceptron
MPT	modern portfolio theory
MVAR ratio	modified value at risk ratio
PD	probability of default
PF	Project Finance
PILL	local GDP per capita
PMN	positive minus negative words in the news
RAROC	risk-adjusted return on capital
RE	real estate
REITs	real estate investment trusts
RMSE	root mean square error
ROA	Return on Asset
ROAS	Return on Absolute Shortfall
ROE	Return on Equity
ROPS	Return of Probability Shortfall
SALD	net borrowing respect to total revenues
SDEB	expenditure on loans repayment
SEC	Security Exchange Commission
Sharpe	Sharpe index
Sharpe	Omega Sharpe Omega ratio
SIC	Schwarz test
SING or SINT	spending on debt
SME	small and medium enterprises
Sortino	Sortino ratio
SSCA	Supervisory Slotting Criteria Approach
Sterling	Sterling ratio
SUR	seemingly unrelated regressions
SVAR	structural vector autoregression
TA	total assets
TEV	Tracking Error Volatility
TIT	internal transfer rate
UL	unexpected loss
VAR	Value at Risk ratio

Introduction

Alessandro Carretta and Gianluca Mattarocci

Main theory on efficient financial markets assumes that the price of an asset is always related to its fundamental value and any misalignment is driven by noise and so it is unpredictable (Fama, 1965). Literature demonstrates that irrational behaviour characterizes almost all the markets and random price dynamics in the financial market could be used in order to construct profitable investment strategies (i.a. De Long et al., 1990). The current financial crisis shows that market prices do not deviate from a theoretical equilibrium in a random manner and there is a two-way reflexive connection between perception and reality which can give rise to initially self-reinforcing but eventually self-defeating boom-bust processes, or bubbles (Soros, 2008; Carretta et al., 2011).

The beginning of the crisis is ascribed to the real estate bubble and the abuse of financial engineering but, due to the relevance of these ABSs into commercial and investment bank balance sheets, it spreads up rapidly all over the world (Diamond and Rajan, 2009).

The real estate market bubble is recognized as the main driver of the development of the financial crisis that started in the American residential sector due to the excessive amount of real estate lending offered to individuals (Shiller, 2008). The increasing number of household defaults causes a reduction of the credit supply (Miam and Sufi, 2009) that implies a decrease of real estate price due to the significant decrease of the demand.

The real estate crisis became a global crisis due to the liquidity-induced contagion mechanism that reduces the demand of financial instruments, and the increase of the risk-premium required by all investors that trade in the financial markets (Longstaff, 2010). Financial markets show negative performances especially for financial instruments issued by financial intermediaries that have direct exposure on the real estate market or suffer from a lack of liquidity that could be refinanced on the interbank market only by paying higher interest rates (Cecchetti, 2009).

Governments are affected as well by the crisis because in the crisis scenario they have to increase public expenditure for covering expenses related to financial rescue programmes and for supporting economy growth and consumptions (Cecchetti, Mohanty and Zampolli, 2010). The increase in public expenditure implies an increase of the public debt and in a crisis scenario governments may suffer from losses related to the lack of investors' confidence and the related increase of the cost of capital. In such a scenario even the extreme event of Sovereign's default could not be excluded (Reinhart and Rogoff, 2011).

Financial innovations, like innovations generally, are basically not predictable improvements of the technology, instruments and business models adopted in the financial industry (Miller, 1986). Even if the financial innovation is not *per se* a source of systemic risk, during the crisis the lack of knowledge for identifying the value of new and complex financial instruments could be considered one of the main causes of the crisis (Zandi, 2009).

This book proposes new approaches and strategies for the areas that are more affected by the crisis for overcoming the main limits that affected the financial industry during the crisis. The volume presents separately topics related to the asset management industry, the public sector and real estate.

The analysis of the financial markets considers the role of the information in the investment selection process, the market integration and volatility and the performance of the investment vehicles.

The analysis of the value of the information available looks at both the effect of media sentiment on stock prices (Chapter 1) and the information-based investment strategies (Chapters 4 to 6). For the former, the impact of media sentiment on the stock market reactions is enhanced/moderated by the level of attention of investors and the attention is driven also by past trading volumes. For the latter, portfolio construction and market timing portfolio rebalances allow the achievement of higher performance if qualitative information or views are considered for defining the investment strategy.

During the last years, markets have increased their level of integration through merger and acquisitions between the main stock markets worldwide (Chapter 3). One of the main effects of the integration is the increase of correlation between market performance that could cause an increase of the overall volatility and a higher risk of crisis development. The analysis of the relationship among different types of markets demonstrates that the increase of sophistication of the financial instruments traded does not imply an increase of volatility because derivatives are prevalently used for hedging purposes instead of speculative ones (Chapter 2).

Investment vehicles represent an instrument for indirect investment in the financial market and its ownership and governance could affect significantly the performance achieved and the return for the investors (Chapter 7).

Before the crisis the real estate market was affected by a price bubble that offered the opportunity to create profits and value for all the stakeholders involved due to an increasing demand for buildings and the correlated increase of the prices. The new scenario reduces significantly the profit opportunities available and demonstrates the usefulness of more detailed analysis of the information available for both direct and indirect investment. In order to evaluate the direct investment opportunities, normally a preliminary evaluation of the investment profitability is released comparing the performance of indexes with the expected performance of the investment available even if frequently there are significant misalignments among different information sources (Chapter 8). The analysis of the indirect investment opportunities has to consider both the characteristics of the investment selection process and the performance achieved. For the former a detailed analysis of the investment selection process shows some misalignments between the expected portfolio allocation and the real one that allows fund managers to create extra-value for investors (Chapter 9). For the latter the main problem is related to the identification of the proper risk measure and the choice of the risk measure could affect significantly the ranking of investment opportunities available and so the investment strategies adopted by individual investors (Chapter 10).

The financial crisis raises the attention of the financial markets to public expenditure and stresses the role of the rating agencies in evaluating the risk of default in the sovereign sector, the relevance of a correct management and the financial function inside the public entities and the role of new financial instruments in order to reduce the public expenditure and support the development of private–public partnerships for developing infrastructures and public services. The analysis of Sovereign and Municipalities rating criteria shows the role of economic and financial fundamentals in evaluating the risk of the public entities even if the rating assigned by different rating agencies could be misaligned due to the different choices made in the rating evaluation procedure (Chapter 11). The development of the financial function in the public sector is normally driven by law changes and especially during the financial crisis some countries revise significantly the regulatory framework in order to define new rules and controls for avoiding the misuse of the structured finance products and derivatives (Chapter 12).

The lack of public resources for developing infrastructures and offering public services incentives for the development of alternative financing solutions, like project financing, and financial intermediaries involved in the transaction are currently facing a new regulatory framework defined in order to measure correctly the risk exposure related to such transactions (Chapter 13).

Over time a stronger integration among financial markets and institutions has occurred but solutions available to improve performance/risk equilibria should be fitted into the peculiarities of each market and situation. It is a hard way to create value in finance today.

References

Carretta, A., V. Farina, F. Fiordelisi, D. Martelli and P. Schwizer (2011) 'The impact of corporate governance press news on stock market returns', *European Financial Management*, 17, 100–119.

Cecchetti, S. G. (2009) 'Crisis and responses: The Federal Reserve in the early stages of the financial crisis', *Journal of Economic Perspectives*, 23, 51–75.

Cecchetti, S. G., M. S. Mohanty and F. Zampolli (2010) 'The future of public debt: Prospects and implications', BIS Working Paper No. 300, http://www.bis.org (home page), date accessed 1 July 2012.

De Long, J. B., A. Shleifer, L. H. Summers and R. J. Waldmann (1990) 'Noise trader risk in financial markets', *Journal of Political Economy*, 98, 703–38.

Diamond, D. W. and R. Rajan (2009) 'The credit crisis: Conjectures about causes and remedies', *American Economic Review*, 99, 606–10.

Fama, E. (1965) 'The behaviour of stock-market prices', *Journal of Business*, v. 38, i. 1, 34–105.

Longstaff, F. A. (2010) 'The subprime credit crisis and contagion in financial markets', *Journal of Financial Economics*, 97, 436–50.

Miam, A. and A. Sufi (2009) 'The consequences of mortgage credit expansion: Evidence from the U.S. mortgage default crisis', *Quaterly Journal of Economics*, 124, 1449–96.

Miller, M. (1986) 'Financial innovation: The last twenty years and the next', *Journal of Financial and Quantitative Analysis*, 21, 459–71.

Reinhart, C. M. and K. S. Rogoff (2011) 'From financial crash to debt crisis', *American Economic Review*, 101, 1676–706.

Shiller, R. J. (2008) *The Subprime Solution: How Today's Global Financial Crisis Happened, and What to Do About It* (Princeton: Princeton University Press).

Soros, G. (2008) *The New Paradigm for Financial Markets* (New York: PublicAffairs).

Zandi, M. (2009) *Financial Shock* (Upper Saddle River: FT Press).

Part I

Asset Pricing during the Crisis

1

Does Investor Attention Influence Stock Market Activity? The Case of Spin-Off Deals

Alessandro Carretta, Vincenzo Farina, Elvira Anna Graziano and Marco Reale

1.1 Introduction

One of the most important research streams in finance is to understand the determinants of stock market dynamics. According to the theory of efficient financial markets (Fama, 1970), stock prices should reflect all available information. However, the evidence of an autocorrelation of stock returns at short horizons (Jegadeesh and Titman, 1993; Moskowitz and Grinblatt, 1999; Hong et al., 2007) suggests that that stock prices do not fully adjust to new information.

In recent times, a number of studies have been conducted to explain stock market underreaction/overreaction to new information. In particular, these models rely on underreaction due to investor sentiment and conservatism when adjusting beliefs (Barberis et al., 1998), variations in investor confidence arising from biased self-attribution (Daniel et al., 1998) and slow information diffusion (Hong and Stein, 1999).

The only way to test these models is to consider market sentiment as a measure of investor expectation about future stock returns and attention allocation as a proxy for either investors' cognitive biases or information diffusion.

In this regard, market sentiment is made up by different sources of information: press releases, analysts' comments and mass media are just a few examples. An intriguing literature provides interesting evidence of the impact of these different sources on various stock market variables, such as returns, trading volumes, and price volatility (Dell'Acqua et al., 2010; Doukas et al., 2005; Antweiler and Frank, 2004; Coval and Shumway, 2001).

Dell'Acqua et al. (2010) find evidence that voluntary disclosure following the introduction of the Regulation Fair Disclosure, included in the Selective Disclosure and Insider Trading Act issued by the SEC, reduces price volatility of high-tech firms listed in the US market. Doukas et al. (2005) find that positive excess analyst coverage, raising investors' optimism, is associated with overvaluation and low future returns. Antweiler and Frank (2004) find evidence of a relationship between message activity and both trading volume and return volatility. Similarly, Coval and Shumway (2001) establish that the ambient noise level created by traders in a futures pit is linked to volume and volatility, but not to returns. In addition, Tetlock et al. (2008) find that some news exerts an effect in a relatively short period and other news in the medium and long term (for example, news regarding core aspects of firm management).

As shown by various cognitive studies (Baumeister et al., 2001; Rozin and Royzman, 2001; Fiske and Taylor, 1991; Brief and Motowidlo, 1986), positive and negative news have different impacts on people's perceptions, and negative news also exerts a stronger impact than positive news. Moreover the emotion aroused by news is likely to influence investors' behaviour (Carretta et al., 2011). Shoemaker and Reese (1996) argue that newspapers generally tend to put a certain emphasis in the news in order to make it more engaging to the public. As a consequence, financial journalists may tend to 'dramatize' corporate events in order to make their articles more interesting for the public of investors.

Theoretically, one could expect a variation in stock market activity as a consequence of a shock in the levels of attention (Daniel et al., 1998; Hong and Stein, 1999). Various empirical studies document this impact (Chemmanur and Yan, 2009; Da et al., 2009; DellaVigna and Pollet, 2009; Barber and Odean, 2008; Cohen and Frazzini, 2008; Peng et al., 2007; Fehle et al., 2005; Huberman and Regev, 2001).

Chemmanur and Yan (2009) find that an increased level of investor attention is associated with a larger contemporary stock return and a smaller future stock return. Da et al. (2009) find investor attention to be correlated with the large first-day return and the long-run underperformance of IPO stocks.

DellaVigna and Pollet (2009) compare the response of stock returns to earnings announcements on Friday, when investors are more likely to be inattentive, and on other weekdays. They find that the volume reaction and two-day stock price reaction to news that is released to the media on Fridays are much weaker than when news is released on other days of the week. Barber and Odean (2008) test and confirm the hypothesis that individual investors are net buyers of attention-grabbing stocks, e.g., stocks in the news, stocks experiencing high abnormal trading volume, and stocks with extreme one-day returns. Therefore individual investors are more prone to search for information when they are buying since they have to choose from a large set of available alternatives.

Cohen and Frazzini (2008) put in evidence that in the presence of investors subject to attention constraints, stock prices do not promptly incorporate news about economically related firms. Peng et al. (2007) find support for the hypothesis that investors shift their (limited) attention to processing market-level information following an increase in market-wide uncertainty and then subsequently divert their attention back to asset-specific information. Fehle et al. (2005) examine whether companies can create attention effects through advertising. Investigating stock price reactions and trading activity for firms employing TV commercials in 19 Super Bowl broadcasts over the period 1969–2001, they find significant positive abnormal returns for firms which are readily identifiable from the contents.

Huberman and Regev (2001) compare the effect of an information diffuse by the popular *New York Times* versus the effect of the same information diffuse by the journal *Nature* and by various popular newspapers (including *The Times*) more than five months earlier. Results show that newspaper content can affect stock prices even if the content does not provide genuine information thus confirming the important role exercised by investor attention.

This chapter aims to test whether and how market sentiment (arising from mass media) and investor attention play a role in influencing the performance of spin-off deals, back in fashion due to the recent financial crisis. We use data from a sample of 16 spin-off deals published between 2004 and 2010 in the *Wall Street Journal*, the US's second-largest newspaper by circulation. In detail, we expect that media sentiment and investor attention will influence investor reaction around the date of various spin-off deals and on the subsequent days.

From a theoretical point of view, we broaden the literature on stock market reaction to spin-off deals. Firms on the world's stock markets have spun off bits of themselves as separate listed companies worth a total of $54 billion in all of 2010 (source: *Economist*, 2011). One of the main reasons for the starburst is that companies seeking buyers for parts of their business are not getting good offers from other firms, or from private equity. Another driving force is the 'conglomerate discount' when stock markets value a diversified group at less than the sum of its parts.

Existing studies on this topic consider investor reaction and performance in relation to (Chemmanur et al., 2010; Veld and Veld-Merkoulova, 2009; Chemmanur and Yan, 2004; Veld and Veld-Merkoulova, 2004; Desai and Jain, 1999; Daley et al., 1997; Cusatis et al., 1993; Rosenfeld, 1984; Schipper and Smith, 1983; Miles and Rosenfeld, 1983; Hite and Owers, 1983): (i) spin-off size, (ii) improvement of industrial focus, (iii) information asymmetry, (iv) regulatory and tax advantages, (v) anti-takeover provisions.

From a methodological point of view, we consider mass media content as a measure of investor expectation about future stock returns and attention allocation as a proxy for either investor cognitive biases or information diffusion.

Moreover, we define a direct measure of investor attention using data from Google Insights for Search. Since internet users commonly use a search engine to collect information, aggregate search frequency in this search engine could be considered a direct and unambiguous measure of attention (Da et al., 2011).

Finally, we examine the statistical relation between investors' attention and stock market variables using a dynamic model built as a sparse structural vector autoregression (SVAR) and adopting an approach based on graphical modelling (Reale and Tunnicliffe Wilson, 2001).

The rest of this chapter is organized as follows. In the next section we present data and variables. Section 1.3 lays out methods and estimation results. Finally, Section 1.4 concludes.

1.2 Data and variables

Our sample includes 16 spin-off deals (Table 1.1) traded on the New York Stock Exchange (NYSE) and published between 2004 and 2010 in the *Wall Street Journal*, the US's second-largest newspaper by circulation (according to *Editor & Publisher*, in 2010 it reported a circulation of just over two million weekday copies).

1.2.1 Media sentiment

We define media sentiment as the degree to which *Wall Street Journal* news regarding each spin-off firm before the deal has a positive or negative meaning. This financial newspaper is considered a natural choice for a data source that reflects and influences investor sentiment since it has a large diffusion and a strong reputation among the financial community (Tetlock, 2007).

Table 1.1 Sample of spin-off deals considered for the analysis

Spin-off	Parent company
Acco Brand Corp. (Acco World Corp.)	Fortune Brands Inc
Ameriprise Financial Inc.	American Express Co
AOL	Time Warner
Broadridge Financial Solutions Inc	Automatic Data Processing Inc
CareFusion Corp	Cardinal Health Inc.
Cenovus Energy	EnCana Corp
Covidien PLC	Tyco International Ltd
Discover Financial Services	Morgan Stanley
Live Nation Entertainment Inc.	Clear Channel Communications Inc.
Mead Johnson Nutrition Co.	Bristol-Myers Squibb Co.
Motorola Mobility Holding Inc	Motorola Inc (Motorola Solution Inc)
Philip Morris International Inc.	Altria Group Inc
Primerica Inc.	Citigroup Inc
Spectra Energy Corp	Duke Energy Corp.
Teradata Corp	NCR Corp
Time Warner Cable Inc.	Time Warner Inc.

First, all the news regarding *Wall Street Journal* spin-off deals are extracted from the database Factiva, which provides access to more than 10,000 sources, including newspapers, magazines, news agencies and information sites.

Second, we apply computer aided text analysis (Stone et al., 1966) using the linguistic dictionary Harvard IV Psycho Social and the software Wordsmith 4 (Scott, 2004).

Operationally, Wordsmith 4 counts the number of words in each news item that falls within the *positive* and *negative* categories of the Harvard IV Psycho Social Dictionary. In fact, each category contains a list of words and word senses. However, since some words in this list (such as mine, cancer or capital) are more likely to identify a specific industry segment than reveal negative financial events we used the revised list of Loughran and McDonald (2011) including words that typically have implications only in a financial sense. For example, the negative category is the largest, with 2,337 entries of words/phrases denoting a negative sense, while the positive category has 353 words with a positive sense. Using lists of words of different size could influence the skew of the distributions for news content. This choice is due to the following reasons. First, using a standard text analysis dictionary allows for the stability and the reproducibility of results. Second, the problem is limited by considering the number of times different words of each category (positive/negative) are repeated in the text of the news.

Finally, the positive or negative sense of the news is determined by: P - N where P and N are, respectively, the number of positive and negative words in the news.

1.2.2 Investor attention

To define a direct measure of investor attention, we used daily data from Google Insights for Search (http://www.google.com/insights/search/) for the considered sample of spin-offs. In fact, according to Da et al. (2009), if someone searches for something in a search engine, he is certainly paying attention to it. Moreover the percentage of global internet users visiting Google is 50.03 per cent of internet users visiting at 30 March 2011 (source: www.alexa.com).

Choi and Varian (2012) provide evidence that search data on Google may predict home sales, automotive sales and tourism. Another study of Ginsberg et al. (2008) finds that search data for 45 terms related to influenza predicted flu outbreaks one to two weeks before official reports. In detail, this tool analyses a portion of worldwide Google web searches from all Google domains to compute how many searches have been done for the terms one has entered, relative to the total number of searches done on Google over time.

We applied the category filter Finance and Insurance in order to download the time series showing the monthly change of the searches over time expressed as a percentage of growth, with respect to the first date on the graph (or the first date that has data).

Finally investor attention is defined as a percentage of growth of aggregate search frequency in Google, with respect to the average value in the previous five days and for a period of three months from the deal.

1.2.3 Stock market

Data regarding stock market activity come from Datastream Database. In detail, the daily returns for each spin-off are calculated from the adjusted close prices. The variation in volumes is computed as the logarithmic difference with the previous day. Volatility is calculated as the standard deviation of spin-off returns. The daily market returns are based on the Dow Jones Industrial Average (DJIA) index.

1.3 Analysis

1.3.1 Descriptive analysis

Some interesting evidence comes from descriptive analysis. First, we analyse the relation between media sentiment and spin-off returns. Figure 1.1 summarizes the main findings.

We observe that the set of spin-offs anticipated with a positive sentiment have a positive variation of returns after the first day of 0.24 per cent on average, while the set of spin-offs anticipated with a negative sentiment have a negative variation of returns after one day from the deal equal to 1.09 per cent. This is coherent with the hypothesis that media sentiment, measured as semantic content of the news, affects the investor behaviour around the spin-off date.

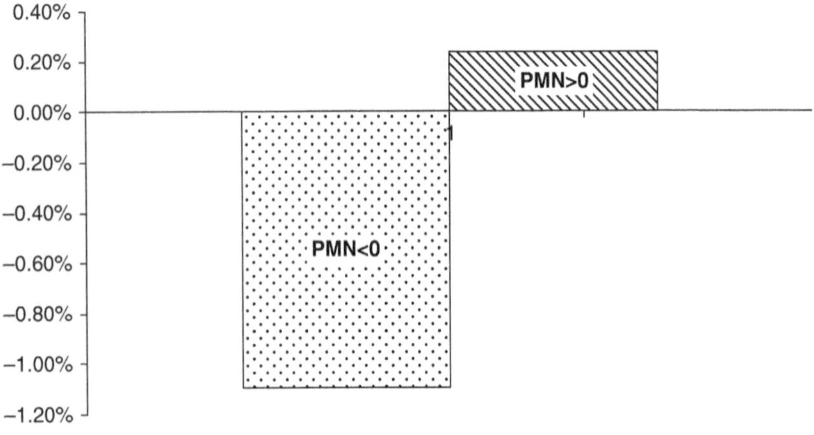

Figure 1.1 Media sentiment and the percentage variation of spin-off returns one day after the deal

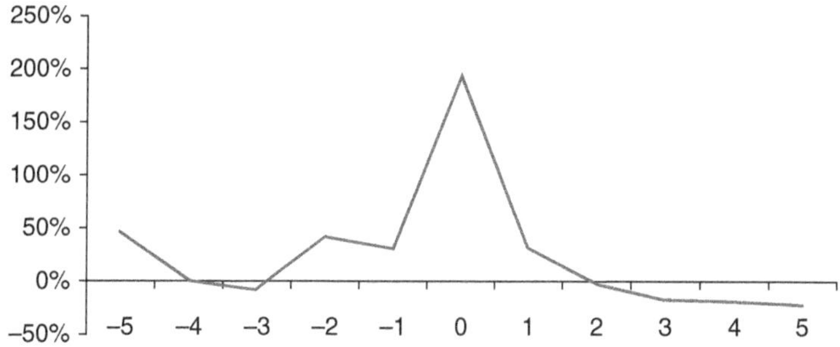

Figure 1.2 The change in attention indicator series around the date (–5gg, +5gg) of spin-off deals

Second, we assess the change in investors' attention around a spin-off deal. Figure 1.2 confirms that there are significant changes in attention level around the date of the spin-off deal (day 0).

There is a significant upward trend in the attention level starting three days prior to spin-off day, and there is a significant jump (nearly 200 per cent) during the day prior to the date of the spin-off deal and the day of the spin-off deal, reflecting a surge in public attention for the stock. Interestingly, the shift in attention is not permanent: the attention level reverts to its pre-spin-off level the day following the deal.

Third, we analyse the relation between change in investors' attention and spin-off returns, finding that the set of spin-offs with low attention during the week prior to the deal have first-day returns of –0.40 per cent on average, while the set of spin-offs with high attention have much lower first-day returns of –2.9 per cent on average (Figure 1.3). The difference between the two average first-day returns is due to an increase in the spin-off with high attention returns higher than the spin-off with low attention on the date of the deal.

Fourth, the change in attention level has an impact also on trading volumes. In Figure 1.4, we observe a significant slump in the volumes of spin-off with high attention the day following the deal. The trading volumes of the set of spin-offs with high attention on the deal-date are higher than the trading volumes of the set of spin-offs with low attention, producing a greater fall the day following the deal.

Fifth, we analyse the relation between investor attention and stocks volatility. Figure 1.5 displays that a week after the date of the deal, the volatility (at various dates) of spin-off stocks with high attention is higher than the volatility of the spin-off stocks with low attention.

Finally, Figure 1.6 shows that investor attention amplifies the effect of media sentiment on spin-off returns. The returns related to the spin-off with high attention and positive (negative) media sentiment have a higher positive

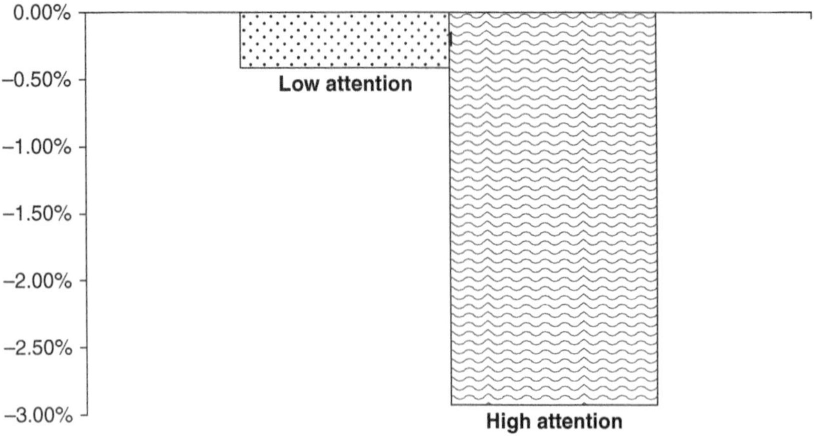

Figure 1.3 The attention level and the percentage variation of spin-off returns one day after spin-off deals

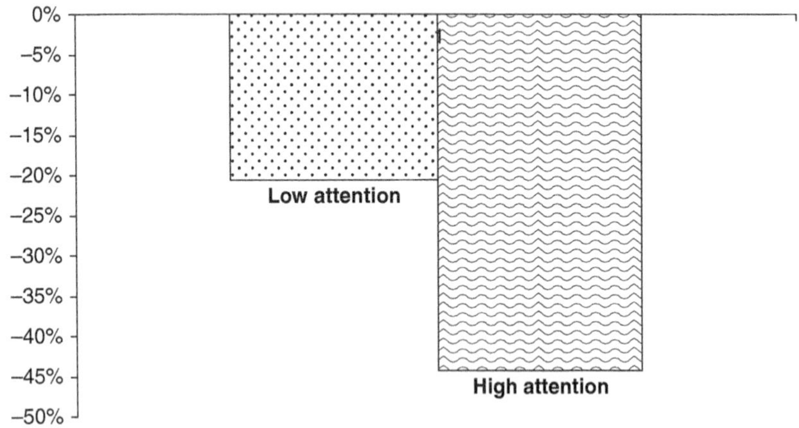

Figure 1.4 The attention level and the percentage variation in trading volumes one day after spin-off deals

(negative) reaction with respect to the set of the spin-off with low attention and positive (negative) media sentiment.

1.3.2 Evidence from a dynamic model

In order to understand the dynamic interaction of the attention with other relevant variables we consider a dynamic model which includes the returns of the spin-offs (R), their variation in volumes traded on the market (V), the change in attention indicator (A) and the average returns of the market (D).

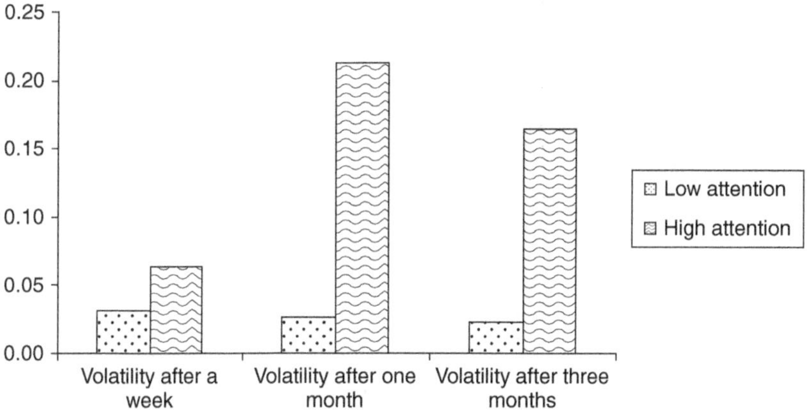

Figure 1.5 The attention level in relation to volatility over the time horizon considered

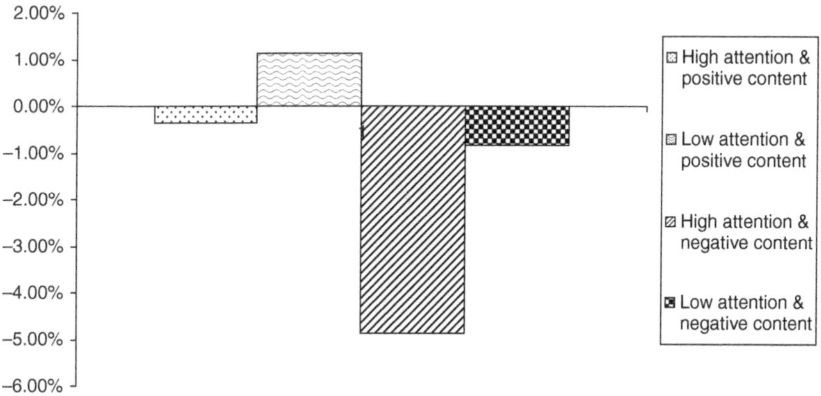

Figure 1.6 The media sentiment, the change in attention indicator and the percentage variation of spin-off returns one day after the deal

All the variables regarding each spin-off refer to a period of three months from the deal-date and are averaged.

This dynamic model is built as a sparse structural vector autoregression (SVAR). To build such a model we adopt an approach based on graphical modelling (Reale and Tunnicliffe Wilson, 2001).

This approach effectively identifies the relationship between the variables at time t, e.g., the current values of the time series; moreover it provides a sparse structure, where only the significant relationships between variables are considered. Its advantage is that it identifies such relationships without prior constraints. A SVAR model of order p, indicated as SVAR(p) can be

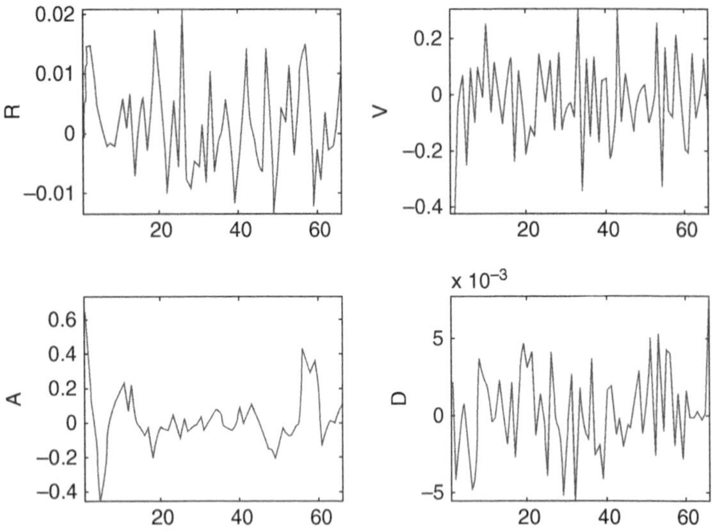

Figure 1.7 Time plots of the variables considered in the dynamic model

written as

$$\Phi_0 x_t = \Phi_1 x_{t-1} + \Phi_2 x_{t-2} + \cdots + \Phi_p x_{t-p} + \varepsilon_t \tag{1.1}$$

where

$$x_{t-j} = [x_{1,t-j}, x_{2,t-j}, \ldots, x_{m,t-j}]^T \quad j = 0, \ldots, p$$

is a vector of time series states at lag j, when $j = 0$ we have the current states of the time series. In our case, a visual inspection of all our m = 4 time series in Figure 1.7 suggests they are stationary, however the approach we follow would be valid even if the time series were $I(1)$ independently from any cointegration (Reale and Tunnicliffe Wilson, 2008) although obviously the interpretation of the results would require more care in such a context.

The errors' vector

$$\varepsilon_t = [\varepsilon_{1,t}, \varepsilon_{2,t}, \ldots, \varepsilon_{m,t}]^T \tag{1.2}$$

is a multivariate white noise with general diagonal covariance matrix W. The working assumption is that the series are Gaussian but the method we apply is applicable under wider conditions, such as ε_t being I.I.D., presented for example in Anderson (1971).

This model is attractive because its estimation from a sample $x_{i,1}, x_{i,2}, \ldots, x_{i,n}$ with $i = 1, \ldots, m$, by least squares applied separately to each component $x_{i,t}$ of x_t is straightforward. The properties of the estimates given by the regression are reliable, and the estimate of W is independent of the estimates of Φ_j, the matrices of the coefficients of x_{t-j}. The approach we

Table 1.2 SVAR order identified by different information criteria

AIC	CAIC	HIC	SIC
1	4	1	1

follow will lead to sparse identification and estimation of all these matrices, including Φ_0.

There are various approaches to multiple time series modelling which seek either to transform models such as a vector autoregression (VAR) to a form which includes contemporaneous relationships among the variables, or to identify directly such a form, see for example Box and Tiao (1977) and Tiao and Tsay (1989).

Our approach in this chapter is similar: we consider the structural autoregressive model of the same form as a VAR but with the addition of contemporaneous dependence through the coefficient matrix coefficient Φ_0. We require this matrix to represent a recursive (causal) dependence of each component of x_t on the others. This is equivalent to the existence of a re-ordering of the elements of x_t such that Φ_0 is triangular with unit diagonal.

The first step in the specification of our model is the identification of the order p of the SVAR. This identification can be done by various methods, including the inspection of the multivariate partial autocorrelation functions (Reinsel, 1993) or by the minimization of an order selection criterion such as AIC (Akaike, 1973), CAIC (Hurvich and Tsai, 1989), HIC (Hannan and Quinn, 1979) and SIC (Schwarz, 1978). Table 1.2 provides the order selected by the different criteria for a SVAR containing our four variables.

We opted for the order $p = 1$, suggested by AIC, HIC and SIC, that leads to the model involving eight variables (R, V, A and D at time t and at time $t-1$). We then use pair-wise sample partial correlations, conditioning on all remaining variables, to construct the conditional independence graph (CIG) of the eight variables, following procedures presented for example in Edwards (2000). As Swanson and Granger (1997) remark, the structural form of dependence between the variables is naturally expressed by (and is equivalent to) a directed acyclic graph (DAG), in which nodes representing variables are linked with arrows (directed edges) indicating the direction of any causal dependence. A DAG implies a single CIG for the variables, but the possible DAGs which might explain a particular CIG may be several or none. The point is that, subject to sampling variability, the CIG is a constructible quantity and a useful one for expressing the data-determined constraints on permissible DAG interpretations.

The CIG consists of nodes representing the variables, two nodes being without an edge if and only if they are independent, conditional upon all the

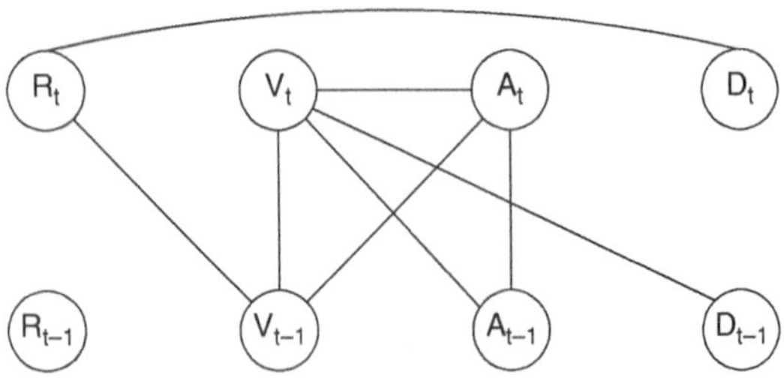

Figure 1.8 Conditional independence graph for the variables in a SVAR(1)

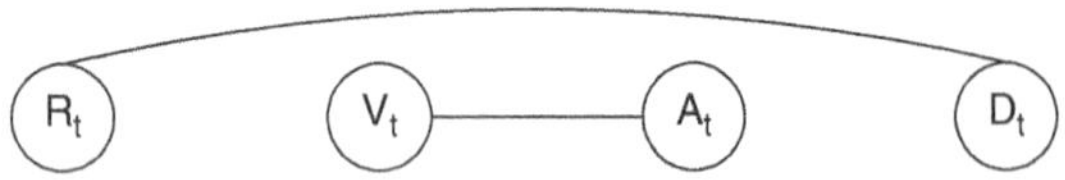

Figure 1.9 Sub-graph of the CIG including just the current variables

remaining variables. In a Gaussian context this conditional independence is indicated by a zero partial correlation.

In the wider linear least squares context, defining linear partial correlations as the same function of linear unconditional correlations as in the Gaussian context, still usefully indicates lack of linear predictability of one variable by the other given the inclusion of all remaining variables. We tested the significance of the partial correlations representing the edges (relationships) at a type 1 error probability threshold of 0.05. The resulting CIG is presented in Figure 1.8.

The CIG considers only edges linking to current variables, as we are interested in specifying a model forx_t. However, using the appropriate sample properties (Reale and Tunnicliffe Wilson, 2002), we could also test for significant edges between lagged variables. This sometimes could be useful even in the identification of a model for justx_t. As we have already mentioned, there are several possible DAGs that can explain a CIG, so we need now to identify the more likely DAG of the several possible ones consistent with the CIG we obtained from the data. This practically resolves into finding the more likely direction of the edges that so far are undirected. In this task the flow of time comes to our help and we can reasonably assume the direction from lagged variables to the current ones. Hence we just need to concentrate on possible links between current variables. If we consider the sub-graph of the CIG considering the edges between the current variables, illustrated in Figure 1.9, we can think of four possible DAGs, illustrated in Figure 1.10, leading to four different models named model 1, model 2, model 3 and model 4.

We are now left with the decision to choose one of the four possible models; at this stage both financial theory and statistical evidence can guide us. From

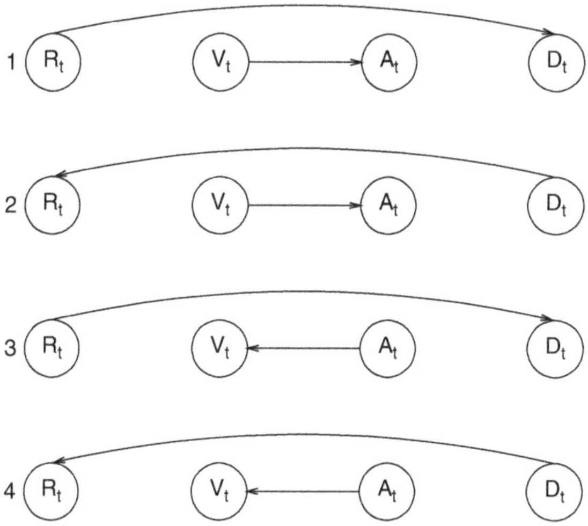

Figure 1.10 All the possible DAGs explaining the CIG between current variables

Table 1.3 Number of parameters and values of information criteria for different models

Model	Parameters	AIC	HIC	SIC
1	8	−1961.00	−1954.10	−1943.60
2	8	−1962.50	−1955.60	−1945.10
3	8	−1962.70	−1955.80	−1945.30
4	8	−1964.20	−1957.30	−1946.80
Saturated	22	−1950.90	−1932.00	−1903.00

the statistical point of view we can use penalized likelihood selection criteria, like the ones used to select the SVAR order, for this choice.

In Table 1.3 we report the number of parameters and the values of AIC, HIC and SIC for the four models and also for the saturated model, which is the model with non-zero coefficients as a control. The direction of the edges in the saturated model is irrelevant as all the different models with different non-cyclical direction of the edges have the same likelihood. At this stage we could operate further simplification by subset regression excluding non-significant parameters for the four models initially selected, but in our case all the parameters were significant and no further simplification could be done.

A first observation arising from an analysis of the results reported by the table is that all 4 models perform better than the saturated model; second, all the different selection criteria, that have a different penalization for the number of parameters, give the same order of preference for the four models

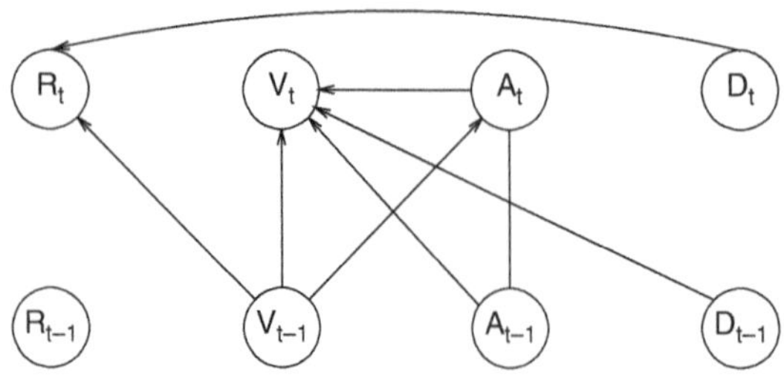

Figure 1.11 DAG of model 4

as they have the same number of parameters; the last observation is that model number 4 is the best model from the statistical point of view but it is also convincing from a financial theory point of view. The DAG for model 4 is shown in Figure 1.11.

We eventually can describe this model with a system of three equations, as $D_t$results as exogenous, providing both coefficients and the corresponding *t-values* in round brackets. The equations are:

$$R_t = 0.00 + \underset{(4.09)}{1.28}\, D_t - \underset{(-1.88)}{0.01}\, V_{t-1} \tag{1.3}$$

$$V_t = -0.02 + \underset{(2.73)}{0.39}\, A_t - \underset{(-3.19)}{0.33}\, V_{t-1} - \underset{(-3.28)}{0.42}\, A_{t-1} - \underset{(-3.82)}{22.50}\, D_{t-1} \tag{1.4}$$

$$A_t = 0.03 + \underset{(2.13)}{0.18}\, D_t + \underset{(7.70)}{0.61}\, A_{t-1} \tag{1.5}$$

According to the model, the stock market returns (D_t) and the lagged volumes (V_{t-1}) are significantly related to current-day spin-off returns (R_t). However, the relation between the lagged volumes and the current-day spin-off returns is negative, because generally the returns react to the trading volumes at the same time. However since high volumes show that investors are interested in both buying and selling a stock, we cannot confirm Barber and Odean's (2008) conjecture that individual investors are net buyers of attention-grabbing stocks.

The current-day spin-off volumes (V_t) are significantly and positively affected by the current-day attention indicator (A_t): this is consistent with the hypothesis that an increased attention level, due to a spin-off deal, has a contemporaneous effect on the trading volumes, enhancing them. On the other hand both the lagged volumes (V_{t-1}) and the lagged attention indicator (A_{t-1}) have a negative impact on current-day volumes: a growth of Google searches, as a proxy of the attention level, involves an increase of trading volumes thus reducing the spin-off returns of the following day. This may well be consistent with the framework of Daniel et al. (1998) in which high attention results in downward pressure on stock market returns. The lagged stock market returns (Dt-1) also negatively affect the current-day spin-off volumes.

Finally, we find that the lagged volumes (V_{t-1}) and the lagged attention indicator (A_{t-1}) significantly and positively affect the current-day attention indicator (A_t). The investors may start to pay attention to a stock and search it in Google the day previous to the spin-off date, leading to a significant jump in attention level on the deal day: we observe that individual investors' attention is grabbed by stocks experiencing high trading volumes on the previous day.

1.4 Conclusion

This chapter investigates empirically the nature of the interactions between mass media, investor attention and the stock market. In particular we provide some preliminary evidence about the impact of media-provided information and the level of investor attention in the spin-off deals market.

The contribution of this study is manifold. First of all, our results show the existence of a significant upward trend in the attention level starting three days prior to spin-off day and a significant jump during the day of the spin-off deals.

Subsequently, our findings support the general argument that the characteristics of information provided by mass media influence investor choices about spin-off firms. In this perspective, we evidence that mass media information is important not only for its novelty, but also for its effects on investor sentiment. As one could expect, media sentiment, measured as semantic content of the news, influences the investors' preferences, and therefore returns, around the spin-off deals' date. In particular a positive (negative) media sentiment in news spread before spin-off deals is associated with positive (negative) short-term returns.

We find also that an increase in investor attention determines an increase of trading volumes and volatility of spin-off firms in both the short and the long run. Nevertheless, results show that investor attention enhances/moderates the effect of media sentiment: the returns related to the spin-off with high attention and positive (negative) media sentiment have a higher positive (negative) reaction with respect to the set of the spin-off with low attention and positive (negative) media sentiment.

Finally, results of our dynamic model show that an increased attention level, due to spin-off deals, has a contemporary effect on the trading volumes, enhancing them. In addition, we observe that individual investors' attention is grabbed by stocks experiencing high trading volumes in the previous day. However since high volumes show that investors are interested in both buying and selling a stock, we cannot confirm Barber and Odean's (2008) conjecture that individual investors are net buyers of attention-grabbing stocks. Besides, results seem to be consistent with the theoretical framework of Daniel et al. (1998) in which high attention results in downward pressure on stock market returns and volumes.

As a note of attention, we are aware that differences in relative levels of expertise, risk, and other types of investment preferences of different types of investors may exert a role in different ways. Therefore, a challenge for future researches is to comprehend if, and under what conditions, the characteristics of the investors influence information use and processing.

References

Akaike, H. (1973) 'A new look at statistical model identification?' *IEEE Transactions on Automatic Control*, 19, 716–23.

Anderson, T. W. (1971) *The Statistical Analysis of Time Series* (New York: Wiley).

Antweiler, W. and M. Z. Frank (2004) 'Is all that talk just noise? The information content of internet stock message boards', *Journal of Finance*, 59, 1259–93.

Barber, B. M. and T. Odean (2008) 'All that glitters: The effect of attention and news on the buying behavior of individual and institutional investors', *Review of Financial Studies*, 21, 785–818.

Barberis, N., A. Shleifer and R. Vishny (1998) 'A model of investor sentiment', *Journal of Financial Economics*, 49, 307–43.

Baumeister, R. F., E. Bratslavsky, C. Finkenauer and K. D. Vohs (2001) 'Bad is stronger than good', *Review of General Psychology*, 5, 323–70.

Box, G. E. P. and G. C. Tiao (1977) 'A canonical analysis of multiple time series', *Biometrika*, 64, 355–365.

Brief, A. P. and S. J. Motowidlo (1986) 'Prosocial organizational behaviours', *Academy of Management Review*, 11, 710–25.

Carretta, A., V. Farina, D. Martelli, F. Fiordelisi and P. Schwizer (2011) 'The impact of corporate governance press news on stock market returns', *European Financial Management*, 17, 100–19.

Chemmanur, T. J. and A. Yan (2004) 'A theory of corporate spin-offs', *Journal of Financial Economics*, 72, 259–90.

——(2009) 'Advertising, attention, and stock returns', http://www.ssrn.com (homepage) date accessed 01 July 2012.

Chemmanur, T. J., B. D. Jordan, M. H. Liu and Q. Wu (2010) 'Antitakeover provisions in corporate spin-offs', *Journal of Banking and Finance*, 34, 813–24.

Choi, H. and H. Varian (2012) 'Predicting the present with Google trends', *Economic Record*, 88, 2–9.

Cohen, L. and A. Frazzini (2008) 'Economic links and predictable returns', *Journal of Finance*, 63, 1977–2011.

Coval, J. D. and T. Shumway (2001) 'Is sound just noise?' *Journal of Finance*, 56, 1887–910.

Cusatis, P., J. Miles and J. Woolridge (1993) 'Restructuring through spinoffs: The stock market evidence', *Journal of Financial Economics*, 33, 293–311.

Da, Z., J. Engelberg and P. Gao (2011) 'In search of attention', *Journal of Finance*, 66, 1461–99.

Daley, L., V. Mehrotra and R. Sivakumar (1997) 'Corporate focus and value creation: Evidence from spinoffs', *Journal of Financial Economics*, 45, 257–81.

Daniel, K. D., D. Hirshleifer and A. Subrahmanyam (1998) 'Investor psychology and security market under- and overreactions', *Journal of Finance*, 53, 1839–85.

Dell'Acqua, A., F. Perrini and S. Caselli (2010) 'Conference calls and stock price volatility in the post-reg FD era', *European Financial Management*, 16, 256–70.

Della Vigna S., and J. Pollet (2009) 'Investor inattention and Friday earnings announcements', *Journal of Finance*, 64, 709–749.

Desai H., and P. C. Jain (1999) 'Firm performance and focus: Long-run stock market performance following spinoffs', *Journal of Financial Economics*, 54, 75–101.

Doukas, J. A., C. F. Kim and C. Pantzalis (2005) 'Two faces of analyst coverage', *Financial Management*, 34, 99–125.

Economist (2011) 'Starbursting breaking up companies is back in fashion', http://www.economist.com (homepage) date accessed 01 July 2012.

Edwards, D. (2000) *Introduction to Graphical Modelling* (New York: Springer).

Fama, E. F. (1970) 'Efficient capital markets: A review of theory and empirical work', *Journal of Finance*, 25, 383–417.

Fehle, F. R., S. Tsyplakov and V. M. Zdorovtsov (2005) 'Can companies influence investor behaviour through advertising? Super bowl commercials and stock returns', *European Financial Management*, 11, 625–47.

Fiske, S. T. and S. E. Taylor (1991) *Social Cognition* (New York: McGraw-Hill).

Ginsberg, J., M. H. Mohebbi, R. S. Patel, L. Brammer, M. S. Smolinski and L. Brilliant (2008), 'Detecting influenza epidemics using search engine query data', *Nature*, 457, 1012–14.

Hannan, E. J. and B. G. Quinn (1979) 'The determination of the order of an autoregression', *Journal of the Royal Statistical Society*, Series B, 41, 190–5.

Hite, G. and J. Owers (1983) 'Security price reactions around corporate spinoff announcements', *Journal of Financial Economics*, 12, 409–36.

Hong, H. and J. C. Stein (1999) 'A unified theory of underreaction, momentum trading, and overreaction in asset markets', *Journal of Finance*, 54, 2143–84.

Hong, H., W. Touros and R. Valkanov (2007) 'Do industries lead stock markets?' *Journal of Financial Economics*, 83, 367–96.

Huberman, G. and T. Regev (2001) 'Contagious speculation and a cure for cancer', *Journal of Finance*, 56, 387–96.

Hurvich, C. M. and C. L. Tsai (1989) 'Regression and time series model selection in small samples', *Biometrika*, 76, 297–307.

Jegadeesh, N. and S. Titman (1993) 'Returns to buying winners and selling losers: Implications for stock market efficiency', *Journal of Finance*, 48, 65–91.

Loughran, T. and B. McDonald (2011) 'When is a liability not a liability? Textual analysis, dictionaries, and 10-Ks', *Journal of Finance*, 66, 35–65.

Miles, J. and J. Rosenfeld (1983) 'The effect of voluntary spinoff announcements on shareholder wealth', *Journal of Finance*, 38, 1597–1606.

Moskowitz, T. J. and M. Grinblatt (1999) 'Do industries explain momentum?' *Journal of Finance*, 54, 1249–90.

Peng, L., W. Xiong and T. Bollerslev (2007) 'Investor attention and time-varying comovements', *European Financial Management*, 13, 394–422.

Reale M., and G. Tunnicliffe Wilson (2001) 'Identification of vector AR models with recursive structural errors using conditional independence graphs', *Statistical Methods and Applications*, 10, 49–65.

——(2002) 'The sampling properties of conditional independence graphs for structural vector autoregressions', *Biometrika*, 89, 457–61.

——(2008) 'The sampling properties of conditional independence graphs for structural vector autoregressions', *Journal of Time Series Analysis*, 29, 802–10.

Reinsel, G. C. (1993) Elements of Multivariate Time Series. (New York: Springer-Verlag).

Rosenfeld, J. (1984) 'Additional evidence on the relation between divestiture announcements and shareholder wealth', *Journal of Finance*, 39, 1437–48.

Rozin, P. and E. Royzman (2001) 'Negativity bias, negativity dominance, and contagion', *Personality and Social Psychology Review*, 5, 296–320.

Schipper, K. and A. Smith (1983) 'Effects of recontracting on shareholder wealth: The case of voluntary spinoffs', *Journal of Financial Economics*, 12, 437–67.

Schwarz, G. (1978) 'Estimating the dimension of a model', *The Annals of Statistics*, 6, 461–4.

Scott, M. (2004) *WordSmith Tools Version 4* (Oxford: Oxford University).

Shoemaker, P. and S. Reese (1996) *Mediating the Message: Theories of Influence on Mass Media Content* (New York: Longman).

Stone, P. J., D. C. Dunphy, M. S. Smith and D. M. Ogilvie (1966) *The General Inquirer: A Computer Approach to Content Analysis* (Cambridge: MIT Press).

Swanson, N. R. and C. W. J. Granger (1997) 'Impulse response functions based on a causal approach to residual orthogonalization in vector autoregressions', *Journal of the American Statistical Association*, 92, 357–67.

Tetlock, P. C. (2007) 'Giving content to investor sentiment: The role of media in the stock market', *Journal of Finance*, 62, 1139–68.

Tetlock, P. C., M. Saar-Tsechansky and S. Mackassy (2008) 'More than words: Quantifying language to measure firms' fundamentals', *Journal of Finance*, 63, 1437–67.

Tiao, G. C. and R. S. Tsay (1989) 'Model specification in multivariate time series', *Journal of the Royal Statistical Society*, Series B, 51, 157–213.

Veld, C. and Y. Veld-Merkoulova (2004) 'Do spin-offs really create value? The European case', *Journal of Banking and Finance*, 28, 1111–35.

——(2009) 'Value creation through spin-offs: A review of the empirical evidence', *International Journal of Management Reviews*, 11, 407–20.

2
The Effects of Derivatives Trading on Stock Market Volatility and Market Efficiency: Some Evidence from European Markets

Giovanni Liccardo

2.1 Introduction

The impact of derivative trading on the volatility of the underlying assets is an issue that has long interested academics, regulators and investors. In particular, media and policy makers are concerned about how futures and options may affect the underlying spot market. In fact, it is believed that derivatives' trading attracts speculators who can destabilize spot prices, allowing them to use the leverage and requiring only a margin of the entire position held. It has been demonstrated that most of the speculative activity has shifted from the cash market to the derivatives market that, for the reasons given above, provides more facilities for speculation. These concerns support the idea that greater regulation of the derivatives market is needed. However, first of all it is important to understand if there is a causal link between the introduction of derivative instruments and the volatility of the underlying stock market.

The debate in literature on this subject has not led to unequivocal conclusions and it is open nowadays. There are two main arguments related to the topic. On the one hand are those who claim that the introduction of derivatives trading increases the volatility of the underlying asset price. The assumption is that derivative markets attract uninformed traders that may destabilize the spot market through the use of leverage. On the other hand are those who argue that the volatility of stock returns decreases following the introduction of trading in futures and options. This school of thought assigns to derivatives a role in transmitting information into the markets: according to this idea derivatives would help the speed at which prices adjust toward equilibrium, hence leading to a greater stability (or, translated, to a reduced volatility) of equity markets. Some other studies highlight the lack of correlation.

The above-mentioned debate is also addressed to the empirical evidence. Even here opinions are fragmented. In conclusion, therefore, obvious and consistent considerations cannot be drawn.

The aim of this work is to examine the causal link between derivatives trading and the volatility of the spot market. Many studies on spot market volatility have been carried out by different academicians. As mentioned earlier they give controversial results about the effect of derivatives listing on the underlying spot market. It is argued that the different results depend on the country examined or the methodology applied in the study. Most of them are focused on the USA market or some other single countries, but very few studies have been conducted comparing several countries. To my best knowledge this is the first study that has been conducted taking into account the major European markets together. In particular, the work will focus on the following markets of the Euro-zone: France, Germany, Holland, Italy, Spain and the United Kingdom. In analysing the relationship between the introduction of derivatives trading and underlying assets volatility, the present chapter attempts to contribute to the existing literature in the following manner. First, the present study examines the impact of derivatives listing on the volatility of the main European stock markets, whereas most of the past studies focused on single countries. This will also allow determining which stock market is more efficient and stable than others. Secondly, employing the GARCH technique to capture the volatility explains not only if the introduction of derivatives determines an impact on volatility but also if there is a change in the structure of volatility before and after the listing of futures and options contracts. The contribution from this research is important for regulators, stock exchange officials and market participants.

The chapter is organized as follows. Section 2 presents the theoretical framework concerning the impact of futures trading and summarizes the main results of the previous empirical studies. Section 3 describes data, the econometric model and the methodology used in the analysis. Section 4 discusses the empirical findings and the final section provides conclusions and further developments for future research in this area.

2.2 Literature review

The impact of derivatives trading on underlying assets is a debate that has long interested both theoretical and empirical studies. The main question is whether the introduction of derivatives trading affects or does not affect the underlying spot markets. Several theoretical arguments have been used to explain the consequences of the futures introduction in the spot market. Overall, two opposing arguments prevail in the existing literature. Some researchers argue that derivatives trading increases stock market volatility due to speculation use. In particular, Cox (1976) found that uninformed speculators participating in the derivatives markets destabilize the spot market prices; while Hellwig (1980) argues that futures markets tend to destabilize the cash markets because of their higher degree of leverage. Cagan (1981) and Stein (1987) also confirm that derivatives' markets attract uninformed traders because of low transaction costs and a higher degree of leverage. This destabilizing role of derivatives recalls a greater need for stronger regulations in order to avoid negative effects. On the other hand, other researchers support the idea that derivative instruments play an important role in reducing price volatility and hence in stabilizing markets, due to price discovery and risk sharing (Danthine, 1978; Schwarz and Laatsch, 1991). Ross (1976), among others, claimed that option contracts help in price discovery, improve the market efficiency and reduce asymmetry information of the cash market. So, derivatives markets may decrease the level of volatility of underlying assets because they provide an improvement in the way of transmitting information. Moreover, derivative contracts provide the possibility of hedging risky investments and this leads to greater demand that is an increase in the trading volume in the spot market and thus a decrease in the volatility (Damodaran and Subrahmanyam, 1992).

The same debate is also opened in empirical research. Bessembinder and Seguin (1992) analyse the relationship between the stock index futures market and the relative S&P500 index volatility demonstrating a decrease in the volatility of the equity index due to derivative trading. In a study on the Italian stock market, Bologna and Cavallo (2002) concluded that the introduction of the stock index futures trading is associated with a decrease in the volatility of the underlying index. The same conclusion was reached by Pilar and Rafael (2002) in their study concerning the Spanish stock market and by A. Kasman (2008) and S. Kasman (2008) in their analysis of the Turkish stock market. On the other side, many other studies suggest that derivative contracts are responsible for the increased volatility of the underlying spot markets. Figlewski (1981) examined the impact of futures trading in the Government National Mortgage Association and concluded that the introduction of futures markets leads to an increase in the volatility of the underlying asset. Among others, Gulen and Mayhew (2000) based on 25 countries found that derivatives' listing is associated with an increase in volatility in the USA and Japan indexes, but no significant change in volatility for the others. Antoniou and Holmes (1995), in their study of UK market found that the introduction of stock index futures caused an increase in spot market volatility in the short run while there was no significant change in volatility in the long run. Finally, some other studies found no significant changes in the volatility of the spot market, concluding that the introduction of derivatives does not destabilize the underlying market (Santoni, 1987; Edwards, 1988).

As highlighted so far, the results regarding the effect of the introduction of derivatives' trading on spot market volatility are mixed and controversial. The question about the relationship between trading on derivatives and spot market volatility is far from being clear. The differences may depend on the nature of stock markets, the time period and the methodology employed as well as the economic conditions.

2.3 Data and methodology

In the present analysis the daily closing prices of the main European equity indexes are used. A list of the European countries and their indexes is given in Table 2.1.

The period analysed covers from the first day of availability of each index data to September 2011.

Futures on individual stock market indexes were introduced between 1988 and 1994. All data were provided by Thomson-Financial (Datastream) and daily returns have been computed using the following expression:

$$R_t = Log(p_t / p_{t-1}) \tag{2.1}$$

That is the logarithmic price changes, p_t being the closing price of the relative index on day t.

Several stock indexes were introduced in order to support the futures contracts on their introductions. Hence, in order to compare pre- and post-derivatives periods, proxies computed by Thomson-Financial (Datastream) for some stock indexes had to be used. In particular, for the Italian market data the FTSE MIB cannot be used as the index has been introduced specifically to support stock index futures contracts. So, given the lack of data regarding the pre-derivative period, it was preferred to use the FTSE Historycal MIB computed by Thomson-Financial (DataStream). The high correlation between the two indices ensures that the results will not be affected significantly by this approximation.

Table 2.1 List of equity indexes and data period

Country	Underlying index	Data period	Introduction date
France	CAC 40	09 July 1987 – 21 September 2011	03 October 1988
Germany	DAX	31 December 1964 – 21 September 2011	23 November 1990
Italy	FTSE MIB	03 January 1975 – 21 September 2011	28 November 1994
Netherlands	AEX	03 January 1983 – 21 September 2011	26 October 1988
Spain	IBEX 35	05 January 1987 – 21 September 2011	20 April 1992
United Kingdom	FTSE 250	31 December 1985 – 21 September 2011	25 February 1994

In order to understand which methodology best fits with our data, preliminary analysis of historical series was done (Table 2.2).

Although descriptive statistics does not contribute much to the purposes of this study, they provide a useful framework about the characteristics of the series distribution. From the values reported, it can be noted that all the historical returns do not show a normal distribution. All the series present excess kurtosis (namely, leptokurtic distribution) which seems to mitigate in the post-derivatives period. Similar results are also given by the skewness statistics, which measures the asymmetry of the distribution around its mean. All series are characterized by a negative skewness in both pre- and post-derivative period although in many cases it seems to converge towards zero after the derivative trading introduction. Jarque-Bera statistic confirms that we must reject the hypothesis of normality at a significance level of 1 per cent. Concluding, the statistical properties of the stock indexes returns have changed since the introduction of derivatives. After this date there has been a greater flattening with a thickening of the tails. This could contribute to the structure of volatility and its persistence level. This evidence confirms econometric GARCH techniques to be one of the best-performer models. The reasons why the GARCH model is often used in financial literature are different: first, it does not require the assumption that the error variance is homoskedastic. In fact, in financial time series it is more likely that the variance is not constant over time and therefore it makes more sense to use a model that does not assume homoskedasticity of variance a priori. Second, the model is consistent with the volatility clustering often seen in financial returns data, where the current volatility tends to be positively correlated with the level assumed in the immediately preceding periods. That is, periods of high (low) volatility tend to be followed by periods of high (low) volatility. Finally, as discussed above, the GARCH model proves to be very parsimonious in financial time series that show a leptokurtic distribution, as in our case. The GARCH (p,q) model developed by Bollerslev (1986) will be used to capture the variation in volatility after the derivatives markets have been introduced in France, Germany, Italy, Netherlands, Spain and the United Kingdom. The following equations represent the most commonly used implementation of the Bollerslev model:

$$y_t = \beta X_t + \varepsilon_t \tag{2.2}$$

$$\varepsilon_t \big| \Phi_{t-1} \sim \mathrm{N}(0,\mathrm{h_t}) \tag{2.3}$$

$$h_t = \alpha_0 + \sum_{i=1}^{p} \alpha_i \varepsilon_{t-i}^2 + \sum_{j=1}^{q} \beta_j h_{t-j} \tag{2.4}$$

Given the restrictions $\alpha_0 > 0$; $\beta_j \geq 0$. Equation (2.3) is the conditional mean equation and Equation (2.4) is the conditional variance equation.

Table 2.2 Descriptive statistics pre- and post-derivatives

	France-CAC		Germany-DAX		Italy-FTSE MIB		Netherlands-AEX		Spain-IBEX 35		UK-FTSE 250	
	Pre	**Post**	**Pre**	**Post**	**Pre**	**Post**	**Pre**	**Post**	**Pre**	**Post**	**Pre**	**Post**
Mean	0.00	0.00	0.00	0.00	0.00	0.00	0.00	0.00	0,00	0.00	0.00	0.00
Median	0.00	0.00	0.00	0.00	0.00	0.00	0.00	0.00	0.00	0.00	0.00	0.00
Mode	0.00	0.00	0.00	0.00	0.00	0.00	0.00	0.00	0.00	0.00	0.00	0.00
St. Dev.	0.02	0.01	0,018	0.01	0.01	0.01	0.01	0.01	0.01	0.01	0.01	0.01
Skewness	−1.01	−0.07	−0.48	−0.17	−0,43	−0.51	−0.65	−0.19	−0.65	−0.02	−1.71	−0.38
Kurtosis	9.06	5,13	12.34	5.33	6.34	4.65	14.36	7.02	11.23	5.71	23.91	8.11
Minimum	−0.10	−0.09	−0.14	−0.10	−0.10	−0.10	−0.13	−0.10	−0.09	−0.10	−0.11	−0.38
Maximum	0.08	0,11	0.09	0.11	0.09	0.08	0.11	0.10	0.09	0.13	0.08	0.08
Jarque-Bera	1114.99	6551.51	43027.65	6438.50	8829.29	4130,201	13037.01	12288.69	7279.98	6865.13	39788.8	5102.72
Obs.	321	5993	6755	5434	5191	4388	1516	5976	1379	5068	2127	4584

Log likelihood ratio tests have been implemented to choose as the specific model the GARCH (1,1). By many, the GARCH (1,1) model specification is considered to be the most parsimonious representation of conditional variance, being able to better describe the statistical properties for most financial time series. The specification of the GARCH (1,1) model is:

$$h_t = \alpha_0 + \alpha_1 \varepsilon_{t-1}^2 + \alpha_2 h_{t-1} \tag{2.5}$$

Where ε_{t-1}^2 is the one-lag of the squared residual from the mean equation (the ARCH term) and h_{t-1} is the last period's forecast variance (the GARCH term).

In order to examine the effect of the introduction of derivatives on the volatility a dummy variable has been included in the conditional variance equation that indicates the introduction of derivatives. This dummy variable assumes value 1 after the introduction of derivative contracts and value 0 before this date. The significance of the dummy variable introduced in the model will provide evidence about the impact of the introduction of derivative markets on the volatility of the underlying stock market. In addition, one necessary step concerns removing market-world influences on the volatility of the underlying indexes. Therefore, the daily returns of the world equity index (MSCI World Index) have been included in the mean equation to isolate the effect on stock index volatility. Again, since the study is interested in isolating only the impact arising from the introduction of derivatives markets, the mean equation will also consider the *day of the week* effect. The regression estimated will assume the following expression:

$$R_t = \beta_0 + \beta_1 MSCI_t + \sum_{j=2}^{5} \beta_j DAY_J + \varepsilon_t \tag{2.6}$$

$$\varepsilon_t \middle| \Phi_{t-1} \sim \mathrm{N}(0, \mathrm{h_t}) \tag{2.7}$$

$$h_t = \alpha_0 + \alpha_1 \varepsilon_{t-1}^2 + \alpha_2 h_{t-1} + \gamma DF \tag{2.8}$$

where R_t is the daily change in log prices for each equity index, $MSCI_t$ is the daily change in log prices for the World Equity Index, DAY_J is a dummy variable that identifies the day of the week from Tuesday to Friday and DF is a dummy variable with value 0 for the pre-derivatives period and 1 for the post-derivative period.

One of the main limits of the GARCH model is that it imposes a non-negativity restriction on the parameters, so they must be positive. In this way, the model is not able to take into account the asymmetric effects that appear in the financial series. In fact, Engle and Ng (1993) observed that a negative shock in returns causes more volatility than a positive shock of the same magnitude; so the GARCH model under-predicts the amount of volatility following bad news and over-predicts the amount of volatility following good news. To overcome these weaknesses, the EGARCH model developed by Nelson (1991) has also been used. Since the conclusions do not differ, in the interests of brevity the results of the EGARCH model employed have not been reported. They are available on request from the author.

The regressions will be performed for every single stock market index. In order to analyse the effect of index futures trading on stock market volatility, two approaches will be used. The first approach will consist in applying the GARCH model to the whole period of analysis. This will allow the determining of the effect of derivative trading on the volatility of the underlying spot market. The second approach will compare return index volatility before and after the introduction of futures trading. The whole samples will be divided into two periods of analysis: pre-derivative period and post-derivative period. This will allow figuring out the changing in the structure of volatility after the derivatives markets are introduced.

2.4 Results

In this study a GARCH model is employed in order to examine if derivatives listing impact on returns volatility in the underlying spot market index. So that the GARCH model can be used, the time series data do not have to show a trend that means they have to be stationary in mean. A unit root test has been tested by Augmented Dickey Fuller and Phillips–Perron on the single index returns. As shown in Table 2.3, all the return distributions are stationary at level for the period considered. The results of the GARCH model for the whole sample are as follows.

Table 2.4 reports the results of the mean and variance equation for the whole period of the samples considered.

As it arises from the coefficient values, the stock indexes, on average, have statistically significant higher returns on Friday, except for Netherlands. This result is consistent with the evidence from other markets studied in previous

Table 2.3 Test for unit root in level

	France-CAC	Germany-DAX	Italy-FTSE MIB	Netherlands-AEX	Spain-IBEX 35	UK-FTSE 250
ADF	−49.04	−79.65	−45.46	−87.09	−76.02	−72.68
PP	−79.75	−107.78	−82.52	87.09	−75.92	−74.23

Notes: The critical value for unit root test are: −3,96 and −3,41 respectively for 1% and 5% level. The above series imply stationarity at 1% level. In testing the equation, trend and intercept have been included.

ADF = Augmented Dickey Fuller PP = Phillips–Perron

Table 2.4 Estimates of the GARCH

		France-CAC	Germany-DAX	Italy-FTSE MIB	Netherlands-AEX	Spain-IBEX 35	UK-FTSE 250
Constant	$\beta 0$	−0.00	−7.92E-05	−0.00	0.00	0.00	−0.00
		(0.00)	(0.00)	(0.00)	(0.00)	(0.00)	(0.00)
MSCI Index	$\beta 1$	1.12	0.72	0.56	0.97	0.96	0.63
		(0.01)	(0.01)	(0.01)	(0.01)	(0.01)	(0.01)
Tuesday	$\beta 2$	0.00	0.00	5.48E-05	−0.00	−0.00	0.00
		(0.00)	(0.00)	(0.00)	(0.00)	(0.00)	(0.00)
Wednesday	$\beta 3$	0.00	0.00	0.00	−0.00	−0.00	0.00
		(0.00)	(0.00)	(0.00)	(0.00)	(0,00)	(0.00)
Thursday	$\beta 4$	0.00	0.00	0.00	−0.00	−9.95E-05	0.00
		(0.00)	(0.00)	(0.00)	(0.00)	(0.00)	(0.00)
Friday	$\beta 5$	0.00	0.00	0.00	−0.00	3.35E-05	0.00
		(0.00)	(0.00)	(0.00)	(0.00)	(0,00)	(0.00)
Constant	$\alpha 0$	4.64E-06	2.09E-06	2.71E-06	4.62E-06	1.71E-06	2.46E-06
		(1.08E-06)	(1.46E-07)	(2.12E-07)	(3.83E-07)	(2.16E-07)	(2.61E-07)
ARCH	$\alpha 1$	0.11*	0.07*	0.08*	0.11*	0.10*	0.12*
		(−0,01)	(0.00)	(0.00)	−0.01	(0.00)	(0.00)
GARCH	$\alpha 2$	0.88*	0.91*	0.91*	0.87*	0.89*	0.85*
		−0,01	(0.00)	(0.00)	−0.01	(0.00)	(0.00)
DummyF	γ	−2.94E-06**	−6.49E-07*	−1.77E-06*	−3.06E-06*	−4.23E-07**	−2.35E-07
		(1.02E-06)	(9.85E-08)	(1.66E-07)	(2.96E-07)	1.67E-07	(1.97E-07)

Notes: Significance levels: * = 1%, ** = 5%, *** = 10%. Standard errors are presented in brackets.

works. Significance is also indicated by the coefficient MSCI World indicating that the world stock markets have an important effect on the European markets, especially on the French, Netherlands and Spanish markets. The coefficients α_1 and α_2 are statistically significant and they show the dependence of volatility on its past behaviour. The estimated coefficients γ of the dummy variable *DF* are negative and statistically significant for all stock indexes except the FTSE 250 index, supporting the hypothesis that the introduction of stock index futures in the main European markets has produced a decrease in the level of conditional volatility of the underlying markets. These evidences are in line with those of other academic studies.

Table 2.5 contains the GARCH estimates for the two periods (pre- and post-derivatives).

The first evidence in comparing results for before and after the listing of futures trading is that the introduction of derivatives has led to a change in the structure of volatility. According to Antoniou and Holmes (1995) α_1 is considered to be a coefficient of reactivity: the higher the value of the coefficient the greater will be the readiness of volatility to react to the market

Table 2.5 Estimates of GARCH before and after the introduction of derivatives

	France-CAC		Germany-DAX		Italy-FTSE MIB	
	Pre	Post	Pre	Post	Pre	Post
Const. $\alpha0$	5.93E-06	1.50E-06	1.50E-06	1.16E-06	4.14E-06	7.47E-07
	(3.10E-06)	(2.18E-07)	(2.58E-07)	(1.71E-07)	(4.09E-07)	(1.03E-07)
ARCH $\alpha1$	0.156*	0.10*	0.10*	0.09*	0.07*	0.09*
	(0.04)	(0.01)	(0.00)	(0.01)	(0.00)	(0.01)
GARCH $\alpha2$	0.82*	0.88*	0.89*	0.90*	0.90*	0.91*
	(0.05)	(0.01)	(0.01)	(0.01)	(0.01)	(0.01)
$\alpha1+\alpha2$	0.97	0.99	0.99	0.99	0.97	1.00
$\alpha0/1-\alpha1-\alpha2$	0.00	0.00	0.00	0.00	0.00	0.00
	Netherlands-AEX		**Spain-IBEX 35**		**UK-FTSE 250**	
	Pre	Post	Pre	Post	Pre	Post
Const. $\alpha0$	9.25E-06	1.35E-06	5.38E-06	1.09E-06	5.89E-06	1.34E-06
	(1.53E-06)	(1.56E-07)	(8.81E-07)	(1.67E-07)	(7.35E-07)	(1.87E-07)
ARCH $\alpha1$	0.09*	0.11*	0.21*	0.09*	0.18*	0.09*
	(0.01)	(0.01)	(0.01)	(0.01)	(0.01)	(0.01)
GARCH $\alpha2$	0.83*	0.87*	0.76*	0.90*	0.74*	0.89*
	(0.02)	(0.01)	(0.02)	(0.01)	(0.02)	(0.01)
$\alpha1+\alpha2$	0.92	0.99	0.97	0.99	0.92	0.98
$\alpha0/1-\alpha1-\alpha2$	0.00	0.00	0.00	0.00	0.00	0.00

Notes: Significance levels: * = 1%. Standard errors are presented in parentheses.
$\alpha0/1-\alpha1-\alpha2$ is unconditional variance.

movements, defined as 'news'; while α_2 represents a coefficient of persistence: a high value of this coefficient indicates that the effect of a positive or negative shock on conditional variance will take a long time to die out, thereby measuring the persistence on volatility of the 'old news'. Derivatives' supporters argue that the introduction of equity index derivatives increases the efficiency of markets. It is therefore expected that in the period after the derivatives listing α_1 shows higher values as the news should be reflected in prices more quickly thanks to derivatives. On the other hand, a reduction of α_2 is also expected due to the fact that the speed at which new information is spread on the markets would substantially reduce the importance of old news.

Looking at the results in Table 2.5, it can be noted that from the pre-derivatives to post-derivatives period the values α_1 have gone significantly down while α_2 are significantly up. In addition, it can be observed that all the variable coefficients in the variance equation are significant at 1 per cent. It was expected that the impact of recent incoming news would have increased with the introduction of stock index futures. But this is rejected by the decrease of α_1 that suggests a reduction in the speed at which information is incorporated into stock prices. On the other side, α_2 has gone up in the post-derivative period. So the uncertainty about previous news has grown due to the decrease of information flow. Therefore old news still plays an important role in determining the current volatility of the stock market. Another result that indicates a decrease in the market efficiency in the post-derivative period is the growing persistence of shocks from the pre-derivative to the post-derivative period, measured by $\alpha_1 + \alpha_2$, which value significantly increased in every single stock market. Finally, the unconditional variance also indicates higher market volatility after stock index futures introduction for some of the European Stock Exchanges. Since α_1 is defined as the rate of speed at which the actual information is reflected in market price, a decrease of α_1 means increase in market frictions. Therefore, α_1 can be perceived as a direct measure of the market operation efficiency. According to this efficiency measure, the UK stock market turns out to be the most efficient European market, followed by the French one.

Again from Table 2.5 it can be observed that the value of α_1 for all the markets analysed has decreased in the post-derivative period. Hence, there is a decrease in the market efficiency after the introduction of index futures. Further, it can be seen from Table 2.5 that the decrease in efficiency is substantially significant at a confidence level of 99 per cent. Evidence shows that the volatility of index returns decreases as operation efficiency of a market gets worse.

2.5 Conclusion

The impact of derivatives trading on the volatility of underlying assets is a debate that has long interested both theoretical and empirical studies. One school of thought asserts that futures trading increases stock market volatility because of their higher degree of leverage. On the other side, supporters claim that derivatives markets enhance market efficiency through price discovery and risk transferring.

The present study, using the GARCH model, examines whether the introduction of derivatives trading does affect or not the underlying spot assets in the main European markets. The results show that after the introduction of derivatives markets there has been a decrease in volatility of the spot markets and hence, it has stabilizing effects. To enforce our findings the results have been adjusted for exposition to other market factors (represented by the World Stock Market Index) which may impact on market volatility. These findings however have to be taken with caution. They support the idea that the reduction in volatility experienced by the major European Stock Exchange is not attributable to external market factors, but it does not exclude the possibility that it could be attributed to some other internal factor.

Finally, the introduction of derivatives is also associated with a reduction in efficiency due to the lower rate at which prices move toward equilibrium. These results should be important for market regulators and supervisors. A suitable market policy should make efforts to improve market efficiency, reducing market frictions, but still preserving market stabilization.

References

Antoniou, A. and P. Holmes (1995) 'Futures trading, information and spot price volatility: Evidence for the FTSE-100 stock index futures contract using GARCH', *Journal of Banking and Finance*, 19, 117–29.

Bessembinder, H. and P. J. Seguin (1992) 'Futures-trading activity and stock price volatility', *Journal of Finance*, 47, 2015–34.

Bollerslev, T. (1986) 'Generalised autoregressive conditional heteroschedasticity', *Journal of Econometrics*, 33, 307–27.

Bologna, P. and L. Cavallo (2002) 'Does the introduction of stock index futures effectively reduce stock market volatility? Is the "futures effect" immediate? Evidence from the Italian stock exchange using GARCH', *Applied Financial Economics*, 12, 183–92.

Cagan, P. (1981) 'Financial futures markets: Is more regulation needed?' *Journal of Futures Markets*, 1, 169–90.

Cox, C. C. (1976) 'Futures trading and market information', *Journal of Political Economy*, 84, 1215–37.

Damodaran, A. and M. G. Subrahmanyam (1992) 'The effects of derivative securities on the markets for the underlying assets in the United States: A Survey', *Financial Markets, Institutions and Instruments*, 1, 1–22.

Danthine, J. (1978) 'Information, futures prices and stabilizing speculation', *Journal of Economic Theory*, 17, 79–98.

Edwards, F. R. (1988) 'Does futures trading increase stock market volatility?' *Financial Analysts Journal*, 44, 63–9.

Engle, R. and V. Ng (1993) 'Measuring and testing the impact of news on volatility', *Journal of Finance*, 48, 1749–78.
Figlewski, S. (1981) 'Futures trading and volatility in the GNMA market', *Journal of Finance*, 36, 445–56.
Gulen, H. and S. Mayhew (2000) 'Stock index futures trading and volatility in international equity markets', *Journal of Futures Markets*, 20, 661–85.
Hellwig, M. (1980) 'On the aggregation of information in competitive markets', *Journal of Economic Theory*, 22, 477–98.
Kasman, A. and S. Kasman (2008) 'The impact of futures trading on volatility of the underlying asset in the Turkish stock market', *Physica A*, 387, 2837–45.
Nelson, D. B. (1991) 'Conditional heteroskedasticity in asset returns', *Econometrica*, 59, 347–70.
Pilar, C. and S. Rafael (2002) 'Does derivatives trading destabilize the underlying assets? Evidence from the Spanish stock market', *Applied Economics Letters*, 9, 107–10.
Ross, S. (1976) 'Options and efficiency', *Quarterly Journal of Economics*, 90, 75–89.
Santoni, G. J. (1987) 'Has programmed trading made stock price more volatile?' *Federal Reserve Bank of St. Louis Review*, 69, 8–29.
Schwarz, T. and F. Laatsch (1991) 'Price discovery and risk transfer in stock index cash and futures markets', *Journal of Futures Markets*, 11, 669–83.
Stein, J. C. (1987) 'Information externalities and welfare-reducing speculation', *Journal of Political Economy*, 95, 1123–45.

3
How Much Globalization Is There in the World Stock Markets and Where Is It?

Gianni Nicolini and Ekaterina Dorodnykh

3.1 Introduction

The effects of globalization in the world economy, and its role within financial markets, were widely analysed in the literature (Shahrokhi, 1998; Aggarwal, 1999; Kearney and Poti, 2006; Eun and Lee, 2010; Aggarwal et al., 2010). The pros and cons of international economic and financial framework, featured by common trends and higher similarities, were considered from different perspectives. Moreover, different concepts and definitions of globalization were provided as well. In the literature, the hypothesis that globalization is growing within world economies is commonly adopted by many scholars, however, there are only a few papers that tried to analyse this phenomenon in a comprehensive manner. Thus, if the presence of globalization in financial markets could be considered as commonplace, the need to evaluate the relevance and the developing path of this phenomenon is quite clear. In this paper, the authors try to fill this gap, providing both (1) a measure of globalization within financial markets around the world in order to understand the main trends, and (2) an analysis of single geographical areas in order to understand if globalization is developing as a homogeneous phenomenon or if, on the contrary, globalization effects are stronger in some stock markets than in others.

Data from 53 stock markets around the world are analysed by a correlation analysis. If correlation is usually considered as a basic statistical tool, it was chosen in order to minimize the hypothesis of the model, enhancing the strength of results. In fact, as the aim of the chapter is not related to an explanation of globalization, but to an evaluation of the tendency of different stock markets to float in a common sense, a correlation analysis is compliant with this goal. Returns of stock indexes have been collected on a weekly basis from 1995 to 2010. Correlation matrices were estimated and summarized annually (using average indexes) in order to highlight the tendency of globalization to affect both local and global single market correlations.

The chapter is organized as follows. A review of the literature on globalization and financial market integration is provided in order to analyse these concepts and to highlight the results from previous studies. A description of the data and an explanation of the methodology will follow, while results of the analysis will be provided and discussed in the result section. In the final section, some conclusions and remarks are provided.

3.2 Literature review

The meaning of globalization was widely analysed in the literature from both economic and non-economic perspectives. Due to the huge interest in this topic and the different possible manners to analyse it, there is the need to provide a clear definition of this phenomenon and a specific perspective of the analysis. A wide economic definition of globalization is provided by Bhagwati (2004). The author defines globalization as a process of integration of national economies into an international economy through trade, foreign direct investments, capital flows, migration and the spread of technology. The different aspects taken into account highlight how much globalization is a complex phenomenon and suggest the need to focus on a specific topic. In this chapter the authors analyse the financial aspects of globalization and refer to the integration of stock exchange markets. However, as Carrieri et al. (2007) pointed out, globalization concerns both economic and financial aspects and it cannot be ignored that equity market integration is a part of a bigger reform effort that includes the financial sector and the economy as well as political processes. For instance, Friedman and Shachmurove (2005) provide evidence of further integration of European stock markets after the introduction of the Euro. Recently Aggarwal et al. (2010) showed that equity market integration is driven by market forces but constrained by regulatory barriers.

In order to analyse the financial aspect of globalization in terms of stock exchange integration a clear definition is useful. Starting from definition, Trichet (2005) on behalf of the ECB announced that stock market integration is a market condition where all potential market participants with the same relevant characteristics face a single set of rules when dealing with financial instruments or services, have equal access to financial instruments or services, and are treated equally when they are active in the market. If this definition could be seen from a global financial consumer perspective, a more country-specific definition can be proposed as well. Pieper and Vogel (1997), talking about integrated markets, refer to a status of markets where investors can buy and sell equities that are issued within the same country or across country borders without restriction and as a result identical securities are issued and traded at the same price across markets (after adjustment for foreign exchange rates). Hence, the authors highlight the relevance of cross-country trading and recall macroeconomic principle as the 'law of one price'. Another similar definition of stock market integration was proposed by Bekaert and Harvey (2003). For these authors, in integrated equity markets, domestic investors are able to invest in foreign assets and foreign investors in domestic assets; hence, assets with identical risks show the same expected return, regardless of trading location. This perspective is coherent with the concepts of integration from Bhalla and Shetty (2006). They argue that when two or more markets are integrated, events in one market will have its impact felt by the other ones. For these authors integration should be related and measured by the effectiveness of information in the price, changing more than the presence of trading barriers within different exchanges.

The great interest by the literature on financial market integration and globalization is justified by the positive effects that integrated financial markets could provide. Many authors studied these effects related both to economic and financial topics. For example, Prasad et al. (2003) highlight that international financial integration can promote growth in developing countries and also helps countries to reduce macroeconomic volatility, while Beck et al. (2000) support the view that better functioning financial intermediaries improve resource allocation and accelerate total factor productivity growth with positive repercussion for long-run economic growth. Furthermore, the results of Bagella et al. (2003) suggest that economic integration and monetary unions by reducing export portfolio risk imported from neighbouring partners may have significant effects on growth. Armanious (2005) highlights how an increasing globalization of the world economy should obviously have an impact on the behaviour of national stock markets, which in turn will push the stock exchanges to merge together in order to create economic growth. In a more financial perspective Erdogan (2009) provided evidences that, due to the integration of stock markets, the firms' cost of capital decreases, helping them to solve capital raising problems. Finally, according to Hasan et al. (2010) stock exchange industry is as a key component of financial markets, where the global exchange integration activities may well promote the efficiency of cross-border capital flows and increased governance standards, and thus have the potential to create value for their shareholders.

If common financial market integration and, in particular, stock market integration seems to be quite desirable, the need to have some parameters in order to measure these phenomena are required as well. Economic integration was widely analysed by the literature and many globalization measures have been proposed, but less interest has been devoted to financial and stock market integration. From an economic perspective Leamer (1988) and Agénor (2003) propose to use the presence of tariff barriers as a degree of economic integration within countries, while Moser et al. (2004) and Quinn and Toyoda (2008) use the presence of capital account restriction or, in the contrary, capital account liberalization rules as parameters of financial globalization. Besides, Campero (2001) and Lawrence and Ishikawa (2005) evaluate economic globalization by the ratio of inward FDI stock (foreign direct investments) over GDP. Even the trade openness, measured as the sum of imports and exports (excluding oil related transactions) over GDP, has been analysed as an integration measure (Lane and Milesi-Ferretti, 2003; Walti, 2005 and Arribas et al., 2006).

Analysing financial integration from the issuer's perspective in terms of stock market integration, Pagano et al. (2001) through the cross-listing of European companies, show that European and North American stock exchanges from 1986 to 1997 provide a growing trend to cross-list or foreign-listing. Taking into account that cross-listing enhances the integration within markets, the ratio between the number of foreign listed firms and the domestic firms can be considered as a measure of stock market integration. Using the same parameter, Sarkissian and Schill (2004) found that about 20% of internationally listed stocks are listed in more than one foreign market, suggesting following connection between markets. Furthermore, many authors have investigated stock market integration from a traders' perspective, using correlations within market indexes as a parameter to evaluate the integration of financial markets. Longin and Solnik (1995) documented an increase in the correlation of stock returns from various developed markets over the 1960 to 1990 periods. Hassan and Naka (1996) reported that in co-integrated markets, price movements in one market immediately influence other markets: this result is consistent with efficient information sharing and free access to markets by domestic and foreign investors. The same correlation approach has been used by Karolyi and Stulz (2003). The authors provide evidences that correlations between equity markets are not constant over time, reacting to market changes. Using monthly data on the five largest stock markets from 1958 to 1996 Longin and Solnik (2000) found that correlation is not related to market volatility but to the market trend. The same authors found that correlation increases in bear markets, but not in bull markets.

From a geographic point of view, the recent study of Schindler and Voronkova (2010) provide that co-integration relationships are much stronger between national markets within one economic and geographic region that between national markets located in different regions. Hence, the authors' results suggest the possibility that integration could not be a homogenous path and highlight the role of geographic features.

The aim of this chapter is to provide some evidences on how much 'globalized' are financial markets by an analysis of stock markets around the world. Using a trend analysis of correlation of stock market indexes during 1995 to 2010, both the level and the trend of globalization in financial market are analysed. Moreover, the comparison of different geographical areas is done in order to highlight the homogeneous (or heterogeneous) path of this phenomenon.

3.3 Data and methodology

Our sample includes general price indexes of 53 national stock markets between 1995 and 2010. The data source is Datastream (Thomson Financial). The data is all in US dollars. Moreover, the chapter uses returns of 18 stock market exchanges involved in integration projects in order to investigate the relationships between M&A operations and the integration of stock market exchanges. The use of weekly data provides more than 800 observations for each index. Some indexes have fewer observations than others due to the fact that the index was introduced after 1995. The use of weekly data was done in order to remove daily noise from the data. From the time series of price indexes, continuously compounded returns for all the 53 stock indexes have been calculated as:

$$R_t = \ln P_t - \ln P_{t-1} \tag{3.1}$$

The list of stock market indexes and the geographic areas they belong to are reported in Table 3.1.

Table 3.1 Geographical distribution of stock market indexes

Geographical areas	Indexes
North America and Canada	S&P 500 (US), Nasdaq Composite (US), Nyse Composite (US), S&P/Tsx Composite (Can);
Latin America	Bovespa (Brazil), Merval (Argentina), Igbc (Colombia), Ipc (Mexico), Ipsa (Chile), Igbvl (Peru);
Oceania and Asia	Nzsx 30 (New Zealand), S&P/Asx 200 (Australia); Sse Composite (Shanghai), Szse Composite (Shenzhen), Hang Seng (Hong Kong), S&P Cnx Nifty 50 (National India), Bse Sensex 100 (Bombay), Jakarta Composite, Ta – 100 (Tel-Aviv), Nikkei 225 (Tokio), Ftse St (Singapore), Kospi (South Korea);
Africa and Middle East	Egx 30 (Egypt), Tasi (Saudi Arabia), Ftse/Jse Top 40 (Johannesburg);
Western Europe	Euronext 100, Bel 20 (Brussels), Cac 40 (Paris), Aex (Amsterdam), Psi-20 (Lisbon), Dax (Frankfurt), Atx (Vienna), Smi (Swiss), Ftse Mib (Milan), Ftse 100 (London), Oseq 20 (Ireland), Luxx (Luxembourg), Athex Composite (Athens), Ibex 35 (Spain), Bcn Global 100 (Barcelona), Igbm (Madrid), Igbv (Valencia), Bilbao 2000;
Northern Europe	Omxn 40, Omx Stockholm 30, Omxh25 (Helsinki), Omx Copenhagen 20, Obx (Oslo);
Eastern Europe	Px (Czech Republic), Wig 20 (Poland), Bet (Romania), Rts (Moscow), Bux (Hungary).

The 53 indexes represent most of the stock exchanges in the world. All the following geographic areas are represented: Europe, North America, Latin America, Africa and Middle East, Asia-Pacific and Oceania. Full descriptive statistics for data (number of observations, minimum and maximum values, standard deviation, skewness, kurtosis and Jarque-Bera tests) are reported in the Appendix.

The data shows that the NYSE Composite Index (US market) and the OBX Index (Norway) are respectively the indexes with the lowest and highest standard deviation. All indexes show a negative skewness, suggesting the lack of data symmetry and indicating that left-tail is longer and the mass of distribution is concentrated on the right. OMX Copenhagen 20 (Denmark) demonstrate especially negative skewness. Significantly positive kurtosis is shown by all indexes, with a clear 'fat-tails' effect. This means that there is a non-normal and 'peaked' distribution of index returns, as Jarque-Bera test confirms.

The analysis of the data started from a correlation analysis. The correlation coefficient is a practice usual measurement of stock market co-movements of stock returns in a given time period, and is widely exploited by the literature (Longin and Solnik, 1995; Hassan and Naka, 1996; Longin and Solnik, 2001; Karolyi and Stulz, 2003; Walti, 2005; Schindler and Voronkova, 2010). According to the Pearson product-moment correlation coefficient (the 'Pearson's correlation'), the correlation index has been calculated by dividing the covariance of two index returns by the product of their standard deviations:

$$\rho_{X,Y} = corr\,(X,Y) = \frac{cov\,(X,Y)}{\sigma_X * \sigma_Y} = \frac{E\,[(X-\mu_X)\,(Y-\mu_Y)]}{\sigma_X * \sigma_Y} \tag{3.2}$$

where E is the expected value operator, *cov* means covariance and *corr* is a widely used alternative notation for Pearson's correlation.

From time series of weekly index returns 17 correlation matrixes were estimated for the 1995 to 2010 period. The values of the average correlation for each year were used as a measure of integration within stock markets. Furthermore, the trend of correlation values was used in order to investigate the dynamic of integration and to estimate its speed over time.

The first hypothesis was formulated as follows:

Hypothesis 1: Positive gap between the domestic correlation and foreign correlation during the observed period can be interpreted as the presence of the globalization effect in a highly integrated geographical region.

The analysis of possible geographical features of integration is done by annual estimation of the average correlations of stock index returns within the same region (internal average correlation index) and the average correlation of these markets with the rest of the sample (external average correlation index). The distance between these data and its trend over time was used in order to highlight if integration in the international stock market is a homogeneous phenomenon or not. If results from hypothesis tests (T-test) for a region will show a domestic average correlation index close to its foreign one, the hypothesis that integration is following a homogeneous path will be supported. Otherwise, the presence of some set of markets that show a more correlated path compared to other markets have to be highlighted, and a heterogeneous path of stock market integration will arise. The lack of hypothesis in the correlation analysis avoids the risks of model manipulations, enhancing the strength of results.

The choice of the authors to employ this methodology is based on the fact that it fits well with the goal of the paper, that does not investigate the causes of integration but provides a measure of the phenomenon and highlights its trend over time.

3.4 Results

The results from the correlation analysis in the 1995 to 2010 periods are summarized in Table 3.2.

The means of the data from annual correlation matrices show an increasing trend. Hence, the hypothesis that globalization within financial markets has been growing over the last two decades is supported by empirical evidence. The trend is positive, and the data from 2005 suggests that integration within financial markets is growing faster than before. The effect of the Asian financial crisis that occurred from 1997 to 1998 and the global financial crisis that started in 2007 on the world financial markets can explain the downward data during these years. Thus, the evidence about how much globalization is affecting world stock markets results is confirmed, where the analysis of correlation within a single geographic region will help to understand the homogeneous or heterogeneous nature of the phenomenon.

Table 3.2 Average correlation between stock markets from 1995 to 2010

Year	Average correlation or weekly returns between stock market indexes	Year	Average correlation or weekly returns between stock market indexes
1995	0.16	2003	0.30
1996	0.16	2004	0.47
1997	0.29	2005	0.37
1998	0.34	2006	0.51
1999	0.16	2007	0.52
2000	0.30	2008	0.66
2001	0.32	2009	0.60
2002	0.32	2010	0.63

The following tables show the domestic average correlation index in different regions: Western Europe, Northern Europe, Eastern Europe, North America, Latin America, Asia and Oceania, Africa and Middle East. Using the data, an analysis of the strength of the integration within a single geographical region is feasible.

Table 3.3 shows the correlation averages for each Western European country with other Western European markets. Hence, this data does not take into account the correlations with non-Western European markets, and it is useful in order to understand if the integration within Western Europe is stronger than the integration with other international markets. The last two columns summarize this gap with data of domestic and foreign average correlation indexes. From the correlation matrix of a specific year, the domestic average correlation index has been calculated as the mean of the correlation matrix data of single Western European markets versus the other Western European markets. From the same annual matrix, the correlation mean of the same Western European markets versus other international markets has been used to calculate the foreign average correlation index. Thus, the wider the gap between domestic and foreign indexes, the stronger the geographical effect is on the integration dynamic and the higher the heterogeneity of globalization is in the financial markets.

The upward trend of correlations of Western European stock markets is quite clear. Data from both single countries and the domestic average correlation index shows the increasing values. The Western European domestic average correlation was equal to 0.451 in 1995, and it grew to 0.857 in 2010. The gap between the domestic and foreign correlation index is positive in each year. This data suggests that the integration process within Western Europe is stronger than integration with other countries. Thus, a geographical bias in the integration process arises. These results confirm high integration of Western European stock markets as expected by previous studies. The high development of ICT in European stock exchanges (Aggarwal, 1999), the introduction of the Euro (Friedman and Shachmurove, 2005) and the demutualization of stock exchanges (Aggarwal, 2006) should have been able to foster financial market integration within Europe.

Table 3.4 shows the correlation averages for each Northern European country with other Northern European markets.

Data from Northern Europe confirms both the upward trend of integration and the presence of a geographical bias. In this case, the data of the domestic correlation index in the late 1990s highlights how a geographical effect was already present in this region, suggesting that Northern Europe was a homogeneous financial area even in the early stage of the analysed period. The foreign average correlation index shows that this region seems to be more integrated with the rest of the world, due to the fact that the gap in the domestic correlation index from 2005 and beyond is close to zero.

Table 3.5 shows the correlation averages for Eastern European markets.

Table 3.3 Average correlation of weekly indexes in Western Europe

	Year															
	1995	1996	1997	1998	1999	2000	2001	2002	2003	2004	2005	2006	2007	2008	2009	2010
Amsterdam	0.29	0.29	0.39	0.51	0.31	0.45	0.50	0.50	0.41	0.65	0.55	0.64	0.65	0.77	0.74	0.76
Brussels	0.27	0.21	0.26	0.45	0.24	0.19	0.42	0.44	0.38	0.63	0.51	0.65	0.64	0.75	0.72	0.74
Paris	0.19	0.28	0.34	0.48	0.31	0.45	0.53	0.49	0.46	0.65	0.56	0.65	0.66	0.78	0.74	0.76
Lisbon	0.19	0.10	0.38	0.45	0.13	0.43	0.36	0.37	0.33	0.60	0.42	0.57	0.52	0.74	0.69	0.70
Euronext	–	–	–	–	–	0.47	0.53	0.51	0.47	0.66	0.57	0.67	0.67	0.78	0.75	0.76
Vienna	0.20	0.24	0.34	0.40	0.24	0.19	0.28	0.23	0.20	0.63	0.47	0.66	0.63	0.76	0.72	0.72
Zurich	–	0.18	0.35	0.44	0.23	0.39	0.46	0.44	0.37	0.60	0.53	0.64	0.62	0.71	0.69	0.74
Milan	–	–	–	0.42	0.29	0.42	0.51	0.52	0.41	0.63	0.55	0.66	0.63	0.77	0.73	0.71
London	0.23	0.23	0.36	−0.08	−0.07	0.35	0.50	0.43	0.42	0.63	0.53	0.66	0.66	0.76	0.69	0.74
Dublin	–	–	–	0.41	0.22	0.25	0.40	0.36	0.36	0.02	0.41	0.59	0.54	0.60	0.67	0.72
Frankfurt	0.24	0.16	0.21	0.42	0.08	0.34	0.47	0.33	0.23	0.61	0.47	0.66	0.64	0.74	0.68	0.70
Luxembourg	–	–	–	–	0.14	0.26	0.44	0.34	0.34	0.62	0.51	0.6	0.6	0.75	0.71	0.73
Athens	0.13	0.02	0.26	0.42	0.12	0.15	0.34	0.34	0.27	0.56	0.42	0.55	0.62	0.7	0.66	0.59
Barcelona	–	–	–	–	0.12	0.44	0.48	0.47	0.46	0.62	0.52	0.65	0.59	0.77	0.72	0.68
Madrid	0.29	0.31	0.37	0.53	0.34	0.47	0.49	0.5	0.48	0.04	0.54	0.66	0.6	0.77	0.73	0.68
Valencia	–	0.28	0.36	0.51	0.32	0.42	0.49	0.49	0.47	0.62	0.54	0.66	0.6	0.77	0.73	0.69
Bilbao	–	–	–	–	–	0.462	0.442	0.471	0.471	0.622	0.542	0.659	0.584	0.767	0.734	0.659
IBEX 35	0.29	0.31	0.36	0.52	0.33	0.46	0.49	0.49	0.47	0.62	0.54	0.66	0.58	0.77	0.73	0.68
Domestic average	0.45	0.34	0.47	0.57	0.27	0.51	0.71	0.59	0.53	0.68	0.75	0.79	0.72	0.83	0.85	0.86
Foreign average	0.23	0.22	0.33	0.42	0.21	0.37	0.45	0.43	0.39	0.56	0.51	0.64	0.61	0.75	0.71	0.71

T-test 11.5964 (The null hypothesis should be rejected at 5% level of significance)

Table 3.4 Average correlation of weekly indexes in Northern Europe

	Year							
	1995	1996	1997	1998	1999	2000	2001	2002
Norway	0.32	0.22	0.33	0.41	0.27	0.38	0.46	0.43
Sweden	0.22	0.29	0.43	0.47	0.29	0.42	0.49	0.48
Finland	0.23	0.22	0.41	0.46	0.25	0.41	0.41	0.50
Denmark	0.27	0.21	0.26	0.34	0.16	0.35	0.46	0.41
Nordic 40*	–	–	–	–	–	–	–	0.48
Domestic average	0.53	0.40	0.58	0.70	0.37	0.55	0.53	0.76
Foreign average	0.26	0.23	0.36	0.42	0.24	0.39	0.45	0.46
	Year							
	2003	2004	2005	2006	2007	2008	2009	2010
Norway	0.38	0.59	0.45	0.58	0.54	0.70	0.67	0.75
Sweden	0.45	0.62	0.51	0.64	0.63	0.76	0.67	0.73
Finland	0.42	0.64	0.55	0.63	0.65	0.77	0.72	0.73
Denmark	0.35	0.62	0.44	0.61	0.63	0.78	0.66	0.71
Nordic 40*	0.45	0.64	0.52	0.65	0.66	0.77	0.71	0.75
Domestic average	0.67	0.84	0.79	0.67	0.66	0.77	0.79	0.81
Foreign average	0.41	0.62	0.50	0.62	0.62	0.75	0.68	0.73

T-test 6.8119 (The null hypothesis should be rejected at 5% level of significance)

* Nordic 40 is a stock index related to all Scandinavian stock markets (Norway, Sweden, Finland, Denmark)

If Western Europe and Northern Europe seem to be homogeneous regions with a strong geographic bias in markets correlations, data from Eastern Europe highlights a different situation. The domestic correlation index was quite low in the early stage of the analysed period and it never exceeded 0.7. The findings suggest that countries from Eastern Europe do not have similarities in their stock market returns, supported by the fact that from 2005 and beyond the foreign correlation index is even higher than the domestic one.

Table 3.6 shows the correlation averages for North American markets.

The gap between the domestic and foreign correlation indexes of North America and the single annual data is typical of highly integrated stock market regions. In fact, the internal correlation in 2010 is equal to 0.871, highlighting the strong relationship within North American stock markets. Moreover, the increasing correlation with other foreign markets can be interpreted as an impact of the globalization effect.

Table 3.7 shows the correlation averages for Latin American markets.

Data from Latin America presents a clear evidence of a heterogeneous area. Unlike other regions, the negative gap between domestic and foreign average correlations highlights the fact that most of the South American stock

Table 3.5 Average correlation of weekly indexes in Eastern Europe

	Year							
	1995	1996	1997	1998	1999	2000	2001	2002
Czech Republic	0.12	0.10	0.09	0.38	0.06	0.24	0.11	0.09
Poland	0.06	-0.00	0.28	0.45	0.29	0.37	0.29	0.27
Romania	–	–	–	0.22	–0.05	–0.01	0.07	–0.12
Hungary	0.12	0.11	0.33	0.44	0.29	0.36	0.41	0.27
Russia	0.05	0.13	0.37	0.40	0.15	0.27	0.19	0.30
Czech Republic	0.16	0.20	0.49	0.47	0.22	0.25	0.17	0.13
Domestic average	0.09	0.08	0.27	0.38	0.15	0.25	0.21	0.16
Foreign average	0.12	0.10	0.09	0.38	0.06	0.24	0.11	0.09
	Year							
	2003	2004	2005	2006	2007	2008	2009	2010
Czech Republic	0.25	0.58	0.43	0.61	0.64	0.74	0.62	0.71
Poland	0.28	0.55	0.48	0.58	0.56	0.70	0.54	0.70
Romania	0.07	0.49	0.35	0.40	0.49	0.64	0.59	0.65
Hungary	0.19	0.56	0.42	0.57	0.58	0.69	0.66	0.68
Russia	0.10	0.48	0.29	0.49	0.50	0.58	0.56	0.62
Czech Republic	0.18	0.65	0.47	0.52	0.50	0.65	0.58	0.62
Domestic average	0.18	0.53	0.39	0.53	0.55	0.67	0.59	0.67
Foreign average	0.25	0.58	0.43	0.61	0.64	0.74	0.62	0.71

T-test 1.8307 (The null hypothesis should be rejected at 5% level of significance)

Table 3.6 Average correlation of weekly indexes in North America

	Year							
	1995	1996	1997	1998	1999	2000	2001	2002
USA (S&P 500)	0.17	0.26	0.40	-0.03	0.22	0.35	-0.26	0.39
USA (NASDAQ)	0.13	0.26	0.35	0.42	0.22	0.36	0.36	0.44
USA (NYSE)	0.15	0.25	0.41	0.44	0.23	0.30	0.45	0.38
Canada (Toronto)	0.15	0.23	0.40	0.48	0.27	0.31	0.45	0.47
Domestic average	0.52	0.71	0.84	0.28	0.78	0.76	0.15	0.77
Foreign average	0.15	0.25	0.39	0.33	0.24	0.33	0.25	0.42
	Year							
	2003	2004	2005	2006	2007	2008	2009	2010
USA (S&P 500)	0.41	0.57	0.42	0.58	0.56	0.69	0.65	0.70
USA (NASDAQ)	0.35	0.54	0.38	0.51	0.54	0.70	0.61	0.68
USA (NYSE)	0.44	0.62	0.50	0.65	0.62	0.74	0.68	0.73
Canada (Toronto)	0.43	0.60	0.44	0.54	0.61	0.74	0.71	0.67
Domestic average	0.75	0.88	0.77	0.65	0.70	0.91	0.74	0.87
Foreign average	0.41	0.58	0.44	0.57	0.58	0.72	0.67	0.70

T-test 5.3643 (The null hypothesis should be rejected at 5% level of significance)

Table 3.7 Average correlation of weekly indexes in Latin America

	Year							
	1995	1996	1997	1998	1999	2000	2001	2002
Argentina	0.15	0.21	0.38	0.40	0.13	0.33	0.20	0.14
Brazil	0.18	0.17	0.36	0.30	0.18	0.36	0.31	0.24
Chile	0.15	0.11	0.34	0.32	0.18	0.27	0.30	0.23
Colombia	–	–	–	–	–	–	0.14	0.11
Mexico	0.16	0.19	0.40	0.37	0.16	0.40	0.42	0.35
Peru	0.11	0.15	0.32	0.22	0.07	0.08	0.03	0.31
Domestic average	0.51	0.29	0.58	0.51	0.34	0.32	0.22	0.27
Foreign average	0.15	0.17	0.36	0.32	0.14	0.29	0.23	0.23
	Year							
	2003	2004	2005	2006	2007	2008	2009	2010
Argentina	0.19	0.52	0.27	0.56	0.62	0.71	0.66	0.58
Brazil	0.27	0.57	0.39	0.58	0.66	0.74	0.67	0.67
Chile	0.31	0.44	0.12	0.13	0.41	0.63	0.52	0.55
Colombia	0.20	0.03	0.13	0.17	0.34	0.47	0.31	0.37
Mexico	0.28	0.58	0.42	0.57	0.61	0.73	0.65	0.69
Peru	-0.01	0.24	0.04	0.28	0.29	0.39	0.26	0.27
Domestic average	0.18	0.35	0.21	0.28	0.40	0.59	0.44	0.53
Foreign average	0.21	0.40	0.23	0.38	0.49	0.61	0.51	0.52

T-test 1.504 (The null hypothesis should be rejected at 5% level of significance)

markets are more correlated with non-South American markets than with domestic ones. From a global perspective, the low average level of the correlation indexes (both domestic and foreign) suggests that globalization in this region is lower than in North America and Western Europe.

Table 3.8 shows the correlation averages for Asia-Pacific and Oceanic markets.

The above conclusions for the Latin American region can be used as well for the Asia-Pacific and Oceanic regions. Accordingly, the comparison between domestic and foreign correlation indexes shows a low level of correlation both within and outside this region.

Table 3.9 shows the correlation averages for Africa and Middle East markets.

If the Latin American, Asian and Oceanic regions cannot be considered as integrated regions, data from Africa and the Middle East are even sharper. The foreign correlation index is constantly close to zero in the period from 1995 to 2007, even if data from the 2008–10 period highlights an upward trend. In fact, in 2009 and in 2010 the average correlation of the African and Middle Eastern stock markets with other non-region markets is equal to 0.33; however, low correlation data for the domestic correlation index shows negative values several times. If the economic, geographical and cultural

Table 3.8 Average correlation of weekly indexes in Asia-Pacific and Oceania

	Year															
	1995	**1996**	**1997**	**1998**	**1999**	**2000**	**2001**	**2002**	**2003**	**2004**	**2005**	**2006**	**2007**	**2008**	**2009**	**2010**
Australia	0.21	0.19	0.38	0.34	0.18	0.42	0.44	0.40	0.34	0.62	0.40	0.55	0.59	0.76	0.71	0.72
New Zealand	0.23	0.15	0.32	0.37	0.12	0.27	0.36	0.24	0.25	–	–	–	–	–	–	–
Indonesia	0.08	0.18	0.16	0.25	0.19	0.04	0.05	0.13	0.27	0.44	0.24	0.51	0.53	0.56	0.49	0.54
China (Shanghai)	−0.04	−0.05	−0.14	0.09	−0.03	0.00	0.04	0.14	0.09	0.16	0.25	0.19	0.22	0.04	0.18	0.45
China (Shenzhen)	−0.06	−0.08	−0.13	0.12	−0.01	−0.01	0.07	0.15	0.08	0.01	0.25	0.14	0.13	0.03	0.13	0.35
Hong Kong	0.15	0.17	0.32	0.29	0.25	0.38	0.41	0.40	0.26	0.54	0.31	0.46	0.55	0.69	0.64	0.58
India (Bombay)	0.00	0.12	0.19	0.17	0.13	0.31	0.33	0.20	0.19	0.05	−0.05	0.44	0.45	0.61	0.55	0.62
India (NSE)	–	0.05	0.20	0.12	0.12	0.35	0.31	0.12	0.15	0.48	0.33	0.45	0.48	0.62	0.57	0.63
Japan (Tokyo)	0.22	0.15	0.20	0.24	0.13	0.14	0.21	0.36	0.25	0.47	0.36	0.54	0.48	0.67	0.52	0.50
Singapore	–	–	–	–	0.15	0.28	0.42	0.31	0.34	0.57	0.33	0.59	0.59	0.73	0.61	0.68
Korea (Seoul)	0.00	0.00	0.19	0.20	−0.04	0.36	−0.20	0.29	0.34	0.04	−0.00	0.04	0.23	0.57	0.51	0.68
Domestic average	0.12	0.08	0.19	0.22	0.09	0.32	0.20	0.23	0.26	0.28	0.21	0.37	0.37	0.45	0.44	0.60
Foreign average	0.09	0.09	0.17	0.22	0.11	0.23	0.22	0.25	0.23	0.34	0.24	0.39	0.42	0.53	0.49	0.57

T-test −0.9152 (The null hypothesis should be rejected at 5% level of significance)

Table 3.9 Average correlation of weekly indexes in Africa and Middle East

	Year							
	1995	1996	1997	1998	1999	2000	2001	2002
Egypt	–	–	–	–	–	–	–	–
South Africa	−0.00	0.00	0.09	0.10	−0.07	0.02	0.05	−0.05
Israel	0.11	0.11	0.26	0.33	−0.01	0.32	0.34	0.24
Saudi Arabia	–	–	–	0.10	0.08	0.05	0.23	0.10
Domestic average	−0.15	−0.30	0.15	0.06	−0.02	0.26	0.20	−0.06
Foreign average	0.05	0.06	0.18	0.18	−0.00	0.13	0.21	0.10
	Year							
	2003	2004	2005	2006	2007	2008	2009	2010
Egypt	–	0.04	0.04	0.21	0.18	0.51	0.32	0.30
South Africa	−0.03	0.01	−0.06	0.07	−0.04	0.07	−0.04	−0.09
Israel	0.16	0.45	0.16	0.38	0.51	0.53	0.60	0.62
Saudi Arabia	0.17	0.27	0.04	0.12	−0.19	0.63	0.45	0.50
Domestic average	0.07	0.04	−0.08	0.03	−0.00	0.23	0.14	0.23
Foreign average	0.10	0.19	0.04	0.19	0.12	0.43	0.33	0.33

T-test −4.2187 (The null hypothesis should be rejected at 5% level of significance)

distances between the countries of this group can explain these results, the conclusion about a very low integrated financial area is clear.

3.5 Conclusion

Using the indexes from 53 international stock exchanges, correlation analysis was applied in order to highlight the relevance of globalization and its geographical trend within financial markets. A comparison between average correlation values for single geographical areas from the 1995 to 2010 period highlighted that correlation between markets around the world is growing over time. Furthermore, the results confirm the hypothesis that globalization of financial markets in the past few years is quite stronger than in the previous ones, suggesting that the globalization effect on the correlation matrices is speeding up.

Data from single geographic regions shows that globalization of financial markets is quite far from being a homogeneous phenomenon. Findings from the stock markets of Western Europe, Northern Europe and North America suggest that these areas are much more 'locally than globally' integrated. Even if correlations with non-region 'foreign' countries are positive, the significant higher values for the domestic correlation index highlight the tendency of globalization to evolve in a clustered manner. Meanwhile, data

Table 3.A1 Summary statistics of weekly data from 30 December 1994 to 31 December 2010

Variable	N°Obs	Mean	Max	Min	SD	Skew	Kurt	J- Bera
S&P 500	835	0.00	0.12	−0.18	0.03	−0.53	8.21	984,40
Nasdaq Composite	835	0.00	0.19	−0.25	0.04	−0.56	8,190.92	980.60
Nyse Composite	835	0.00	0.13	−0.20	0.03	−0.67	1,003.26	1,783.00
S&P/Tsx Composite	835	0.00	0.18	−0.23	0.03	−0.84	1,021.75	1,910.00
Bovespa	835	0.00	0.29	−0.29	0.06	−0.24	5,522.32	229.10
Merval	835	0.00	0.27	−0.29	0.05	−0.27	7,244.60	636.80
Igbc	494	−0.01	0.09	−0.45	0.06	−3.47	1,662.89	4,812.00
Ipc	835	0.00	0.16	−0.26	0.04	−0.62	5,934.10	352.70
Ipsa	832	−0.01	0.18	−0.46	0.07	−5.40	3,509.05	4.0*e*+04
Igbvl	835	0.00	0.21	−0.31	0.04	−0.16	1,179.62	2,696.00
Nzsx 30	470	0.00	0.10	−0.09	0.03	−0.12	4,265.13	32.39
S&P/Asx 200	835	0.00	0.15	−0.29	0.03	−1.31	1,423.01	4625
Sse Composite	835	0.00	0.12	−0.20	0.04	−0.31	5,106.55	167.4
Szse Composite	835	0.00	0.36	−0.91	0.06	−5.39	9,054.72	2.7*e*+05
Hang Seng	835	0.00	0.15	−0.18	0.04	−0.18	5,501.21	222.30
S&P Cnx Nifty 50	835	0.00	0.20	−0.18	0.04	−0.13	473.39	98.05
Bse Sensex 100	766	0.00	0.22	−0.90	0.05	−61.50	1,073.15	3.8*e*+05
Jakarta Composite	833	−0.00	0.17	−0.44	0.05	−1.95	1,486.98	5,420.00
Ta – 100	835	0.00	0.16	−0.16	0.04	−0.41	4,612.53	114.00
Nikkei 225	835	0.00	0.14	−0.20	0.03	−0.06	5,358.65	194.10
Ftse St	591	0.00	0.20	−0.19	0.03	−0.25	8,279.30	692.60
Kospi	833	−0.00	0.12	−0.46	0.05	−3.53	2,835.59	2.4*e*+04
Egx 30	340	0.00	0.13	−0.21	0.05	−0.80	6,113.33	174.00
Tasi	591	0.00	0.17	−0.22	0.04	−1.20	9,267.78	1,109.00
Ftse/Jse Top 40	809	0.00	0.12	−0.18	0.04	−0.73	5,155.92	227.80
Euronext 100	574	0.00	0.14	−0.24	0.03	−0.86	9,362.93	1,039.00
Bel 20	835	0.00	0.13	−0.25	0.03	−0.93	9,727.57	1,696.00
Cac 40	835	0.00	0.15	−0.24	0.03	−0.61	8,367.89	1,055.00
Aex	835	0.00	0.15	−0.27	0.03	−0.77	9,911.24	1,745.00
Psi-20	835	0.00	0.18	−0.20	0.03	−0.68	876.92	1,221.00
Omxn 40	470	0.00	0.16	−0.21	0.04	−0.66	7,174.48	375.30
Omx Stockholm 30	835	0.00	0.22	−0.21	0.04	−0.17	7,073.09	581.00
Omxh25	835	0.00	0.18	−0.20	0.04	−0.48	6,187.75	385.80
Omx Copenhagen 20	835	0.00	0.14	−0.22	0.03	−1.15	1,013.71	1,955.00
Obx	835	0.00	0.23	−0.25	0.04	−0.53	9,507.61	1,512.00
Dax	835	0.00	0.08	−0.21	0.03	−1.16	974.29	1,770.00
Atx	835	0.00	0.21	−0.30	0.04	−1.05	1,311.48	3,712.00
Smi	678	0.00	0.10	−0.15	0.04	−0.67	5,058.15	169.80
Ftse Mib	678	0.00	0.21	−0.23	0.04	−0.53	9,700.78	1,300.00
Ftse 100	835	0.00	0.17	−0.24	0.03	−0.76	1,351.67	3,928.00

from Eastern Europe, Latin America, Asia and Oceania show a lower level of integration. Furthermore, Africa and Middle Eastern countries seem to show no similarities in their stock market returns. Hence, the findings highlight the presence of a 'local globalization' at the geographical level prior to a 'common globalization' of all geographical areas and international markets.

Furthermore, the findings are consistent with results provided in the literature by previous papers (Kearney and Poti, 2006; Mendes et al., 2007; Cheng et al., 2007) and provide additional evidence about the reasons why the advanced economies of Europe and North America have experienced the impact of the financial crisis more strongly and dramatically as their financial markets were highly linked and the effects of the crisis were easily transmitted to the real economies (Berkmen et al., 2010; Ahmedov and Bessler, 2011; Schmukler and Zoido-Lobatón, 2011). In any case, in previous studies the authors have analysed the single market area, whereas in this paper, thanks to (1) the big number of exchanges, (2) the world perspective and (3) the almost 20-years long analyses, the authors investigate globalization in financial stock exchange markets from a new macroeconomic perspective in terms of risk-transmission. Obtained results can be interesting for both academics and practitioners. Awareness about how globalization is developing around the world can be useful in order to explain its role in different countries' phenomena (exchange rates, imports and exports, and so on). Moreover, due to the relevance of globalization in the asset allocation process, adopted by mutual funds and other investors, data on the globalization effect in different regions can be useful in order to understand if a geographical criterion (Europe, Asia, North America, and so on) or an industry-based criterion (goods and services, telecommunication, oil and gas, and so on) is the most effective in a portfolio diversification approach.

References

Agénor, P. R. (2003) 'Does globalization hurt the poor?' http://www.worldbank.org (homepage) date accessed 01 July 2012.

Aggarwal, R. (1999) 'Technology and globalization as mutually reinforcing forces in business', *Management International Review*, 39, 83–104.

——(2006) 'Demutualization and public offerings of financial exchange', *Journal of Applied Corporate Finance*, 18, 96–106.

Aggarwal, R., B. Lucey and C. Muckley (2010) 'Dynamics of equity market integration in Europe: Impact of political economy events', *Journal of Common Market Studies*, 48, 641–60.

Ahmedov, Z. and D. A. Bessler (2011) 'Structure of interdependencies among international stock markets and contagion patterns of 2008 global financial crisis', http://ageconsearch.umn.edu (homepage) date accessed 01 July 2012.

Armanious, A. (2005) 'Globalization effect On stock exchange integration', http://www.ssrn.com (homepage) date accessed 01 July 2012.

Arribas, I., F. Perez and E. Tortosa-Ausina (2006) 'Measuring international economic integration: theory and evidence of globalization', http://www.fbbva.es (homepage) date accessed 01 July 2012.

Bagella, M., L. Becchetti and I. Hasan (2003) 'The benefits Of economic integration and monetary unions: the negative impact on growth of "export portfolio volatility" ', http://ideas.repec.org/ (homepage) date accessed 01 July 2012.

Beck, T., R. Levive and N. Loeysa (2000) 'Finance and the sources of growth', *Journal of Financial Economics*, 1–2, 261–300.

Bekaert, G. and C. Harvey (2003) 'Emerging markets finance', *Journal of Empirical Finance*, 10, 3–55.

Berkmen, S. P., G. Gelos, R. Rennhack and J. P. Walsh (2010) 'The global financial crisis: Why were some countries hit harder?' *Finance & Development*, 47, 29–31.

Bhagwati, J. (2004) *In Defense of Globalization* (Oxford: Oxford University Press).

Bhalla, B. and A. Shetty (2006) 'Interest rate linkages and capital market integration: evidence from the Americas', http://www.bnet.fordham.edu (homepage) date accessed 01 July 2012.

Campero, G. (2001) 'Trade union responses to globalization: Chile' http://library.fes.de (homepage) date accessed 01 July 2012.

Carrieri, F., V. Errunza and K. Hogan (2007) 'Characterizing world market integration through time', *Journal of Financial and Quantitative Analysis*, 42, 915–40.

Cheng, H. F., M. Gutierrez, A. Mahajan, Y. Shachmurove and M. Shahrokhi (2007) 'A future global economy to be built by BRICs', *Global Finance Journal*, 18, 143–56.

Erdogan, B. (2009) 'How does European integration affect the European stock markets?' http://hayek.diw.de/ (homepage) date accessed 01 July 2012.

Eun, C. and J. Lee (2010) 'Mean-variance convergence around the world', Working paper, *Journal of Banking and Finance*, 34, 856–70.

Friedman, J. and Y. Shachmurove (2005) 'European stock market dynamics before and after the introduction of the Euro', http://economics.sas.upenn.edu/ (homepage) date accessed 01 July 2012.

Hasan, I., H. Schmiedel and L. Song (2010) 'Growth strategies and value creation: What works best for stock exchanges?' http://www.ecb.int/ (homepage) date accessed 01 July 2012.

Hassan, M. K. and A. Naka (1996) 'Short-run and long-run dynamic linkages among international stock markets', *International Review of Economics and Finance*, 5, 387–405.

Karolyi, G. A. and R. M. Stulz (2003) 'Are financial assets priced locally or globally?', in G.M. Constantinides, M. Harris and R.M. Stulz (eds), *Handbooks of the Economics and Finance. Financial Markets and Asset Pricing* (San Diego: Elsevier).

Kearney, C. and V. Poti (2006) 'Correlation dynamics in European equity markets', *Research in International Business and Finance*, 20, 305–21.

Lane, P. and M. G. Milesi-Ferretti (2003) 'International financial integration', http://www.cepr.org (homepage) date accessed 01 July 2012.

Lawrence, S. and J. Ishikawa (2005) 'Social dialogue indicators trade union membership and collective bargaining coverage: Statistical concepts, methods and findings', http://www.ssrn.com/ (homepage) date accessed 01 July 2012.

Leamer, E. (1988) 'Measures of openness', in R. E. Baldwin (ed.), *Trade Policy Issues and Empirical Analysis* (Chicago: University of Chicago Press).

Longin, F. and B. Solnik (1995) 'Is the correlation in international equity returns constant: 1970–1990', *Journal of International Money and Finance*, 14, 3–26.

——(2001) 'Extreme correlation of international equity markets', *Journal of Finance*, 56, 646–76.

Mendes, B., R. Leal and A. Carvalhal-da-Silva (2007) 'Clustering in emerging equity markets', *Emerging Markets Review*, 8, 194–205.

Moser, G., W. Pointner and J. Scharler (2004) 'International risk sharing in Europe: Has anything changed?' In K. Liebscher, P. Mooslechner, and D. Ritzberger-Grünwald (eds), *The Economic Potential of a Larger Europe* (Northampton: Edward Elgar Publishing).

Pagano, M., O. Randl, A. Röell and J. Zechner (2001) 'What makes stock exchanges succeed? Evidence from cross-listing decisions', *European Economic Review*, 45, 770–82.

Pieper, P. and R. Vogel (1997) 'The stock market integration in Latin America', http://www.cid.harvard.edu (homepage) date accessed 01 July 2012.

Prasad, E., K. Rogoff, S. J. Wei and M. A. Kose (2003) 'The effects of financial globalization on developing countries: Some empirical evidence', http://www.imf.org/ (homepage) date accessed 01 July 2012.

Quinn, D. and A. M. Toyoda (2008) 'Does capital account liberalization lead to growth?' *The Review of Financial Studies*, 21, 1403–49.

Sarkissian, S. and M. Schill (2004) 'The overseas listing decision: New evidence of proximity preference', *The Review of Financial Studies*, 17, 769–809.

Schindler, F. and S. Voronkova (2010) 'Linkages between international securitized real estate markets: Further evidence from time-varying and stochastic cointegration', http://www.zew.de/ (homepage) date accessed 01 July 2012.

Schmukler, S. L. and P. Zoido-Lobatón (2011) 'Financial globalization: Opportunities and challenges for developing countries', http://www.worldbank.org (homepage) date accessed 01 July 2012.

Shahrokhi, M. (1998) 'Global financial challenges for the new millennium', *Global Finance Journal*, 9, 1–4.

Trichet, J. C. (2005) 'Reflections on the international financial system', http://www.bis.org/ (homepage) date accessed 01 July 2012.

Walti, S. (2005) 'The macroeconomic determinants of stock market synchronization', *Journal of International Banking Law*, 11, 436–41.

4
Financial Analyst Recommendation Driven Funds: A Risk Adjusted Measure Analysis

Giuseppe Galloppo

4.1 Introduction

Financial analysts are important information intermediaries in the capital markets. They gather and evaluate information from public and private sources, generate forecasts on companies' earnings and future prospects, and make recommendations that lead to buying or selling of the companies' securities by investors. So they provide valuable research to investors and facilitate optimal capital allocation. Indeed financial analyst research aims at forecasting future earnings, stock price (target price) and giving a recommendation of buying or selling for any given company. This information seems to be relevant, especially for unsophisticated investors who may incorporate it to drive their investment decisions.

Studies that provide evidence of the investment value of analysts' research include Gleason and Lee (2003) on earnings forecasts, and Barber et al. (2007) on target prices, among others. Since the 1990s evidence shows that, on average, recommendations contain valuable information for investors (Stickel, 1995; Womack, 1996) with significant abnormal returns observed following the issuance of a research report.

At the same time, their coverage benefit followed companies through reducing information asymmetries. These benefits to investors and followed companies and the resulting benefits to brokerage firms employing financial analysts in the form of increased trading commissions and investment banking fees likely underlie the increasing influence and presence of financial analysts on the capital markets in recent years.

The increasing influence and presence of financial analysts indicates the importance of understanding the informativeness of their reporting process, particularly the process of issuing stock recommendations.

This chapter investigates this issue in the context of the market impact of stock recommendations.

Unlike analysts' earnings forecasts, which are short-term point estimates, analysts' recommendations can be considered more analogous to capital budgeting decisions. We choose to analyse stock recommendations because they are important research outputs of financial analysts. Furthermore, they represent "one of the few cases in evaluating information content where the forecaster is recommending a clear and unequivocal course of action rather than producing an estimate of a number, the interpretation of which is up to the user' (Elton et al., 1986).

This chapter focuses on the profitability of an investment strategy based on stock recommendations issued by analysts. We present a strategy which, by using research reports created by financial analysts, mimics a fund manager asset allocation process.

Our chapter contributes to the literature on financial analysts by studying the role of financial analysts' reports in helping institutional investors make better investment decisions. In summary, we not only provide new evidence on the informativeness of analyst recommendations, but we also offer significant insights into the question of how to use them in an asset allocation context.

Our results show that, on average, stock recommendations give better returns than a simple buy and hold strategy.

The remainder of the chapter is organized as follows. The second section gives a brief summary of prior research on the profitability of asset allocation strategy based on analyst recommendations and on the value of analyst research. The third one describes the construction of the dataset and the sample selection criterion. The fourth section explains the procedure followed to build the portfolios on the basis of the stock recommendations issued by the analysts, and outlines the methodology used to estimate returns. The fifth section evaluates the return predictability of asset allocation activities based on analyst stock recommendations. The chapter finishes by summarizing the main conclusions.

4.2 Literature review

Over the past two decades, the predictive power of analysts has been the subject of empirical and experimental studies. Two important papers published in the early 1990s provide perspectives on the literature in this area, one appeared in *Accounting Horizons* (Schipper, 1991) and the other appeared in the *International Journal of Forecasting* (Brown, 1993).

Recent papers classify the information in analysts' research reports into four categories: earnings forecasts, target price forecasts, investment recommendations, and conceptual arguments supporting the forecasts and recommendations. Analyst recommendations generally fall into three categories, strong buy, buy and hold, with sell and strong sell categories used much less frequently (McNichols and O'Brien, 1997).

At the base of recommendations there is a question: what models do analysts use to convert their forecasts into value judgements? Womack (1996) suggests that analysts develop explicit (or implicit) valuation models. If the market price is sufficiently below the true value indicated by the model, the stock is accorded a buy recommendation; when the market price is above the model value, the stock is given a sell recommendation. Some empirical research contradicts the view that analyst recommendations are based primarily on fundamental valuation models.

Bradshaw (2004) examines approximately 100 analysts' research reports from Investext, dated (primarily) in 1998 or 1999, and finds that analysts most frequently justify their recommendations with references to P/E ratios and long-term growth rate forecasts. Thus, it appears that analysts combine their long-term growth forecasts with the firm's P/E ratio to reach a valuation and recommendation decision. The PEG ratio, defined as the P/E ratio divided by the long-term growth rate, a popular Street heuristic, suggests that a firm's forward P/E ratio should equal 100 times its long-term growth rate forecast and Bradshaw (2002, 2004) uses this heuristic to create pseudo price targets and finds that these pseudo price targets are highly correlated ($r = 0.39$) with the level of analysts' buy/hold recommendations and with analysts' reported target prices ($r = 0.50$).

Interestingly, although Bradshaw (2004) finds that fundamental valuation models are not reliable predictors of analyst recommendations, he does find that heuristic valuation models have significant explanatory power. In particular he concludes that the PEG ratio, defined as the P/E ratio divided by the long-term growth rate, is an important heuristic used by analysts to convert their earnings forecasts into target prices forecasts and recommendations. This result holds, furthermore, despite the fact that rankings of stock based on PEG ratios are often quite different than rankings based on the ratio of fundamental value to price and despite the fact that PEG ratios are no better predictors of future returns than value-to-price ratios. However, Bradshaw's results are consistent with the survey work of Block (1999). Based on a survey of analysts, Block reports extremely low reliance on valuation methods in the formation of stock recommendations. Furthermore he finds that the PEG ratio is correlated with the level of analyst recommendations.

Bradshaw's results are consistent with the survey work of Block (1999). Based on a survey of analysts, Block reports extremely low reliance on valuation methods in the formation of stock recommendations.

Different authors have developed two main lines of research; the effects of stock recommendations on the share price and the creation of portfolio strategy based on analysts' recommendations. On this last ground in very recent work Ramnath et al. (2008) provide a detailed taxonomy listing and categorize every paper published in 11 research journals since 1992.

Chen and Cheng (2005) show that stock recommendations are not just taken into consideration by individual investors, but are also followed by institutional investors, who increase (reduce) their participations in companies with favourable (unfavourable) recommendations. Investors have also been shown to be slow in responding to analysts' stock recommendations. Barber et al. (2001) revisit Womack (1996) finding that stock recommendations of analysts are associated with abnormal returns both around the recommendation period and in the subsequent six (one) months for downgrades (upgrades). They use a calendar time strategy and find significantly positive abnormal returns in the post-recommendation period to portfolios formed on the basis of analysts' consensus recommendations drawn from the Zacks Investment Research database. However, in additional tests Barber et al. (2001) find that implementing trading strategies based on analysts' stock recommendations involves frequent reshuffling in the portfolio (turnover of over 300 per cent annually) which negates the abnormal returns that can be earned through the strategy. However, they use recommendations of all analysts in their analysis and caution that there may be other strategies that could produce abnormal returns net of transaction costs (for example, picking recommendations of analysts/brokerage houses that have superior past performance). Mikhail et al. (2004) explore this issue. Specifically, they examine whether analysts whose recommendations yielded positive returns in prior periods, command more attention from investors (i.e., elicit bigger price reactions) when they recommend stocks in the future. They find that both the market reaction around the recommendation change as well as the post-recommendation drift are higher, in the direction of the recommendation change, for superior analysts (based on past performance). While the abnormal returns to taking a long (short) position in upgrades (downgrades) of analysts with the best prior performance yields positive abnormal returns, it is insufficient to cover round-trip transaction costs. Thus, Mikhail et al. (2004) find no evidence in support of one of the conjectures in Barber et al. (2001) that differentiating between analysts may alter their conclusions regarding trading on analyst recommendations. Several authors have tried to exploit positive abnormal returns through stock recommendations issued by analysts, generating benchmark-superior portfolio strategies. Womack (1996) finds that stock recommendations are associated with significant abnormal returns on average. Jegadeesh and Titman (2001) compare the investment value of stock recommendations (six-month abnormal returns following consensus recommendations) with that of other variables predictive of future stock returns, such as return momentum, trading volume, valuation multiples, etc. Earlier studies find no evidence of superior investment performance (Bidwell, 1977; Groth et al., 1979). More recent studies, however, show that stock recommendations do hold value (Dimson and Marsh, 1984; Elton et al., 1986; Stickel, 1995; Womack, 1996) suggesting that analysts develop explicit (or implicit) valuation models. If the market price is sufficiently below the true value indicated by the model, the stock is accorded a buy recommendation; when the market price is above the model value, the stock is given a sell recommendation. Some empirical research contradicts the view that analyst recommendations are based primarily on fundamental valuation models. Bradshaw (2004) examines the correlation between analyst recommendations and the ratio of fundamental firm value to market price. Bradshaw calculates fundamental value by substituting analysts' consensus earnings forecasts into the residual income version of the discounted cash flow model developed by Ohlson (1995). Surprisingly, he finds that analysts' recommendations are more (less) favorable for stocks with *low* (*high*) value relative to price. Barber et al. (2001, 2003) analyse the value of trading strategies based on the consensus level of the stock recommendations issued by analysts in the United States. In their 2001 paper, they observe that the trading strategy consisting of buying the most highly recommended stocks and simultaneously selling the least favoured stocks generates abnormal returns, which disappear when the transaction costs are taken into account. In their 2003 paper, they observe that the same strategies give negative returns. The reason seems to be the inclusion of the turbulent 2000 period, when stock prices crashed.

Bradshaw (2002) finds evidence to suggest that the value-to-price ratios are *positively* associated with future abnormal returns but *negatively* associated with the analysts' recommendations. All in all, Bradshaw's evidence suggests that analysts do not use their own earnings forecasts efficiently in making recommendations. Jegadeesh and Kim (2006) use a similar methodology with data on stock recommendations from G7 countries (USA, UK, Canada, France, Germany, Italy and Japan). They reach the conclusion that trading strategies based on the consensus level are not profitable, as the losses from 2000 onwards eliminated the positive returns of previous years. Boni and Womack (2003) create a consensus-based portfolio to examine the competition between analysts. The authors highlight that the returns achievable by buying upgraded stocks and selling downgraded stocks is 1.4 per cent on a monthly basis and 18 per cent on a yearly basis. They also find that analysts' competition reduces the opportunity to make profits from changes of recommendations, portfolios formed with stocks followed by a great number of analysts generate lower returns. Later, Jegadeesh et al. (2004) studied the value of strategies based on consensus changes. Their aim was to study the impact caused by new corporate information on stock recommendations and their effects on the capital market. These authors show that changes in stock recommendations predict future returns, suggesting that they capture qualitative aspects of corporate activity not picked up by other quantitative variables. While Bradshaw (2004) finds that consensus analyst recommendations based on analysts' consensus long-term earnings growth rate forecasts do not predict abnormal returns, he does not examine the association between the relative accuracy of an individual analyst's earnings forecasts and the profitability of the analyst's stock recommendations. Loh and Mian (2006) address this issue. Specifically, they compare the profitability of stock recommendations of relatively accurate earnings forecasters to those of poor earnings forecasters in any given firm-year. Relying on I/B/E/S earnings forecasts and recommendations related to over 32,000 firm-years between 1994 and 1999, they find that monthly abnormal returns on hedge portfolios based on recommendations of analysts in the top (bottom) quintile of earnings forecast accuracy are, on average, approximately 0.74 per cent (−0.53 per cent). The differences are highly significant, both statistically and economically. The authors infer that efforts by analysts to produce accurate earnings forecasts pay off in terms of the profitability of their stock recommendations. Thus, it appears that analysts use their earnings forecasts to produce stock recommendations, with more accurate forecasters providing more profitable recommendations. Jegadeesh et al. (2004) employ long-short portfolios based on analyst recommendations and conclude that recommendations do hold value. In addition they show that changes in, but not levels of, recommendations have value.

4.3 Research design and sample selection

The purpose of this chapter is twofold:

1. the construction (and evaluation) of an equity portfolio through the use of a signalling trading system starting from recommendations provided by IBES,
2. analysis of the association between the convergence of analysts' estimates regarding the future development of the equity and return to maturity associated with it.

Investors and the analyst have an initial belief about the firm value before the analyst acquires a private signal. Based on the signal, the analyst updates her belief about firm value and issues a buy, hold, or sell recommendation.

The investors do not learn what the realized recommendations are, but do know the distribution from which recommendations are drawn. Investors then update their belief about firm value based on the recommendation.

Let the initial belief about firm value follow a normal distribution:

$$\tilde{v} = P_0 + \varepsilon_v \tag{4.1}$$

Where $P_0 = E[\tilde{v}|I_0], \varepsilon_v \sim N(0, \sigma^2)$ and I_0 represent the public information set.

We assume that an analyst has to issue his recommendations of a company at some point during the forecasting period, $t \in [0, T]$, e.g., between the recommendations release of the previous period and the release of the forthcoming recommendation.

Some studies (Conrad et al., 2006, Guttman, 2010) assume that the recommendations of the company which are denoted by π, are the realization of a random variable $\widetilde{\pi_0}$, where

$$\pi_0 \sim N(\widetilde{\mu_\pi 0}, \sigma^2_{\pi 0}) \tag{4.2}$$

At the beginning of the forecasting period (t = 0), the investors have no information about the recommendation on the firm other than the distribution of $\widetilde{\pi_0}$. At the end of the forecasting period, the company publicly reports its recommendation.

We begin by determining for each firm in the recommendations database the beginning and end dates. We limit our study to stocks that are covered by at least one analyst and have returns data available from Datastream. Using these dates to define the time period for the firm, we construct a vector of returns for this period, beginning immediately before the start of the recommendations in the database.

Our data come from two different sources: stock returns from Datastream and Individual analysts' stock recommendations are collected from I/B/E/S.

The term IBES (Institutional Brokers' Estimate System) identifies a collection of estimates made by stock market analysts that refer to the individual companies listed on major world markets. These estimates may refer among others, both on balance account variable (earnings per share) and an opinion about the future profitability of a particular equity (recommendation). I/B/E/S compiles individual analyst recommendations data from hundreds of brokerage houses.

I/B/E/S assigns each analyst a unique code that remains the same even if the analyst switches brokerage firms. Although different brokerage houses have different names for similar recommendations (for example, 'Neutral' or 'Hold'), recommendations in the IBES database are coded as follows: 1 = Strong Buy, 2 = Buy, 3 = Hold, 4 = Sell, 5 = Strong Sell (see Table 4.1).

The 'Detail' recommendation file contains the name of the firm covered by the analyst, the brokerage house, the analyst issuing the report, and a 5-point recommendation rating scale of 1 to 5, along with the issue date of the recommendation.

To conform with the rating scale of I/B/E/S, throughout the chapter we follow the notation that a higher rating indicates a less favourable opinion from financial analysts.

Each analyst can express on a certain date, an opinion on what should be the position that would be appropriate to take on a particular stock. In this way, each analyst can express, on the same time interval, ratings for several

Table 4.1 Recommendation meaning

Recommendation type	Suggested market position
Strong Buy	Strong recommendation to buy
Buy	Recommendation to buy
Hold	Recommendation to hold a stock equity in portfolio
Underperfom	Recommendation to sell
Sell	Strong recommendation to sell

companies and/or on multiple time intervals express more judgements for the same company.

Constrained by the availability of the analyst recommendations data from I/B/E/S, the sample period spans between 1993 and 2003. In the first part of this section it discusses the criteria for generation of equity portfolios. The second part presents the Spearman test of independence about the definition of a possible association between the number of recommendations and harmony in the judgements of the analysts on the future of the assets, part of a portfolio, and the profitability of the same portfolio.

We have analysed 851 companies listed on US Standard & Poor's stock markets. We have selected among all companies that belong to S&P's stock markets, those that have, in the sample period analysed, at least one recommendation for every (sub-sample) holding period taken into account. Overall, there are 372,000 individual Recommendations within the sample period. The returns of the portfolios generated from recommendation (built with the logic shown in the next section) are calculated on a database containing the prices of 851 companies making up our IBES database.

There is some debate as to which statistic, derived from the distribution of analyst forecasts available at each point in time, best reflects the current analyst expectations. Various studies show that consensus forecasts are more accurate than individual forecasts, consistent with the notion that idiosyncratic errors are minimized when sample means are used.[1]

4.4 Portfolio identification

To evaluate the informativeness and profitability of analyst recommendations, we examine the return performance of portfolios composed starting from a ranking methodology, as a function of recommendations of a set of equities. To do so, at the end of each holding period, we sort all stocks according to the rank attributed to a stock as a function of his own recommendation.

A key feature of this research is the signalling use of stock recommendations. By using stock recommendations as opening and closing signals, we expect a portfolio strategy based on recommendations to obtain larger returns than traditional approaches like those one could gain by a buy and hold strategy or by a strategy investing in a free risk asset. The portfolio strategy we build considers each recommendation recorded in a report as a potential buying or short selling signal according to a stock recommendations ranking mechanism.

Regarding the construction of the equity portfolio here we analyse the main steps of our iterative methodology:

- The estimation period
- Number of recommendations

- The criterion for selecting companies to be included in the portfolio
- Stock position (Long / Short)
- Portfolio vector of weights
- Holding period.

The estimation period is how many units of time (daily), back in time, starting from the initial moment of allocation, must be recorded the recommendations from which the portfolio will be built. Regarding the estimation period, we considered six intervals: 20, 30, 40, 60, 120 and 180 days. Recommendation number represents the minimum number of recommendations necessary, for a given estimation period, to consider the possible inclusion of a stock in a portfolio

The criterion for selecting companies for inclusion in the portfolio, is the way to aggregate the different recommendations in order to create a selection of assets to include in a portfolio and also how many of them. Stock position (Long/Short) represents the identification of criteria for determining, after selecting a specific stock, its market position Long or Short, to be taken. The vector of weights, of the securities in a portfolio, i.e., given that a certain stock has been selected, what is the portion of capital to invest in it. Holding period, or for how many units of time a given asset must be kept in the portfolio. The criterion for selecting what asset to include in the portfolio and market position mode of a stock (Long/Short) follows the logic below. First we analyse the number of recommendations for all companies within the estimation period, then we exclude companies that do not show the number of recommendations required (see below the minimum number of recommendation). For the remaining companies we consider the average of the value attributed to recommendation according to an algorithm that converts the qualitative variable in the quantitative values (Table 4.1 for the conversion of qualitative values in recommendation in quantitative values). Then an ascending sort is carried out on the basis of the recommendation converted values. Defined a priori as the number of Long securities (in this application 10 and 20) and the number of Short securities (in this application 10 and 20) stocks are selected from the ordering above exposed, so the first 'n1' society (where 'n1' is the number of Long titles) and the latest 'n2' society (where 'n2' is the number of Short securities). According to this approach every transaction in the portfolio is kept open as long as the holding period is expired.

The minimum number of recommendations varies according to the number of securities to be selected within the portfolio. In fact, for example, given a sub-period of 20 days, setting a minimum number of 20 recommendations, you may not be able to identify a number, equal to or greater, of securities to be held in the portfolio (for example, 10 Long and 10 Short). In fact, if the criterion for selecting companies for inclusion in the portfolio includes the construction of a portfolio of 20 stocks on which to take a position in which

20 Long and 20 shares take a Short position, for a particular sub-sample cannot be a number of securities coupled with a number of recommendations greater or equal to the number of stock requested (20 Long and Short 20). Portfolio vector of weights: here we consider a vector of weights is a vector that gives equal weight to all assets.

About the holding period several authors (see Barber et al., 2001; Jegadeesh et al., 2004; Boni and Womack, 2003) debate the appropriate holding period due to the tradeoff between the frequency of rebalancing and transactions costs. In this article we have considered six intervals: 20, 30, 40, 60, 120, 180 days. The choice of considering multiple time periods relates to the fact that it is not possible to know what was the time interval at which the recommendation was reported. For example, if analyst X issues a rating of Strong Buy on Company Y we do not know the time within which the recommendation would remain valid. For this reason we have different holding periods, namely: 20, 30, 60, 120, 180 and 360 days. The strategy implemented in this chapter rebalances the entire portfolio in every period.

So according to the various holding periods after a period of 20, 30, 40, 60, 120 and 180 days respectively, every position is automatically closed, independently from the achievement of any price level. As seen above, for the purposes of portfolio construction it can be taken, as market position, both Long (buying) and Short position. For every class of transaction we compute the portfolio return as follows:

$$R_{P_{tp}} = \frac{1}{n+m}\left(\sum_{t=1}^{n} R_{L_{TP_{\eta\gamma t}}} + \sum_{i=1}^{n} R_{S_{TP_{\eta\gamma t}}}\right) \tag{4.3}$$

$$R_{L_{P_{\eta\gamma t}}} = \frac{P_{\eta\gamma t+k}}{P_{\eta\gamma t}} - 1, \{\epsilon \{k = 20, 30, 40, 60, 120, 180.\} \tag{4.4}$$

$$R_{S_{TP_{\eta\gamma t}}} = \frac{P_{\eta\gamma t+k}}{P_{\eta\gamma t}} - 1, \{\epsilon \{k = 20, 30, 40, 60, 120, 180.\} \tag{4.5}$$

Where

n: number of long transactions in the portfolio;

m: number of short transactions in the portfolio;

$R_{P_{tp}}$: portfolio return as the mean of all long and short transactions;

$R_{L_{P_{\eta\gamma t}}}$: return on a long transaction related to the report issued by analyst γ on company η in t;

$R_{S_{P_{\eta\gamma t}}}$: return on a short transaction related to the report issued by analyst γ on company η in t;

$P_{\eta\gamma t}$: price of firm η in t.

4.5 Spearman independence test

The test of independence proposed by Spearman allows the calculation of the relationship between two variables through the correlation coefficient computed on ranks and not on variables themselves. It is a nonparametric test, so there are no required assumptions on the distributions of the observed variables. Before the construction of the test it is necessary to define the Spearman correlation coefficient on the ranks. It is none other than the coefficient of linear correlation between the ranks of the original variables as shown in the following formula:

$$Sp_n = Corr(R,S) = \frac{\sum_{i=1}^{n}\left(R_i - \frac{n+1}{2}\right)\left(S_i - \frac{n+1}{2}\right)}{\sqrt{\sum_{i=1}^{n}\left(R_i - \frac{n+1}{2}\right)^2 \sum_{i=1}^{n}\left(S_i - \frac{n+1}{2}\right)^2}} \tag{4.6}$$

Where R_i is the rank of i-th variable X value and S_i is the rank of i-th variable Y. The test constructed according to the formula 3.1 has as hypothesis H_0 the independence between variables X and Y or that $Sp_n = 0$. The v.c. Sp_n tends, with increasing of the sample size to a normal v.c. with mean term 0 and variance equal to $\frac{1}{n-1}$ (where n is the sample size). According to the asymptotic property of the distributions it can be used as distribution functional form of variable. Sp_n a t student distribution with *n–2* (where *n* is the sample size) degree of freedom.[2] In the presentation of the results it will show both versions of the Spearman test.

4.6 Empirical results

In the first part of this section we illustrate the results of equity portfolios generated, according to the methodology presented in the previous section, from recommendations. The second part examines the association between number of recommendations used for the construction of the portfolio and the return obtained from it. It is necessary to stress that our findings are not driven by a specific time period that is included in our sample. We have checked the robustness of our results by performing the sub-sample period analysis: 1993 to 2003.

4.6.1 Portfolio results

Observing the tables presented below, we show the results of the portfolios generated from the proposed procedure in Section 4.3. In order to properly read and interpret the data obtained it is useful to introduce some key readings later reported in tabular form (Figure 4.1).

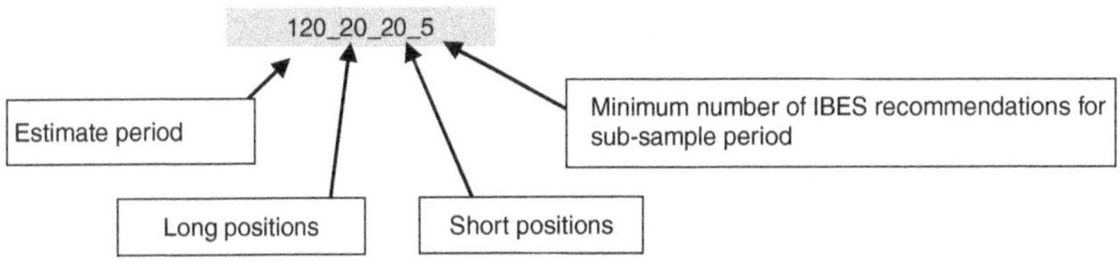

Figure 4.1 Key readings of portfolio labels

In this regard it is noted that in the first column are the identification codes of the portfolios, the criterion of interpretation of each code is shown in figure 4.1:

- The estimation period, number of days starting from which recommendations are collected in order to allow the construction of the portfolio.
- Number of long positions, the number of stock for which the portfolios record a long position.
- Number of short positions, the number of stock for which the portfolios record a short position (short selling).
- Minimum number of recommendations from IBES for a sub-sample period, indicates the minimum number of recommendations, for each stock, starting from which a stock may eventually be selected in the process of portfolio inclusion.

In the second column of Table 4.2 is shown the period of application, or holding period of assets in the portfolio. The third column shows the annual average return of the strategy, then values of standard deviation are shown. They are calculated on an annual basis, the Sharpe ratio, calculated on an annual basis, skewness and kurtosis.[3]

Analysing Table 4.2 as a whole it can be shown that: only 21 per cent of the portfolios constructed exhibit a positive Sharpe ratio to maturity, although the strategies with returns greater than 0 are about 28 per cent. The difference between these two percentages is due to the fact that the average return generated by the portfolios, and particularly, for some of the portfolios that have produced a positive return, is lower than the rate used for the risk-free asset (here 3 per cent per year).[4]

The portfolios that have obtained higher returns to maturity, and also a high value of Sharpe index, are characterized mainly by an estimation period which is relatively high (120 and 180 days). Focusing on the portfolios that have achieved a Sharpe ratio greater than 0, we observe that it seems that there is an association between the estimated range and holding period (sub-sample period, after which, with rolling procedure, it moves to a new portfolio allocation). In fact, the portfolios with higher Sharpe ratio are, on average, characterized by a range period of estimates wider than the

Table 4.2 Portfolio results – holding period: 20 days

Portfolio	Holding period	Annualized mean	Annualized dev. st.	Sharpe ratio	Skewness	Kurtosis
20-10-10-01	20	−20.41%	38.29%	−61.13%	−1.79	12.75
20-20-20-01	20	−20.79%	26.89%	−88.46%	−0.81	2.91
30-10-10-01	20	−16.03%	44.43%	−42.84%	−2.38	13.32
30-20-20-02	20	4.30%	30.25%	4.31%	0.09	6.30
40-10-10-05	20	−29.62%	43.07%	−75.74%	−2.39	9.72
40-20-20-05	20	−23.77%	27.42%	97.64%	−2.94	13.15
60-10-10-08	20	−40.69%	41.08%	106.37%	−2.38	11.62
60-20-20-08	20	−11.59%	22.07%	66.09%	−0.11	−0.21
120-10-10-05	20	0.83%	34.64%	−6.28%	−0.27	1.92
120-20-20-05	20	−5.30%	17.94%	−46.29%	−0.85	1.03
180-10-10-10	20	−0.77%	62.91%	−5.99%	0.48	2.86
180-20-20-10	20	−5.32%	21.72%	−38.33%	−0.83	0.49

Table 4.3 Portfolio results – holding period: 30 days

Portfolio	Holding period	Annualized mean	Annualized dev. st.	Sharpe ratio	Skewness	Kurtosis
20-10-10-01	30	17.72%	33.04%	44.54%	0.14	1.13
20-20-20-01	30	2.04%	27.65%	−3.46%	0.22	1.52
30-10-10-01	30	−8.22%	39.71%	−28.26%	−0.91	5.17
30-20-20-02	30	0.81%	29.50%	−7.42%	0.64	4.14
40-10-10-05	30	−29.69%	45.17%	−72.36%	−3.74	26.44
40-20-20-05	30	−18.60%	25.45%	−84.88%	−3.51	21.54
60-10-10-08	30	19.30%	39.46%	41.31%	0.61	1.46
60-20-20-08	30	2.44%	23.05%	−2.41%	0.13	0.83
120-10-10-05	30	13.78%	41.32%	26.09%	1.09	5.06
120-20-20-05	30	−1.09%	28.30%	−14.50	−0.13	0.26
180-10-10-10	30	106.30%	75.08%	137.59	3.20	12.27
180-20-20-10	30	11.60%	23.87%	36.01	0.25	1.81

range of application or holding period (by comparing values in Tables from 4.2 to 4.7, it showed that, the estimation period of 180 days is coupled, on average, with holding periods of 30 and 40 days).

Furthermore, the portfolios that have achieved a positive return in terms of Sharpe ratio have special characteristics as regards the values of skewness and kurtosis. In fact they tend to show a positive value of skewness and a kurtosis value of greater than 3. This means that the distribution of return strategies show a positive asymmetry, with regard to a normal distribution

Table 4.4 Portfolio results – holding period: 40 days

Portfolio	Holding period	Annualized mean	Annualized dev. st.	Sharpe ratio	Skewness	Kurtosis
20-10-10-01	40	−2.62%	35.52%	15.81%	0.10	2.30
20-20-20-01	40	−11.19%	25.63%	−55.36%	−0.59	0.72
30-10-10-01	40	−14.89%	39.75%	−45.00%	−2.15	8.69
30-20-20-02	40	−4.59%	27.88%	−27.22%	−0.01	1.10
40-10-10-05	40	−25.31%	41.17%	−68.76%	−1.22	2.78
40-20-20-05	40	−20.07%	27.36%	−84.31%	−2.11	9.49
60-10-10-08	40	−22.08%	32.09%	−78.17%	−0.54	0.12
60-20-20-08	40	−9.65%	21.18%	−59.70%	−0.27	0.59
120-10-10-05	40	42.50%	36.75%	107.49%	−0.62	4.14
120-20-20-05	40	19.70%	12.53%	133.26%	−0.14	2.15
180-10-10-10	40	19.43%	57.36%	28.64%	2.05	6.43
180-20-20-10	40	20.91%	24.55%	72.97%	0.01	−0.03

Table 4.5 Portfolio results – holding period: 60 days

Portfolio	Holding period	Annualized mean	Annualized dev. st.	Sharpe ratio	Skewness	Kurtosis
20-10-10-01	60	−8.49%	38.07%	−30.18%	−0.14	1.51
20-20-20-01	60	−11.09%	26.43%	−53.30%	−0.70	1.20
30-10-10-01	60	−12.75%	36.83%	−42.77%	−0.59	2.60
30-20-20-02	60	−6.92%	27.14%	−36.56%	−0.38	1.29
40-10-10-05	60	−14.27%	42.47%	−40.68%	−1.26	3.95
40-20-20-05	60	−7.99%	22.52%	−48.80%	−0.48	2.15
60-10-10-08	60	−24.92%	32.32%	−86.39%	−1.30	3.12
60-20-20-08	60	−11.91%	20.17%	−73.89%	−0.31	−0.21
120-10-10-05	60	14.19%	25.63%	46.43%	−0.26	−0.15
120-20-20-05	60	0.06%	18.94%	−15.54%	0.09	−0.85
180-10-10-10	60	−22.09%	39.95%	−62.81%	−0.43	3.09
180-20-20-10	60	15.68%	19.73%	64.27%	0.31	−1.04

characterized by a mean value and a standard deviation term equal to those exhibited by empirical strategy return distribution.

Buy and Hold returns, represented by the return of the S & P 500 exhibit negative returns for the years 2000–2, but the average return for the entire period of analysis, 1993–2003, is positive.

Until now the analysis of portfolio returns over the period 1/1/1992–31/12/2003 has been conducted omitting the performance of the portfolios in the sub-sample. Table 4.9 shows the excess returns of portfolios with an annual positive Sharpe ratio to maturity.

Table 4.6 Portfolio results – holding period: 120 days

Portfolio	Holding period	Annualized mean	Annualized dev. st.	Sharpe ratio	Skewness	Kurtosis
20-10-10-01	120	−4.10%	36.50%	−19.45%	−0.76	2.64
20-20-20-01	120	−1.89%	23.99%	−20.40%	0.09	1.32
30-10-10-01	120	−2.74%	31.50%	−18.22%	0.08	1.41
30-20-20-02	120	−4.49%	23.86%	−31.37%	−0.16	1.56
40-10-10-05	120	−9.25%	29.73%	−41.20%	−0.65	2.50
40-20-20-05	120	−4.39%	16.41%	−45.05%	−0.10	0.63
60-10-10-08	120	3.83%	31.91%	2.60%	1.14	5.00
60-20-20-08	120	−8.89%	18.35%	−64.81%	−0.24	−0.10
120-10-10-05	120	−11.40%	29.84%	−48.26%	−1.04	1.58
120-20-20-05	120	−15.67%	26.31%	−70.96%	−0.38	2.12
180-10-10-10	120	8.11%	45.74%	11.16%	1.70	7.46
180-20-20-10	120	6.91%	22.14%	17.64%	1.02	0.09

Table 4.7 Portfolio results – holding period: 180 days

Portfolio	Holding period	Annualized mean	Annualized dev. st.	Sharpe ratio	Skewness	Kurtosis
20-10-10-01	180	−7.47%	32.61%	−32.12%	−0.68	2.07
20-20-20-01	180	−10.09%	34.78%	−37.64%	−2.28	−1.93
30-10-10-01	180	−3.78%	28.835	−23.53%	−1.04	2.77
30-20-20-02	180	−1.48%	24.93%	−17.95%	−0.37	1.62
40-10-10-05	180	−9.42%	30.72%	−40.43%	−1.21	4.11
40-20-20-05	180	−6.34%	17.52%	−53.28%	−0.33	0.75
60-10-10-08	180	−6.55%	27.95%	−34.16%	−0.18	0.19
60-20-20-08	180	−9.11%	19.61%	−61.74	0.24	−0.03
120-10-10-05	180	−7.04%	23.63%	−42.48%	−0.10	−0.45
120-20-20-05	180	−6.09%	17.82%	−51.02%	1.24	2.26
180-10-10-10	180	−9.44%	22.84%	−54.48	−0.82	1.07
180-20-20-10	180	−6.27%	19.41%	−47.78	0.33	−0.42

Table 4.8 Standard and Poor's 500 index performance breakdown by year

Year	Return	Year	Return
1993	7.06%	1999	19.53%
1994	−1.55%	2000	−10.14%
1995	30.93%	2001	−13.04%
1996	20.26%	2002	−23.37%
1997	31.01%	2003	26.38%
1998	26.67%		

Table 4.9 Excess return of portfolios with positive Sharpe ratio

Portfolio	Holding period	1993	1994	1995	1996	1997	1998	1999	2000	2001	2002	2003
180-10-10-10	30	−70.09%	3.09%	90.25%	56.85%	166.33%	91.75%	−57.71	184.63%	−47.02%	214.81%	−68.97%
180-20-10-10	40	101.52%	26.90%	−9.87%	32.28%	−22.50%	153.17%	36.68%	−29.20%	9.37%	9.77%	5.80%
180-20-20-10	60	48.35%	108.99%	20.51%	−15.78%	−13.27%	81.23%	50.07%	−24.18%	−27.22%	−9.71%	2.23%
180-20-20-10	30	167.46%	24.55%	−23.44%	42.68%	−58.26%	84.51%	63.64%	−22.27%	0.48%	22.55%	−21.48%
180-10-10-10	40	−71.86%	8.07%	45.80%	−17.04%	19.99	−18.88%	−24.77%	296.75%	−65.26%	−33.47%	−52.83%
180-20-20-10	120	−28.59%	32.44%	−29.35%	0.61%	23.12%	25.25%	49.18%	−15.40%	−10.16%	24.37%	−22.85%
180-10-10-10	120	11.74%	1.13%	62.97%	−26.02%	−30.84%	13.40%	33.19%	166.35%	−64.59%	26.82%	−12.89%
120-20-20-05	40	101.52%	25.01%	37.89%	0.91%	12.33%	71.28%	−9.41%	−20.65%	−9.20%	31.57%	37.97%
120-10-10-05	40	158.57%	129.97%	41.20%	−2.17%	47.31%	103.82%	38.39%	−47.95%	−79.18%	129.63%	360.76%
120-10-10-05	60	149.48%	18.14%	45.48%	27.45%	−9.50%	−6.95%	−6.06%	−35.58%	−6.53%	27.65%	77.91%
120-10-10-05	30	268.56%	10.25%	−1.75%	−5.00%	10.01%	10.35%	−16.65%	53.49%	12.79%	−54.20%	93.36%
60-10-10-08	30	−87.21%	14.60%	52.40%	−11.67%	−24.81%	−28.71%	82.92%	73.825	110.87%	34.63%	−21.08%
60-10-10-08	120	29.94%	−2.30%	−14.17%	24.15%	36.17%	−11.11%	7.91%	−1.89%	39.19%	−36.41%	−20.39%
30-20-20-02	20	34.33%	33.02%	−3.62%	13.92%	6.32%	−60.32%	56.80%	56.52%	−24.52	−18.21%	14.12%
20-10-10-01	30	−77.19%	78.26%	17.48%	−1.15%	15.59%	−4.61%	45.59%	19.14%	11.29%	30.75%	−32.87%

The portfolio returns summarized above, show excess returns with regard to a free-risky asset, particularly high remarkably during the following years: 1993, 1994, 1998 and 2000. In fact, the average returns of various portfolios, calculated over the period 1993–2003 amounted to 23.36 per cent, while for 1993 the average returns of portfolios approximately is doubled (48.44 per cent). Return mean terms exhibiting an increase of 50 per cent compared to the average value calculated over the entire period are shown for the years 1994, 1998 and 2000. The only bad year in terms of the sum of the returns of all portfolios, is 2001 where 60% of the portfolios exhibit a cumulative negative return (−9.98 per cent on average).

4.6.2 Association Spearman test between number of recommendations and portfolio return to maturity

The portfolios generated from the procedure described in the previous section have not always achieved positive returns, many of them have nearly destroyed the capital initially invested. However, in the portfolios with positive performances we have not found an association between the number of recommendation, from which the different portfolios are originated, and positive return. In other words, we are interested to see if by increasing the number of recommendations and therefore the number of analysts producing reports for each portfolio company, it shows some association with a positive return at maturity. In particular, we run a test of association, considering the total number of recommendations for each sub-period (and every portfolio), within each holding period, and the sub-period result in terms of portfolio return. We can synthesize our research as follows: is it worth paying particular attention to those companies for which there is a widespread harmony of judgements in the analyst community? If I were a fund manager would I prefer to invest in those companies that have a high number of recommendations that on average advise me to buy or sell a particular security?

As an example, let the reader pay attention to the following tables. To statistically test the independence of these variables we have used the Spearman test. This particular type of test calculates the correlation coefficient of variables, not on the variable terms but on the corresponding ranks.

The table 4.10 refers to a portfolio constructed with the following parameters (hence the title 60_10_10_8, the same criterion must be adopted to read all the subsequent tables):

- The estimation period: 60 days.
- Equity trading strategy position(Long/Short): 10 Long assets and 10 Short assets.
- Minimum number of recommendations: 8.
- Vector of portfolio weights: assets equally weighed.
- Holding period: 120 days.

Table 4.10 Association Spearman test between number of recommendations and portfolio return to maturity

	Negative	Positive	Total
SumIbes>60	3	2	5
50<SumIbes<60	6	3	9
40<SumIbes<50	3	4	7
30<SumIbes<40	7	6	13
20<SumIbes<30	5	7	12
10<SumIbes<20	3	3	6
SumIbes<10	3	3	6
Total	30	28	58

The strategies that we have considered in this application generate, for each holding period considered, a number of portfolios equal to the number of sub-sample application periods (for example, for a portfolio with 60_10_10_8 with a holding period of 120 days we have 58 sub-sample periods) in line with what is described in Section 4.3, where it shows the rolling portfolio building procedure (iterative process).

The variable SumIbes representing the sum of recommendations starting from the portfolio 60_10_10_8 is constructed for each sub-sample period. In the table it shows the frequencies, for a class distribution of the variable SumIbes, that are coupled with the returns, positive or negative, of each subperiod. It was decided to split the variable 'SumIbes in 7 classes', for example, for Table 4.11, the class (first row) SumIbes>60 identifies those compositions of sub-sample portfolios (for 60_10_10_8 portfolio), for the construction of which have been used over 60 recommendations, in this case we have 5 portfolios (Table 4.11, column 'Total', first line) with more than 60 recommendations which have generated positive returns 2 times (Table 4.11, column 'positive', the first line) and negative returns 3 times (Table 4.11, column 'negative', the first line).

As can be seen from Table 4.11, there is no association between the number of recommendations and positive performance in the sub-sample period portfolios. In fact, as the number of recommendations used in portfolio construction (first column of Table 4.11) increases, the success ratio does not increase, expressed as the ratio of the number of times that the portfolio will achieve a positive return on the total number of cases that are in a certain range class of SumIbes variable. The lack of relationship between two variables is also endorsed by the Spearman correlation index which assumes a value close to 0 (0.101) for the portfolio 60_10_10_8. Even in the following tables, given by way of example, there are no associations between the number of recommendations and positive performance of the portfolio. Even in

Table 4.11 Portfolios with Sharpe ratio greater than zero: Spearman test results

N°	Portfolio	Holding period	Spearman correlation	Test v.c. normal	Test v.c. t student
19	180-10-10-10	30	0.36	Refused	Refused
19	180-20-20-10	40	−0.01	Accepted	Accepted
19	180-20-20-10	60	0.48	Accepted	Accepted
19	180-20-20-10	30	0.00	Accepted	Accepted
19	180-10-10-10	40	0.19	Accepted	Accepted
19	180-20-20-10	120	−0.13	Accepted	Accepted
19	180-10-10-10	120	0.11	Accepted	Accepted
26	120-20-20-05	40	0.32	Refused	Refused
26	120-10-10-05	40	−0.25	Accepted	Accepted
26	120-10-10-05	60	0.31	Accepted	Accepted
26	120-10-10-05	30	0.17	Accepted	Accepted
58	60-10-10-08	30	0.36	Accepted	Accepted
58	60-10-10-08	120	0.10	Accepted	Accepted
99	30-20-20-02	20	0.17	Accepted	Accepted
171	20-10-10-01	30	−0.02	Accepted	Accepted

these cases the Spearman coefficient shows values close to zero, or that do not lead to exclude the null hypothesis of absence of association. In order to prove the absence of relationship between variables below are shown Spearman test results. Please note that the null hypothesis is the absence of relationship (independence) of two variables.

Table results lead us to conclude that selecting assets for which you record a high number of recommendations is not indicative of future profitability of the portfolios generated from them. In fact, for only two portfolios the null hypothesis is rejected, in such cases, however, the sign of the relationship, if any, is discordant, positive for the first and negative for the second relationship.

Notes

1. See, for example, Ashton and Ashton (1985) and Winkler and Makridakis (1983).
2. In this case the v.c. is as follows:

$$t = \frac{Sp_n}{\sqrt{\frac{\left(1-Sp_n^2\right)}{(n-2)}}}$$

3. Asymmetry of a V.C. with mean term μ and variance σ is defined as follows:

$$\gamma = \frac{E(X-\mu)^3}{[(Var(X)]^{\frac{3}{2}}}$$

Kurtosis is defined as follows:

$$\delta = \frac{E(X - \mu)^4}{\sigma^4}$$

where σ^4 stands for the square term of variance of the V.C.

4. In fact, the differential between the strategy mean return and the risk-free rate is the numerator of the Sharpe ratio. It contributes also to determine the sign of the Sharpe coefficient (since the denominator is always positive since it is represented by strategy standard deviation).

References

Ashton, A., R. Ashton (1985) 'Aggregating subjective forecasts: Some empirical results', *Management Science*, 31, 1499–508.

Barber, B., R. Lehavy and B. Trueman (2007) 'Comparing the stock recommendation performance of investment banks and independent research firms', *Journal of Financial Economics*, 85, 490–517.

Barber, B., R. Lehavy, M. McNichols and B. Trueman (2001) 'Can investors profit from the prophets? Security analyst recommendations and stock returns', *Journal of Finance*, 56, 531–63.

——(2003) 'Reassessing the returns of analyst recommendations', *Financial Analysts Journal*, 59, 88–96.

Bidwell, C. M. III (1977) 'How good is institutional brokerage research?' *Journal of Portfolio Management*, 3, 26–31.

Boni, L. and K. Womack (2003) 'Analysts, industries and price momentum', *Journal of Financial and Quantitative Analysis*, 41, 85–111.

Bradshaw, M. (2002) 'The use of target price to justify sell-side analysts' stock recommendations', *Accounting Horizon*, 16, 27–41.

——(2004) 'How do analysts use their earnings forecasts in generating stock recommendations?' *Accounting Review*, 79, 25–50.

Brown, L. D. (1993) 'Earnings forecasting research: Its implications for capital markets research', *International Journal of Forecasting*, 9, 295–320.

Chen, X. and Q. Cheng (2005) 'Institutional holdings and analysts' stock recommendations', *Journal of Accounting, Auditing, and Finance*, 21, 399–440.

Conrad, J., B. Cornell, W. R. Landsman and B. Rountree (2006) 'How do analyst recommendations respond to major news?' *Journal of Financial and Quantitative Analysis*, 41, 25–49.

Dimson, E., and P. Marsh (1984) 'An analysis of brokers' and analysts' unpublished forecasts of UK stock returns', *Journal of Finance*, 39, 1257–92.

Elton, J. E., M. J. Gruber and S. Grossman (1986) 'Discrete expectational data and portfolio performance', *Journal of Finance*, 41, 699–713.

Gleason, C. A., and C. M. C. Lee (2003) 'Analyst forecast revisions and market price discovery', *The Accounting Review*, 78, 123–5.

Groth, J. C., W. G. Lewellen, G. G. Schlarbaum and R. C. Lease (1979) 'An analysis of brokerage house securities recommendations', *Financial Analysts Journal*, 35, 32–40.

Guttman, I. (2010) 'The timing of analysts' earnings forecasts', *Accounting Review*, 85, 513–58.

Jegadeesh, N. and J. Kim (2006) 'Value of analyst recommendations: International evidence', *Journal of Financial Markets*, 9, 274–309.

Jegadeesh, N., J. Kim, S. Krische and C. Lee (2004) 'Analyzing the analysts: When do recommendations add value?' *Journal of Finance*, 59, 1083–124.

Jegadeesh, N., and S. Titman (2001) 'Profitability of momentum strategies: An evaluation of alternative explanations', *Journal of Finance*, 56, 699–720.

Loh, R. and M. Mian (2006) 'Do accurate earnings forecasts facilitate superior investment recommendations?' *Journal of Financial Economics*, 80, 455–83.

McNichols, M. and P. O'Brien (1997) 'Self-selection and analyst coverage', *Journal of Accounting Research*, 35, 167–99.

Mikhail, M. B., B. R. Walther and R. H. Willis (2004) 'Do security analysts exhibit persistent differences in stock picking ability?' *Journal of Financial Economics*, 74, 67–91.

Ohlson, J. (1995) 'Earnings, book values, and dividends in equity valuation', *Contemporary Accounting Research*, 11, 661–87.

Ramnath, S., S. Rock and P. Shane (2008) 'The financial analyst forecasting literature: A taxonomy with suggestions for further research', *International Journal of Forecasting*, 24, 34–75.

Schipper, K. (1991) 'Commentary on analysts' forecasts', *Accounting Horizons*, 5, 105–19.

Stickel, S. E. (1995) 'The anatomy of the performance of buy and sell recommendations', *Financial Analysts Journal*, 51, 25–39.

Winkler, R. and S. Makridakis (1983) 'The combination of forecasts', *Journal of the Royal Statistical Society*, 2, 150–7.

Womack, K. (1996) 'Do brokerage analysts' recommendations have investment value?' *Journal of Finance*, 51, 137–67.

5
Alternative Neural Network Approaches for Enhancing Stock Picking Using Earnings Forecasts

Giuseppe Galloppo and Mauro Aliano

5.1 Introduction

Interest in financial markets has increased in the last couple of decades, among fund managers, policy makers, investors, borrowers, corporate treasurers and specialized traders. Forecasting the future returns has always been a major concern for the players in stock markets and one of the most challenging applications studied by researchers and practitioners extensively. Predicting the financial market is a very complex task, because the financial time series are inherently noisy and non-stationary and more it is often argued that the financial market is very efficient. Fama (1970) defined efficient market hypothesis (EMH) where the idea is a market in which security prices at any time 'fully reflect' all available information both for firms' production–investment decisions, and investors' securities selection. Furthermore, in EMH context no investor is in a position to make unexploited profit opportunities by forecasting futures prices on the basis of past prices. On the other hand, a large number of researchers, investors, analysts, practitioners etc. use different techniques to forecast the stock index and prices. In the last decade, applications associated with artificial neural network (ANN) have drawn noticeable attention in both academic and corporate research. Neural networks have flexible nonlinear function mapping capability, where a variable is explained with a set of explanatory variables without assuming any structural or linear relationship among the variables and is able to approximate any continuous function with arbitrarily desired accuracy. They are also capable of continuous learning through the new information received. In the financial market, it has proved to be a very powerful predictive tool and a reliable instrument with good error tolerance, capable of handling large and complicated information and achieving satisfactory forecasting results. Due to their success in financial forecasting, neural networks have been adopted as an alternative method in the prediction of stock prices, exchange rates etc.

There exist vast literatures which concentrate on the predictability of stock market return. In almost all cases, the performance metrics and the acceptability of the proposed models are measured by the deviations of forecast value from the actual values. The drawback of the previous studies is, none of the studies evaluated the effect of nonlinear predictions on portfolio performances driven by analyst and the question whether these predictions are economically exploitable has been neglected in the literature. This chapter aims to fill the gap, and we think that the results of this study are significant value addition to the trading decisions in the stock index futures. This chapter intends to test the forecasting ability of ANN models in case of Nifty index returns when financial analyst information is taken into account. Quarterly time series data of a stock portfolio is analysed using two layer architecture of the ANN and various input data combinations.

Specifically the major contributions of this study are as follows:

1. to demonstrate financial analyst information contribution in forecasting stock return and in asset allocation decision in a non linear context;
2. to compare the out-of-sample one step forecast of various ANN architectures;
3. whether the length of the investment horizon has a significant impact on the quality of the forecasts and on asset allocation performance.

The different competing models are rigorously compared using two approaches. Firstly, the study examines the out-of-sample forecasts generated by different competing models employing statistical criteria such as goodness of forecast measures (i.e., root mean squared errors (RMSE)). To provide a more complete evaluation of the models, our comparison is based on not only the performance statistics but also the trading profits. Thus, this study develops a set of trading strategies whose performances are compared with those generated by the buy and hold strategy, and the investment strategies guided by the forecasts estimated by a parametric forecasting approach, namely the random walk. Random walk is also used because it is a natural benchmark that is based on the efficient market hypothesis. Many sophisticated forecasting models are not able to outperform the 'naive' random walk model. Given the notion that a prediction with little forecast error does not necessarily translate into capital gain, nevertheless empirical results show that the analyst information ANN-based investment strategies obtain higher returns than other investment strategies examined in this study.

The remaining portion of this chapter is organized as follows. Beside this introduction, utilization of neural networks are researched and results of similar empirical works are presented. Section 5.3 describes the dataset and covers details of how neural networks have been designed to perform the task of forecasting the index returns and how to translate this into an investor's portfolio decision. Then, the results of forecasting are presented and discussed in Section 5.4. Section 5.5 describes the proposed index trading strategies which are driven by the forecasts made by various forecasting models. Finally, Section 5.6 summarizes the main findings with concluding observations.

5.2 Literature review

A survey of the literature has not revealed any papers whose purposes is the testing of artificial neural networks (ANN) for forecast making by using as input, information, recommendations and earnings forecast, derived from financial analysts via IBES data.

Liu and Song (2001) examined analysts' forecast of earnings for internet companies surrounding the market crash in March 2000. They reported that analysts were more optimistic before than after the March 2000 period suggesting that analysts' optimism may have caused the stock market bubble.

O'Brien and Tian (2006) conclude that analysts were more optimistic in their recommendations for Internet companies than non-Internet during the 1990 bubble period.

5.2.1 Evidence of return predictability

There exists considerable evidence showing that stock returns are to some extent predictable. A critical view on return predictability of risky assets is taken by Valkanov (2003), Ang and Bekaert (2007), Goyal and Welch (2003) and Goyal and Welch (2008). Most of the research is conducted using data from well-established stock markets such as the US, Western Europe, and Japan. Ferson and Harvey (1993) examine 18 international equity markets, some of which are found in developing economies. The study provides evidence of returns predictability. Harvey (1995) focuses on emerging markets by looking at the returns of more than 800 equities from 20 emerging markets including Taiwan. He finds that the degree of predictability in the emerging markets is greater than that found in the developed markets. In addition, local information plays a much more important role in predicting returns in the emerging markets than in the developed markets. This characteristic helps to explain the difference in predictability between the two kinds of markets.

For the US, several studies examine the cross-sectional relationship between stock returns and fundamental variables. Variables such as earnings yield, cash flow yield, book-to-market ratio, and size are shown to have some power in predicting stock returns. In earlier studies, during the 1980s, valuation ratios were used to predict future returns, starting with dividend yields. Banz and Breen (1986), Jaffe et al. (1989) and Fama and French (1992) are good examples of this group of research.

Also Campbell and Shiller (1988a, 1988b) found that dividend yields are positively correlated with future returns. More recently Kothari and Shanken (1997), Pontiff and Schall (1998), Lamont (1998), Stambaugh (1999), Lewellen (2004) and Campbell and Yogo (2006) examined the predictability of returns by financial ratios. They show that book-to-market ratios and dividend yields have predictive power for subsequent stock market returns.

5.2.2 Related researches on artificial neural networks

Although a comprehensive review of the literature available on the subject is beyond the scope of this paper, we tried to accommodate the most relevant studies from across the world in respect of the application of ANN models for forecasting index returns. On the whole a number of studies have investigated the neural network model for predicting the stock market and the results support the importance of the model. The first significant application of the concepts of neural network models in a stock market context was initiated for questioning the validity of the efficient market hypothesis by examining the forecasting accuracy of the neural network models on IBM stock's daily returns (White, 1988). The growing interest in the applications of ANN particularly in finance and stock markets started catching the interest of researchers during the early nineties, and eventually became one of the most explored techniques of prediction in stock index returns.

Bengoechea et al. (1996), in their research, used the 240-day trade information of the Santiago Stock Exchange as samples and the indices and transaction volume of the preceding 10 days as the input data, trying to predict the overnight closing indices of the Santiago Stock Exchange through the neural network approach. The result showed that, through the neural network approach, they achieved an accuracy rate of 63.3 per cent in predicting directions in the rising range of the stock market and a 74.7 per cent accuracy rate in the falling range. Another study on the forecasting of stock market prices has been done by Lawrence (1997). This study reveals the ability of the neural network to discover patterns in nonlinear and chaotic systems more accurately that other current forecasting tools.

Tsai et al. (1999), tried to predict the best timing for investment by integrating various technical indices and constructing a stock forecasting model based on neural networks. The result was that, through the cross-utilization of neural network and stop-loss strategies, one can effectively forecast the best timing for stock purchase and achieve better returns from one's investment. Fernandez-Rodrigues et al. (2000) used the Back Propagation Network (BPN) to construct their forecasting model for Madrid Stock Exchange General Indices. The result of their empirical study also showed that the model is an effective forecasting model for the Madrid Stock Exchange General Indices and helped to achieve better investment returns.

Al-Hindi and Al-Hasan (2002) selected seven Saudi Arabian companies from varying sectors and depicted an efficient prediction ability of the neural networks with 2-5-1 structure. By using technical analysis indicators (momentum MACD, etc.), Diler (2003) cooked at predicting the direction of the Istanbul Stock Exchange (ISE) for the following day. The results of the study showed that the direction of the IMKB-100 index could be predicted at a rate of 60.81 per cent.

Pant and Rao (2003) in their work used ANN for estimating the daily return of the BSE Sensex using randomized back propagation. Wu (2004) adopted the back propagation neural network (BPN) for his stock price research, based on the transaction volume, trade price and the technical indices.

While some studies were focused on measuring the forecasting performance of neural network models based on several statistical and financial performance measures, there were some other studies which compared the forecasting performances of neural network models with other statistical forecasting methods (Gencay, 1998; Kim and Chun, 1998; Lim and McNelis, 1998; Lam, 2004; Rodriguez et al., 2005).

Ma (2003) applied the fuzzy neural network technology in his simulated investment in Taiwan's stock market. In his empirical study, he used Taiwan's General Index as input variables. He then compared the results with the actual results of using merely the 12-day moving average. The discovery was that, by adopting the fuzzy neural network approach, one can avoid the misleading effect of cheat lines, which are more likely to happen when merely using the moving average approach. The investment return, also, is significantly better than the return achieved through the buy-hold strategy or the traditional moving average strategy.

Manish and Thenmozhi (2003, 2004, 2005) have used back propagation neural networks and compared this with a linear ARIMA model for forecasting different time series like INR/USD, Stock index return, index future returns etc. Results indicate that the ANN-based forecasting method is superior to the linear ARIMA models.

Kim (2006) proposes an advanced genetic Algorithm approach to instance selection in ANNs for financial data mining. Using this approach the study could avoid the basic limitations of ANNs such as inconsistency, problems in prediction for noisy data, etc. The study produces a satisfactory forecasting in the direction of change on the Korean Stock Price Index (KSPI) using GA-based ANN (GANN).

Furthermore, Avci (2007) investigated the forecasting performance of the back propagation neural network model for the Istanbul Stock Exchange (ISE-100) index with daily frequency. Ince and Trafalis (2007) and Bekiros and Georgoutsos (2008) show that neural network models can be successfully implemented for return predictability. More recently, Hammad et al. (2009) showed that the Artificial Neural Network (ANN) technique provides fast convergence, high precision and strong forecasting ability of real stock prices.

5.3 Data and methodology

5.3.1 Database

The main objective of this study is to determine the predictability of the ANN models in forecasting the returns of the Nifty index making a comparison between two different ANN architectures and making a comparison between the two-layer architecture of the ANN and various input data combinations with particular focus on the financial analyst information contribution in forecasting stock return and in asset allocation decisions in a non-linear context. For the stated purpose, basic variables covered in our database pertain to quarterly average Sp500, Nasdaq100 stock price index. Quarterly average stock price of a portfolio composed by a set of shares quoted in sp500 and NASDAQ market. Other input data are: quarterly average of Barclays Us Treasury 3-5 years free risk index, and of the, actual and forecast E/P ratio, financial analyst recommendations, quarterly by quarterly.

For the composition of the sample of stock, we looked at the database Ibes2 at those companies which had forecast on average more than 20 per year within the full period (obtaining in this way about 1500 stocks, about one-third from the NASDAQ market and the rest from other stock markets). Starting from this sample we have downloaded prices from DataStream.

The data set covers the horizon from January 1997 to June 2003 and is divided into two periods: the first period runs from 31 December 1997 to 1 January 2000 and the second period runs from January 2001 to June 2003. The first period, the in-sample estimation period, is used for model determination (i.e., specifying the model parameters) and validation. The second period is the reserved out-of-sample evaluation period and is used to compare the forecasts and trading performances of various models.

We chose to use as our testing period in this study, a very turbulent period, the so-called dot com bubble period, in order to test in a better way the predictive capabilities of the different ANN schemas and to better highlight the contribution of financial analysts' information that at that time was the subject of very much attention. The use of data in levels in the stock market has many problems: stock market price movements are generally non-stationary and quite random in nature, and therefore not very suitable for learning purposes. To overcome these problems, the stock portfolio series is transformed into rates of return. The data on return are derived from these basic variables. In this study, one-period stock market return at time point t, say Rt , is simply defined as Rt = log(Pt) – log(Pt-1); where Pt is a security price. An advantage of using a returns series is that it helps in making the time series stationary, a useful statistical property.

5.3.2 Artificial neural networks models

The development of ANN models usually encompasses the selection of suitable network topology and the determination of several key parameters associated with training. Among these decision variables are the number of hidden layers, the number of neurons in each of the hidden layers, the number of training cycles in an epoch, the total number of epochs in the complete training session, the learning rate, and the momentum.

The artificial neural networks are non-linear systems formed by neurons (regions where information is processed) which imitate the processing mechanism of the human brain. The connection type, number of entries, layers, exits and the type of training used are aspects which differentiate the types of neural networks.

The most important characteristic of the neural networks, is the ability of learning with its environment and so improving its performance. This is done through an interactive process of adjustments applied to its weights, what is called the training stage. One typical method for training a network is to first separate the data series into two disjoint sets: the training set and the test set. The network is trained (e.g., with back propagation) directly on the training set (i.e. arrive at set of weights between two neurons). The testing set is used to test how well the neural network performs on new data after the network is trained.

The architecture of the neural network is denoted by X-Y-Z. The X-Y-Z stands for a neural network with X neurons in input layer, Y neurons in hidden layer, and Z neurons in output layer. This study resorts to experimentation in the network construction process. The number of input nodes is probably the most critical decision variable for a time series-forecasting problem since it contains important information about the data. In this study, the number of input nodes corresponds to:

- the number of lagged returns observations used to discover the underlying pattern in a time series and to make forecasts for future values;
- financial analyst forecast;
- financial analyst recommendations;
- since this study attempt to forecast the direction of daily price change in the stock price index, technical indicators are used as input variables. Different tools are used in technical analysis, out of which two tools are taken as input parameters as determined by prior research, (Kim and Han, 2000) and (Kim, 2003).

The network construction process has been evaluated with two different architectures, Recurrent MLP and Feedforward Back Propagation, with five levels of the number of input nodes ranging from 1 to 6. The combination of 4 input nodes and two ANN architectures yields a total of 8 different neural network models. These in turn are being considered for each in-sample training set for the portfolio returns.

Only one output node is deployed in the output layer since one-step-ahead forecast is made in this study. The number of input nodes and hidden nodes are not specified a priori. This will be selected through experiment. This study uses one hidden layer. The transfer function used for the output layer was the hyperbolic tangent function. As for the transfer function used for the hidden layer, it was found after some testing that the best effect can be achieved by using Sigmoid Function as the transfer function.

Sigmoid and Hyperbolic tangent function are calculated using the following formulas.

Sigmoid Function: The Output value is between 0 and 1

$$f(n) = \frac{1}{1 + exp^{-n}} \tag{5.1}$$

Hyperbolic Tangent Function: Symmetrical with respect of the origin, with an output value of between −1 and 1

$$f(n) = \frac{e^n - e^{-n}}{e^n + e^{-n}} \tag{5.2}$$

In this study, the researchers have adopted the rollover estimations (moving average window) to generate the 1-step ahead forecast for stock returns for the out of sample period. It means, when a new data is received, the oldest data from the training dataset is dropped and new data is added to the dataset. The advantage of the moving average window is its ability to capture the environmental changes as it utilizes more recent data. Moreover, by utilizing such an approach, the forecasting performance of neural network models would be observed in a continuous manner.

To achieve this end we consider the following strategy: the ANN models are initially trained on a subset of the in-sample data 29 March 1996 to 31 December 2000. The estimated model is then used to generate forecasts for the remaining in-sample-period 1 January 2001 to 31 December 2001.

We adopt stricter criteria for convergence: particularly we stop training condition of MSE of 1 per cent to find the best network during the network training.

Furthermore, as different ranges of value are involved, we need to avoid the situation where the significance of variables with a smaller range is obscured by those with a larger range in the neuron. Under the

circumstances, variables with a larger range of value will dominate the network learning and adversely impact the neural network training results. To avoid this undesirable situation, we need to normalize the range of value of the variables. This will improve the efficiency of the neural network training. The approach is to execute a 'pre-processing' prior to the network input process to ensure that the value will always fall within the specified range of 0–1 (Yen, 1999). All data has to be normalized first before being used. The formula for normalization is as follows:

$$y = \frac{(x - x_{min})}{(x_{max} - x_{min})} \tag{5.3}$$

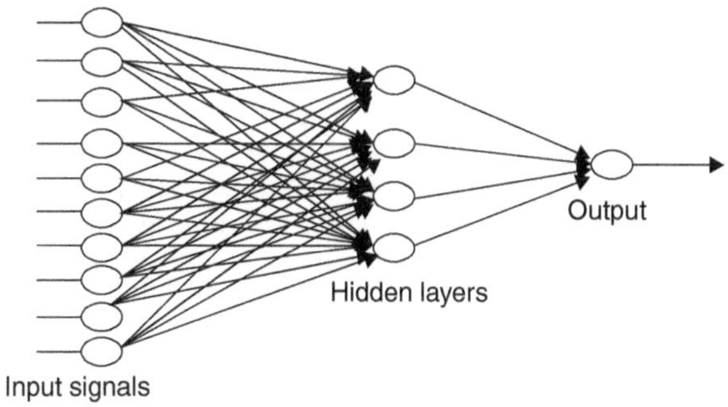

Figure 5.1 ANN architecture: multilayer perceptron

Where x stands for the raw data before normalization; xmin stands for the minimum value of raw data prior to normalization and xmax stands for the maximum value of raw data prior to normalization.

Recurrent MLP model

Although, there are several ANN models have been used for forecasting research, a multilayer perceptron model is mathematically proved to be a universal proxy for any continuous function.[5] Besides, the multilayer perceptron model has become a standard forecasting tool in neural network research, especially in the area of finance and stock markets, as over 80 per cent of the research is carried out using this model (Adya and Collopy, 1998). Other advantages of using this multilayer model are that, it can handle a very high degree of non-linear problem space very efficiently (Roy and Roy, 2008).

Figure 5.1 presents a multilayer perceptron with multiple inputs and outputs. The lines between the nodes indicate the flow of information from one node to the next. In this particular type of neural network, the information flows only from the input to the output (that is, from left-to-right).

The mathematical expression for the MLP(1,8) drawn in Figure 5.1 is given by Equation 5.4, where the subscripts t from the output and input variables are suppressed to ease the exposition. Thus:

$$y = \sum_{j}^{n} a_j x_j + \sum_{j}^{n} b_i f\left(\sum_{j}^{n} c_{i,j} x_j\right) \tag{5.4}$$

where f(.) is the activation logistic cumulative distribution function, a_j are the weights for the direct signals from each of the two input variables to the output variable, b_i is the weight for the signal from each of the hidden units to the output variable, and ci,j, are the weights for the signals from each of the various input variables combinations to the hidden units. The network interpretation of Equation 5.4 is as follows. Input variables, Xj send signals to each of the hidden units. The signal from the j-th input unit to the i-th hidden unit is weighted by some weight denoted by $c_{i,j}$, before it reaches the hidden unit number i. All signals arriving at the hidden units are first summed and then converted to a hidden unit activation by the operation of the hidden unit activation function f (.). The next layer operates similarly with connections sent over to the output variable. As before, these signals are amplified by weights bi and summed. Finally, signals are transmitted directly from the input variables to the output variable with weight a_j.

Feedforward multilayer network

Feedforward network is a collection of interconnected simple processing elements. The most popular and successful one is the backpropagation neural network (BPN). A BPN is typically composed of several layers of nodes. The first or the lowest layer is an input layer where external information is received. The last or the highest layer is an output layer where the problem solution is obtained. The input layer and output layer are separated by one or more intermediate layers called the hidden layers. The units in the network are connected in a feedforward manner, from the input layer to the output layer. Every connection in a neural network has a weight attached to it. In backpropagation algorithm input variables are passed forward to the hidden layer from the input layer and multiplied by their respective weights to compute a weighted sum of total input value to a neuron in the hidden layer. The weighted sum is modified by a transfer function and then sent as input to neurons in the next layer (hidden or output). They stand for the signals thus generated from earlier layers to later layers and the signal finally reaches the output layer. The output layer neuron re-calculates the weighted sum and applies the transfer function to produce the output value of the signal received by it. Finally, an error signal is backpropagated to the hidden layer in a sequence opposite to that of the input variable. The error signal is computed as the difference between the output value of the neural network and the actual output value (also called the target value of the neural network). The weights that connect two layers are adjusted proportionally according to the contribution of each neuron to the forecast error. This is done so as to minimize the mean squared error (MSE). This training process continues until an acceptable MSE target that is specified based on requirement is achieved.

5.3.3 Forecasting accuracy and trading simulation

To compare the performance of the models, it is necessary to evaluate them on previously unseen data. This situation is likely to be the closest to a true forecasting or trading situation. To achieve this, all models were compared for the out-of-sample forecasts using two different approaches, namely an out-of-sample forecasting accuracy measure and an out-of-sample trading performance measure.

This study uses root mean squared errors (RMSE), to evaluate the forecasting capabilities between the various ANN models. RMSE measure the deviation between actual and forecast value. The smaller the values of RMSE, the closer are the predicted time series values to that of the actual value.

Statistical performance measures are often inappropriate for financial applications. In other words, the forecast error may have been minimized during model estimation, but the evaluation of the true merit should be based on the performance of a trading strategy.

We formulate a set of trading rules guided by the returns predicted by various ANN models and then we compare results with B&H and random walk models. The empirical testing takes the form of a trading simulation which closely mimics the timely investment decisions faced by investors in the marketplace. This trading simulation also allows us to evaluate the relative economic profit of the proposed investment strategies. Essentially, the trading simulation investigates the influence of three experimental factors: length of the investment horizon, architecture and input data. The length of the investment horizon is the period of time in which the portfolio stock returns are realized. This is practically the same as the horizon lengths associated with the predicted stock returns. Thus, three month, and twelve month investment horizons are used to implement the forecasts.

We now describe the operational details of the trading simulation.

In this study, we adopted two approaches. The first concerns the choice between a risky and a risk-free asset. By the second approach an investor instead, is able to go long or short on a portfolio of assets depending on market prediction about future performance of the portfolio of stocks.

The trading strategy is to go long on stock portfolio when the model predicts that the average stock portfolio price will rise i.e. the forecast is positive and a sell otherwise. Then the stock portfolio will be held at hand until the next turning point that the model predicts.

The trading performance measures used to analyse the forecasting techniques are: mean annualized return, standard deviation of return, and Sharpe ratio, maximum drawdown and average gain/loss ratio. The Sharpe ratio is a risk-adjusted measure of return, with higher ratios preferred to those that are lower.

5.4 Empirical results

5.4.1 Forecast accuracy

In the first part of this section we will consider the results of the forecast performance of the portfolio taking into account: the time horizon, the network architecture used and the contribution of analysts.

As the forecast accuracy criterion has estimated the two empirical models discussed above and obtained 1-step ahead out-of-sample forecasts for the out-of-sample period, we proceed to evaluate their relative forecast performance comparing the out-of-sample data by calculating the root mean squared errors (RMSE) of out-of-sample predictions. The RMSE is calculated as:

$$RMSE = \sqrt{\frac{1}{T}\sum\nolimits_{t=1}^{T}(y_t - \hat{y}_t)^2} \tag{5.5}$$

In the second part of this section we will discuss the results of certain trading models, constructed using the estimates of the returns provided by the neural network structures, with the results of the models Buy and Hold (starting from Nasdaq100 SP500 stock indexes) and random walk model.

According to the efficient market hypothesis (EMH), asset prices will follow a random walk as news is instantaneously incorporated into prices. The random walk model is therefore a natural theoretical benchmark. Random walk has been used as a benchmark for forecasting ability by numerous studies over the years. The random walk model is a very simple model to use and is often termed the 'naïve model' because it does not involve much technical skill to implement. However, it has been shown to outperform, in terms of forecasting, many sophisticated methods. Therefore, it is a norm in the financial forecasting area to use it as a benchmark. The argument is that any new model that involves the implementation of advanced techniques should at least outperform the random walk model. Otherwise, the random walk model will be preferred since it does not involve much effort. For those reasons, we compare the performance of our ANN models with that of the random walk model. The random walk model assumes that the best forecast is equal to the most recently observable observation.

The results concerning the prediction of performance are set taking into account three elements: the first is the type of architecture used (architecture type A or B), the second refers to the time horizon used for predicting the performance of the portfolio (yearly or quarterly), the third relates to the contribution made by analysts to estimate stock returns. The analysts' contribution is measured by two variables: earnings per share and recommendations.[8]

To better articulate this part of the chapter, it was considered appropriate to adopt the following logical scheme: the results will be presenting to horizon estimation, in which we will analyse the best results for the two network structures used and beyond the contribution made by analysts. Finally, we examine the effect resulting of the time horizon, or in other words we will discuss the best network structures for different time horizons.

The statistical measure used to test the network's ability to predict portfolio returns is given by the RMSE (root mean square error). The RMSE is the root square of the squared sum of the differences between estimated and actual return. In reference to this measure it has been computes also its standard deviation.

Table 5.1 shows the empirical results for the quarterly time horizon. As a first analysis we can observe a tendency of decreasing RMSE, particularly for

Table 5.1 Results for the prediction of returns: quarterly horizon

	RMSE Arch A	Dev. St. Arch A	RMSE Arch B	Dev. St. Arch B	Diff Mean	Diff Dev. st.
Lagged	15.64%	3.07%	20.07%	4.01%	−4.42%	−0.94%
Lagged+at	5.46%	0.69%	4.92%	0.31%	0.54%	0.38%
Lagged+at+forecast	3.65%	0.16%	5.38%	0.32%	−1.74%	−0.15%
Lagged+at +rec	3.17%	0.08%	5.34%	0.16%	−2.17%	−0.07%
Lagged+at +forecast+recc	4.12%	0.16%	4.78%	0.24%	−0.66%	−0.08%
Mean	6.41%	0.83%	8.10%	1.01%	−1.69%	−0.17%

the architecture of type A, according to an increasing amount of information used by the network as input for the estimation of returns.

In particular, the introduction of recommendations and earnings' forecast as ANN inputs leads to a reduction in both the RMSE (RMSE Arch A column and RMSE Arch B column) and the standard deviation of the RMSE itself (Dev. st. Arch A column and Dev. st Arch B Column) than the models lagged and lagged +. at (that stands for lagged variables or technical indicators as input in ANN models). That is, the forecast and recommendations allow, given the forecast quarterly time horizon, to reduce the error in the prediction of return.

Regarding the comparison between architectures, not just dwelling on the best models for the structure (shown in green), one can see how the structure A allows to generate an average RMSE lower than the B structure; this observation is supported not only by the value average reported in the last row of Table 5.1 but also by the values in column 'Diff Mean' which, being almost all negative confirming the point made above.

Finally, by selecting combinations of inputs that have a lower RMSE for the two architectures, we observe how the 'AT + lagged + Recc' is for architecture A that has both the lowest RMSE and the lowest standard deviation, with regard to all other models. The model with the combination of input 'lagged + forecast[9] + at + recc' appears instead to be the best for architecture B.

It should be noted that while for architecture B it is clear that the introduction of joint recommendations and financial analyst forecast leads to a reduction of error of the estimate of return, it is not as clear as the contribution that these two inputs jointly provide for architecture A. For the latter it would seem that, unlike architecture B, the combined effect of recommendations and forecast does not lead to a reduction of RMSE than using them separately. However, even if taken together they allow a reduction of RMSE more than the models 'lagged' and 'lagged + at'.

In conclusion, for the quarterly time horizon the presence of recommendations and of financial analysts' earning forecasts allows, regardless of the network used, a certain reduction of the error in estimating the return of stock portfolio.

Table 5.1 shows a clear contribution from the use of joint recommendations and earning forecasts to the forecast accuracy of ANN models in order to predict the future returns of the equity portfolio. However, it is appropriate to make distinctions, and indeed for structure A the use of disjoint recommendations and earning forecasts leads to greater forecast accuracy of models than the 'lagged' input models (RMSE Arch A column). For architecture B the use of disjoint recommendations and earning forecasts does not lead to a reduction of both RMSE and the standard deviation.

Regarding the comparison between architectures, excluding models with just lagged input variables, the A architecture presents RMSE and standard deviation lower than the B architecture not only on average (last row of Table 5.1) but also for the individual model (excluding the first row of Table 5.1 let you have a look to the columns 'Mean Diff' and 'Diff Dev St'). In this regard the negative differential terms indicate the ability of models with A architecture to have RMSE and standard deviations less high in value than the models with architecture B.

In the comparison between accurate models according to the architecture used it is clear, for both architectures, that one can reach better performance by using networks that consider both recommendations and earning forecasts; in this context the model: 'lagged + forecasts + recc' with A architecture prevails which shows an RMSE and a standard deviation lower than the model with architecture B.

Finally, in reference to the models related to the A architecture of the neural networks it is clear that the recommendations and forecasting, used either separately or together, improves the 'lagged' model in terms of lower RMSE and in terms of lower deviation standard associated with it with respect to ANN models not considering these two input variables. This observation is not valid for models built with architecture B, for which only the joint use of recommendations and earning forecasts, reduces the RMSE and its standard deviation once compared to the model with just lagged variables.

By comparing the model results for the two different time horizons some considerations emerge. First of all, the architecture A with quarterly holding period has identified, on average, a number of models with RMSE and a standard deviation lower than the model with yearly time horizons. The more accurate model was created for the yearly horizon, with the combination: 'lagged + forecasts + recc'. Between these two ANN architectures, architecture B gave rise to models with a higher RMSE on average.

From the analysis previously made and reported in Tables 5.1 and 5.2, one can see how the introduction of recommendations and earning forecast between inputs, in general, can upgrade the error estimates of the models. In particular, for the yearly time horizon the joint use as input nodes of earning forecast and recommendations allows for the greater accuracy of

Table 5.2 Results for the prediction of returns: yearly horizon

	RMSE Arch A	Dev. St. Arch A	RMSE Arch B	Dev. St. Arch B	Diff Mean	Diff Dev. st.
Lagged	9.52%	1.11%	6.21%	0.60%	5.31%	1.01%
Lagged+forecast	3.99%	0.21%	7.40%	0.71%	−3.41%	−0.51%
Lagged+recc	7.05%	0.57%	8.57%	0.89%	−1.52%	−0.32%
Lagged+forecast+recc	3.36%	0.14%	5.16%	0.37%	−1.80%	−0.23%
Mean	5.98%	0.51%	6.33%	0.52%	−0.35%	−0.01%

the forecasting models used. Whereas, for the quarterly holding period, the combined effect has a better result only for architecture B, while for the A architecture the application not contemporary of the earning forecast and recommendations as input nodes achieves models with lower estimation errors on average.

In conclusion, for all time horizons, models that have the lowest RMSE use, jointly or severally, the recommendations and the forecast of financial analysts. Furthermore, considering the overall model and wanting to compare the results based on the architecture used, it is evident that the greater accuracy is offered by the architecture A.

5.4.2 Trading simulation

The first simulation experiment assumes that, at the beginning of each monthly period, the investor makes an asset allocation decision of whether to shift his liquid assets into risk-free bonds or into the stock portfolio fund (*Equity–Bond*[10] *model*). Liquid assets are defined as money that is currently not invested in either the riskfree bonds or the stock portfolio. Further, it is assumed that the money that has been invested in either risk-free bonds or the stock portfolio becomes illiquid and will not become liquid until the end of the investor's chosen investment horizon. In other words, the invested money will become available after the selected investment horizon reaches its maturity. For example, suppose the investor has decided to use an investment horizon of three months. The money that he has invested into either risk-free bonds or the stock portfolio in the last three months is considered to have been 'locked up' in asset allocation. Hence, the asset will not be available for another round of investment decision before the security or portfolio matures.

The second simulation experiment invests exclusively in the stock market with the possibility of short selling on the basket of shares which comprise in the stock portfolio (*Long–Short Model*).

The Equity–Bond model was compiled by the following logic, if $\overline{r_t} > 0$, then it is investing in the Equity Portfolio otherwise it invests in the bond market by buying the free risk index. $\overline{r_t}$ represents the estimated return of the Stock Portfolio made at time t–1. This forecast Questa is provided by various neural network models according to the architecture, combinations of input data and forecast horizon (that correspond also to the holding period) (e.g. Arch A + delayed + at + recc, quarterly). For comparison purposes the same forecast is provided also by a random walk model for which the estimated return at time t corresponds to the return observation at time t-1.

The long–short model, instead, was constructed as follows, if $\overline{r_t} > 0$, then the Equity Portfolio is invested in long position, otherwise it sells short the whole portfolio. As with the Equity Bond model $\overline{r_t}$ represents the estimated return of the Stock Portfolio made at time t-1. This forecast can be provided, in order to implement the trading rules, both from ANN models and random walks or buy and hold strategies.

The testing period runs from January 2001 to June 2003 for a total of 10 quarterly out-of-sample observations. In the trading experiment, it is assumed that, during the initiation period, an investor will invest $1 at the beginning of each month in either risk-free bonds or the stock index fund depending on his chosen investment strategy.

Table 5.3 shows the results of trading patterns not only by analysing the average return on an annual basis (Annualized Mean) and standard deviation on an annual basis (Standard Dev. Annualized) but also a Risk adjusted

Table 5.3 Trading model results: quarterly horizon

Time horizon	Type	Model	Mean annualized	Standard dev. annualized	Sharpe ratio
Quarterly	L/S	Arch A lagged+at +recc	39.67%	22.57%	158.06%
Quarterly	E/B	Arch A lagged+at +recc	25.44%	23.81%	90.03%
Quarterly	E/B	Arch B Lagged+at+recc+ forecast	25.44%	23.81%	90.03%
Quarterly	L/S	Arch B Lagged+at+recc+ forecast	19.20%	29.54%	51.46%
Yearly	E/B	Lagged+rec+forecast	3.77%	0.58%	26.21%
Yearly	L/S	Lagged+rec+forecast	5.16%	2.54%	8.12%
Yearly	E/B	Lagged+rec+forecast	−1.80%	7.30%	−0.99%
Yearly	E/B	Random walk (3–5 years)	−1.80%	7.30%	−0.99%
Yearly	L/S	Lagged+rec+forecast	−1.80%	7.30%	−0.99%
Yearly	L/S	Random walk (3–5 years)	−1.80%	7.30%	−0.99%
Quarterly	E/B	Random walk (3–5 years)	−6.31%	25.40%	−40.57%
Quarterly	L/S	Random walk (3–5 years)	−17.54%	43.61%	−49.39%
		S&P 500 Index	−18.39%	14.51%	−5.07%
		Buy and hold	−8.73%	4.96%	−7.04%

Notes: E/B = Equity/Bond L/S = Long/Short

performance measure like Sharpe Ratio. This indicator allows a comparison of investment strategies with diversified risk and return.

Almost all trading models driven by the estimates of neural networks have seen a better result when compared to the random walk models, not only with respect to the average return but also for the Sharpe Ratio, for all time horizons to estimate analysed. In particular, strategies that use the best models of neural networks and a quarterly time horizon have recorded a very high Sharpe Ratio when compared to the results achieved by the buy and hold portfolio that is composed of 50% from Standard & Poor's 500 index and the remaining 50% from the index BARCLAYS TREASURY U.S. 3-5Y. The strategies employing neural networks with a yearly time horizon of estimate showed a higher Sharpe Ratio compared to the Standard & Poor's 500 Index.

The high performance obtained from the quarterly data models is mainly due to its ability to predict the size and sign of future performance (one step ahead). Furthermore, quarterly data models, since they have a shorter time horizon with respect to models fed with yearly data, show for a same out-of-sample period, a greater number of estimates. It appears that, in almost equal accuracy in return forecasting, the greater number of estimates made during the period 2000 to 2003, by quarterly data models, make true the opportunity to capture a greater number of upward and downward movements of the return portfolio, and in this way make possible a remarkable performance.

5.5 Conclusion

Finance is a promising area for applying the ANN models to forecasting prices, returns and indices. Generally speaking the success of the ANN models depends to a great extent on the selection of explanatory input variables which have a structural and corresponding with the output variable. In the present study, attempts have been made to test the contribution of information related to financial analysts like earnings' forecasts and recommendations and the effectiveness of different ANN architectures. It has also taken into account the forecasting horizon. To pursue this goal the study investigated the effectiveness of various neural network models in prediction of stock returns in the case of a stock portfolio of sp500 and nasdaq100 indexes shares. For the purpose, quarterly data have been obtained from January 1997 to June 2003, and the neural networks are trained with varying sets of input data. Once the training of the neural networks is over, the network has been used to predict the portfolio stock returns for one quarterly ahead. The performances of the various nonlinear models and the linear model were measured statistically and financially via a trading experiment. On the whole the results are quite impressive, in fact the findings of our study support, to a great extent, the effectiveness of the neural network models in stock portfolio return forecasting, when the contribution of financial analysts, is also considered as data input namely earnings' forecasts and stock recommendations.

Furthermore between various ANN schemes used, the Recurrent MLP model has been shown to be particularly useful in predicting portfolio returns. Also the trading experiment shows that the ANN-guided trading strategies, with particular reference to the quarterly horizon forecasting, obtain higher profits than the other investment strategies, namely B&H and random walk trading strategy.

Notes

1. Both indexes are used for a variety of purposes such as benchmarking fund portfolios, index based derivatives and index funds.
2. The data from financial analysts used in this study are obtained from the IBES database.
3. Simple Moving Average of last 3 days closing Nifty values and Relative Strength Index of last 3 observations.
4. The number of hidden nodes plays a very important role too. These hidden neurons enable the network to detect the feature, to capture the pattern in the data, and to perform complicated nonlinear mapping between input and output variables.
5. Multilayer perceptron models are non-linear neural network models that can be used to approximate almost any function with a high degree of accuracy (White, 1992).
   Recurrent MLP model.
6. Feedforward multilayer network.
7. For the quarterly horizon we also used two indicators of technical analysis on returns, namely Relative Strength Index (3) and Moving Average (3).
8. This variable stands for financial analyst earning forecasts as input in ANN models.
9. Barclays US Treasury 3–5 years has been taken into account.

References

Adya, M. and F. Collopy (1998) 'How effective are neural networks at forecasting and prediction? A review and evaluation', *Journal of Forecasting*, 17, 481–95.

Al-Hindi, Z. and F. Al-Hasan (2002) 'Forecasting stock returns with the neural network models', *Journal of King Saud University*, 14, 65–81.

Ang, A. and G. Bekaert (2007) 'Stock return predictability: Is it there?' *Review of Financial Studies*, 20, 651–707.

Avci, E. (2007) 'Forecasting daily and seasonal returns of the ISE-100 Index with neural network models', *Dogus University Journal*, 8, 128–42.

Banz, R. and W. Breen (1986) 'Sample-dependent results using accounting and market data: Some evidence', *Journal of Finance*, 41, 779–93.

Bekiros, S. D. and D. A. Georgoutsos (2008) 'Direction-of-change forecasting using a volatility based recurrent neural network', *Journal of Forecasting*, 27, 407–17.

Bengoechea, G. A., U. C. Ordonez, S. M. Marchant and M. N. Opazo (1996) 'Stock market indices in Santiago de Chile: Forecasting using neural networks', *IEEE International Conference on Neural Networks*, 4, 2172–5.

O'Brien, P. and Y. Tian (2006) 'Financial analysts' role in the 1996-2000 internet bubble', http://accounting.uwaterloo.ca (homepage), date accessed 01 July 2012.

Campbell, J. Y. and R. J. Shiller (1988a) 'The dividend-price ratio and expectations of future dividends and discount factors', *Review of Financial Studies*, 1, 195–228.

——(1988b) 'Stock prices, earnings, and expected dividends', *Journal of Finance*, 43, 661–76.

Campbell, J. Y. and M. Yogo (2006) 'Efficient tests of stock return predictability', *Journal of Financial Economics*, 81, 27–60.

Diler, A. I. (2003) 'ISE national-100 index of the direction of the neural network errors estimation method with propagation backward', *ISE Review*, 25–6, 65–81.

Fama, E. (1970) 'Efficient capital market: A review of theory and empirical work', *Journal of Finance*, 25, 383–417.

Fama, E. and K. French (1992) 'The cross-section of expected stock returns', *Journal of Finance*, 47, 427–65.

Fernandez-Rodrigues, F., C. Gonzalez-Martel and S. Sosvilla-Rivero (2000) 'On the profitability of technical trading rules based on artificial neural networks: Evidence from the Madrid stock market', *Economics Letters*, 69, 89–94.

Ferson, W. E. and C. R. Harvey (1993) 'The risk and predictability of international equity returns', *Review of Financial Studies*, 6, 527–66.

Gencay, R. (1998) 'Optimization of technical trading strategies and the profitability in the stock markets', *Economic Letters*, 59, 249–54.

Goyal, A. and I. Welch (2003) 'Predicting the equity premium with dividend ratios', *Management Science*, 49, 639–54.

——(2008) 'A comprehensive look at the empirical performance of equity premium prediction', *Review of Financial Studies*, 21, 1455–508.

Hammad, A. A. B., S.M.A. Ali and E. L. Hall (2009) 'Forecasting the Jordanian stock price using artificial neural network', http://www.min.uc.edu (homepage), date accessed 01 July 2012.

Harvey, C. R. (1995) 'Predictable risk and returns in emerging markets', *Review of Financial Studies*, 8, 773–816.

Ince, H. and T. B. Trafalis (2007) 'Kernel principal component analysis and support vector machines for stock price prediction', *IEE Transactions*, 39, 629–37.

Jaffe, J., D. Keim and R. Westerfield (1989) 'Earnings yields, market values and stock returns', *Journal of Finance*, 44, 135–48.

Kim, K. J. (2003) 'Financial time series forecasting using support vector machines', *Neurocomputing*, 55, 307–19.

——(2006) 'Artificial neural networks with evolutionary instance selection for financial forecasting', *Expert System Applications*, 30, 519–26.

Kim, K. J. and I. Han (2000) 'Genetic algorithms approach to feature discretization in artificial neural networks for the prediction of stock price index', *Expert System Application*, 19, 125–32.

Kim, S. H. and S. H. Chun (1998) 'Graded forecasting using array of bipolar predictions: Application of probabilistic neural networks to a stock market index', *International Journal of Forecasting*, 14, 323–37.

Kothari, S. and J. Shanken (1997) 'Book-to-market, dividend yield, and expected market returns: A time series analysis', *Journal of Financial Economics*, 44, 169–203.

Lam, M. (2004) 'Neural network techniques for financial performance prediction: Integrating fundamental and technical analysis', *Decision Support Systems*, 37, 567–81.

Lamont, O. (1998) 'Earnings and expected returns', *Journal of Finance*, 53, 1563–87.

Lawrence, R. (1997) 'Using neural network to forecast stock market prices', http://www.yris.ch/ (homepage), date accessed 01 July 2012.

Lewellen, J. (2004) 'Predicting returns with financial ratios', *Journal of Financial Economics*, 74, 209–35.

Lim, G. C. and P. D. McNelis (1998) 'The effect of the Nikkei and the S&P on the all-ordinaries: A comparison of three models', *International Journal of Finance and Economics*, 3, 217–28.

Liu, Q. and F. Song. (2001) 'The rise and fall of Internet stocks: Should financial analysts be blamed?', http://www.sef.hku.hk/ (homepage), date accessed 01 July 2012.

Ma, T. H. (2003) 'The application of neuron–fuzzy to emulate the investment in TAIEX', http://ethesys.lib.cyut.edu.tw (homepage), date accessed 01 July 2012.

Manish, K. and M. Thenmozhi (2003) 'Forecasting daily returns of exchange rates using artificial neural network and ARIMA model', *ICFAI Journal of Applied Finance* 10, 16–36.

——(2004) 'Forecasting nifty index futures returns using neural network and ARIMA models', http://www.actapress.com (homepage), date accessed 01 July 2012.

——(2005) 'A comparison study of selected training algorithms for neural networks to financial time series prediction', http://www.icmis.net/ (homepage), date accessed 01 July 2012.

Mantri, J. K., P. Gahan and B. B. Nayak (2010) 'Artificial neural networks an application to stock market volatility', *International Journal of Engineering Science and Technology*, 2, 1451–60.

Pant, B. and K. S. S. Rao (2003) 'Forecasting daily returns of stock index: An application of artificial neural network', *ICFAI Journal of Applied Finance*, 9, 5–18.

Pontiff, J. and L. D. Schall (1998) 'Book-to-market ratios as predictors of market returns', *Journal of Financial Economics*, 43, 141–60.

Rodriguez, J. V., S. Torra and J. Andrada-Félix (2005) 'STAR and ANN Models: Forecasting performance on Spanish Ibex-35 Stock Index', *Journal of Empirical Finance*, 12, 490–509.

Roy, P. and A. Roy (2008) 'Forecasting daily returns of Nifty index – using the method of artificial neural network', *FFMI 2008 Conference Proceedings* (Kharagpur : Indian Institute of Technology).

Stambaugh, R. (1999) 'Predictive regressions', *Journal of Financial Economics*, 54, 375–421.

Tsai, Y. C., T. M. Chen, T. Y. Yang and C. Y. Wang (1999) 'Neural network used in the investment strategy of stock research', *Web Journal of Chinese Management Review*, 2, 25–48.

Valkanov, R. (2003) 'Long-horizon regressions: Theoretical results and applications', *Journal of Financial Economics*, 68, 201–32.

White, H. (1988) 'Economic prediction using neural networks: The case of IBM daily stock returns', http://weber.ucsd.edu/ (homepage), date accessed 01 July 2012.

Wu, S. H. (2004) 'Applying technical analysis of stock trends to trading strategy of dynamic portfolio insurance', www.atlantis-press.com (homepage), date accessed 01 July 2012.

Yen, Y. C. (1999) 'Application of neural network models with the implementation' (Taipei: Scholars Books).

6

Market Timing with the Black–Litterman Model

Ugo Pomante

6.1 Introduction

The portfolio construction issues have stimulated an intense debate in both academic and practitioner communities. In more than half a century, asset managers and academics have developed a set of almost unlimited asset allocation techniques.

While in the financial literature the investment strategy stems from a scientific process based on the estimation of statistical parameters and the development of mathematical optimization, many portfolio managers deny the usefulness of a quantitative framework, defending the role of their views that, unfortunately, are difficult to process in a mathematical model. Such behaviour, confirmed by empirical evidence, suggests as follows:

a) the construction of mathematical models is disproportionate if compared to their use;
b) the asset managers, often "entrenched" behind their heuristic techniques, are likely to be closer to craftsmen rather than scientists.

Regarding the limited use of quantitative models, a mathematical framework is based on simplified assumptions that make the process of portfolio construction unable to incorporate all the operational issues. In addition, asset managers do not like to delegate investment decisions to a mathematical model that, not being consistent with their operating procedures, leads to portfolios whose weights are often unreasonable. The limited use of quantitative finance is therefore due to its failure to incorporate the asset managers' *modus operandi*.

The transition from a naïve to a scientific methodology is possible if:

- financial operators are available to a cultural change;
- asset allocation models are consistent with the needs of investors and asset managers.

The aim of this chapter is to demonstrate that the Black–Litterman (B–L) model is able to combine theory and practice. However, before introducing the analytics of the B–L approach (Section 6.3) and proposing the application for market timing purposes (Section 6.4), Section 6.2 investigates the reasons underlying the limited use of quantitative finance.

6.2 Barriers to the practical application of quantitative models

Asset managers prefer asset allocation techniques that:

a) lead to reasonable portfolios;
b) are not black-box optimizers;
c) do not require a large amount of inputs.

Apart from the need to maximize the expected return given a targeted risk level, the portfolio composition must be reasonable. For instance, a portfolio aimed at a European investor that consists solely of:

- Emerging Markets equity;
- Pacific excluding Japan equity;
- Emerging Market bonds;

should be considered unreasonable (and therefore dismissed regardless of its risk–return combination), because of the concentration in asset classes that usually have marginal weights.

Unfortunately, many mathematical approaches, including the Markowitz model (Markowitz, 1952; 1959) which is the main reference of many softwares of portfolio construction, share the tendency to build unreasonable portfolios. It is easy to identify the reason why the portfolio compositions are often not reasonable: models aim to identify portfolios that maximize expected return, disregarding the composition of portfolios. In doing so the investors' preferences are focused only on risk-return combinations and all portfolios are assumed eligible. No distinction is made between reasonable and unreasonable portfolios, as the sole relevant inequality is between efficient and inefficient solutions.

However, asset managers do not build corner portfolios, that is, portfolios poorly diversified and heavily concentrated in marginal asset classes. On the contrary, they:

- construct portfolios that are fairly 'faithful' to the financial markets capitalization;
- over-weight local markets (*home bias*).

For this reason, asset managers reject models unable to build portfolios consistent with their *a priori* behaviours.

Referring to black box optimizers, no mathematical model can be used in practice if it will return results that are inconsistent with asset managers' expectations. Unfortunately, in traditional asset allocation models it is very difficult to find a direct link between the input parameters (estimates) and the output (portfolio weights). With a large number of asset classes, the inputs–output connection is so obscure (hence the term *black box*) that any attempt to anticipate the result of the mathematical optimization is useless. In other words, because of the large number of variables involved, any attempt to capture the cause–effect relationship that links estimates and portfolio compositions is useless. Moreover, asset managers tend to act in this way: they first state *generic* views (optimistic, pessimistic or neutral) which are then transformed into *numerical* inputs just to be compliant with the mathematical optimization. Consequently, analysts give greater relevance to the starting qualitative views, rather than the final quantitative inputs. Therefore if the optimizer does not return portfolios consistent with the preferences of asset managers, these would prefer to make changes to the inputs which have proved unable to translate their qualitative views, rather than relying on the results of the model. In conclusion, if the asset manager is facing a crossroads:

- be loyal to the starting ideas (the optimistic, pessimistic or neutral views about market trends);
- make a 'leap of faith' on the optimization that leads to results inconsistent with the starting views;

he will choose the first solution.

In order to increase the operational use of mathematical models, it is crucial to use only those able to avoid numerical inputs (especially for the expected returns). Moreover, this *modus operandi* prevents the use of past data, whose unreliability has been known for decades (Frankfurter et al., 1971; Jobson and Korkie, 1980; Jobson and Korkie, 1981) . Too often, indeed, faced with the need to produce numerical estimates, financial institutions do not make predictions, but rather rely on the 'rearview mirror' rule that prevents the analyst from influencing the portfolio composition.

6.3 The Black–Litterman Model

Because of the problems discussed, the quantitative models are not applied with the expected diligence and techniques with no theoretical justification (often called *naïve portfolio formation rules*) are much more common than expected.

As stated before, the operational failure of quantitative techniques is often due to the inconsistency with the asset managers' behaviour (Black and

Litterman, 1992). To go beyond the theory, an asset allocation model should have the following properties:

- the output should be a set of reasonable and well-diversified portfolios;
- the model should take into account the size (capitalization) of financial markets, in order to incorporate the tendency of managers to deviate from *market neutral* positions only if forecasts are reliable;
- expected return, risk and correlation should incorporate the asset managers' forecast;
- the model should allow the expression of both *relative views*[1] (*market A will over perform market B*) and *absolute view* (*market A will perform well*);
- given the asset classes previously selected, the model should enable asset managers to generate views just for a subset of them (for example, those whose prediction is reliable).

The B–L approach is able to incorporate all the points mentioned, showing a significant balance between methodological precision and usability. Thanks to this rare equilibrium between theory and practice, the Bayesian model by Fisher Black and Robert Litterman (Black and Litterman, 1991, 1992), is an outstanding tool for asset managers who want to apply the Markowitz approach.

Now the analysis focuses on the model analytics.

The asset classes returns (r) are normally distributed with expected returns μ and covariance matrix Σ:

$$r \sim N(\mu, \Sigma) \tag{6.1}$$

Being Bayesian, the B–L model combines two information sets: equilibrium returns (the *prior*), and the asset managers' views.

The intuition behind the model can be summarized as follows: without market forecasts, asset managers should build *market neutral* portfolios 'faithful' to the size of all markets.

The first information set is the following:

- the equilibrium expected returns (Π_{eq});
- the covariance matrix of returns (Σ).

Given the risk-aversion parameter λ (it can be interpreted as the average risk tolerance of the world investors), if Π_{MN} and Σ are used as inputs of a mean-variance optimization, the efficient portfolio is *market neutral*. Without further information (the views) the final expected returns are exactly Π_{eq}: the model suggests not to deviate from a portfolio perfectly consistent with the size of financial markets.

The first information set is synthesized by the distribution of equilibrium returns:

$$r \sim N(\Pi_{eq}, \Sigma) \tag{6.2}$$

While the covariance matrix is often calculated using the time series of returns, the equilibrium expected returns is calculated with a *reverse optimization*, so named since the expected returns (portfolio weights) are not the input (output) but the output (input) of the optimization process. Given:

Π_{eq} = the column vector of the equilibrium expected returns;
Σ = the covariance matrix of returns;
λ = the coefficient of risk aversion;
W_{eq} = the column vector of equilibrium portfolio weights assimilated to the *market portfolio* of the Capital Asset Pricing Model (see Sharpe (1964); Lintner (1965); Mossin (1966));

the equilibrium expected returns are:

$$\Pi_{eq} = (\lambda\Sigma) \cdot W_{eq} \tag{6.3}$$

λ is often estimated as follows:

$$\lambda = \frac{E(R)_{eq} - r_f}{\sigma^2_{eq}} \tag{6.4}$$

where:

$E(R)_{eq}$ = expected return of the *market neutral* portfolio;
r_f = risk-free rate;
σ^2_{eq} = variance of (the returns of) the *market neutral* portfolio.

However, if λ is calculated as described above, $(\lambda\Sigma) \cdot W_{eq}$ are the equilibrium *excess returns* (or risk premiums). The equilibrium expected returns are given by:

$$\Pi_{eq} = r_f \cdot I + (\lambda\Sigma) \cdot W_{eq} \tag{6.5}$$

where I is a column vector with all elements being one and size equal to the number of asset classes.

The Bayesian *prior* is that expected returns (μ) are random variables normally distributed, centred around Π_{eq}:

$$\mu = \Pi_{eq} + \varepsilon^{(I)} \tag{6.6}$$

where $\varepsilon^{(I)}$ is a normally distributed random vector with zero mean and covariance matrix $\tau\Sigma$:

$$\varepsilon^{(I)} = \begin{bmatrix} \varepsilon_1^{(I)} \\ \varepsilon_2^{(I)} \\ \vdots \\ \varepsilon_N^{(I)} \end{bmatrix} \sim \mathrm{N}\left(\begin{bmatrix} 0 \\ 0 \\ \vdots \\ 0 \end{bmatrix}; \quad \tau\Sigma\right) \tag{6.7}$$

Alternatively, we can write:

$$\mu \sim N\left(\Pi_{eq}, \quad \tau\Sigma\right) \tag{6.8}$$

In the literature there is not a common opinion about the value to be attributed to τ. Since the uncertainty of the average returns is lower than the uncertainty of returns, τ should be less than one (usually $\tau \in [0.01; 0.05]$). If the covariance matrix (Σ) is inferred from a sample of past observations of size T, τ is $1/T$. In doing so the properties of the sample means are applied to the equilibrium expected returns. However, τ remains a subjective parameter: the greater the confidence in the market equilibrium condition, the lower the value attributed to τ.

The second information set is composed by the views whose mission is to give asset managers the chance to construct portfolios consistent with their expectations. This model does not assume that markets are in constant equilibrium: equilibrium is a starting point from which the analysts can diverge using reliable expectations.

The B–L model does not require asset managers to express views on all asset classes. Also, as already mentioned, views may be relative or absolute.

Views are expressed as:

$$P \cdot \mu = Q + \varepsilon^{(II)} \tag{6.9}$$

where:

P is a $k \times n$ matrix, where any of the k rows identifies the markets involved in each view (and n is the number of asset classes).

μ is a column vector of size n representing the expected returns of asset classes;

Q is a column vector of size k identifying the *views;*

$\varepsilon^{(II)}$ is a column vector of size k measuring the views' uncertainty (this vector is normally distributed with zero mean – views are unbiased – and covariance matrix Ω).

Alternatively we can write:

$$P \cdot \mu \sim N(Q; \quad \Omega) \tag{6.10}$$

Before discussing the issue of the combination of the two sources of information (the starting equilibrium and the views), it is necessary to analyse the matrix Ω, measuring the uncertainty of the views. Usually Ω is a diagonal matrix, with zero values outside the main diagonal:

$$\Omega = \begin{bmatrix} \varpi_1 & 0 & 0 & 0 \\ 0 & \varpi_2 & 0 & 0 \\ & & \ddots & \\ 0 & 0 & & 0 \\ 0 & 0 & 0 & \varpi_n \end{bmatrix} \tag{6.11}$$

The views are therefore independent of each other and the correlations between them should not be estimated. As the elements on the main diagonal are the error terms from the expressed views, they represent the uncertainty in each view. Perhaps, the estimation of ϖ is the most complex and debated issue.

An efficient solution is to estimate ϖ as follows (see Meucci, 2005):

$$\Omega = \begin{bmatrix} \left(\frac{1}{c_1} - 1\right) \cdot p_1 \cdot (\tau\Sigma) \cdot p_1^T & 0 & 0 & 0 \\ 0 & \left(\frac{1}{c_2} - 1\right) \cdot p_2 \cdot (\tau\Sigma) \cdot p_2^T & 0 & 0 \\ 0 & 0 & \ddots & 0 \\ 0 & 0 & 0 & \left(\frac{1}{c_k} - 1\right) \cdot p_k \cdot (\tau\Sigma) \cdot p_k^T \end{bmatrix} \tag{6.12}$$

$c_1, c_2, \ldots, c_k$ identify the confidence levels that asset managers have towards the k views. These parameters can get values within the interval (0, 100 per cent), bounds excluded:

- if the asset manager has a low confidence, c is close to zero and the probability distribution of the view will be highly dispersed (the view has a poor impact on the final expected returns);
- if the asset manager has a high confidence, c is close to one and the probability distribution of the views will be poorly dispersed (the view has a strong impact on the final expected returns).

In brief, when c is large, expected returns deviate significantly from the equilibrium expected returns (Π_{eq}), leading to optimal portfolios also significantly different from market-neutral position (W_{eq}).

The final expected returns (Π_{BL}) are calculated combining the Bayesian *prior* and the views:

$$\Pi_{BL} = \left[(\tau\Sigma)^{-1} + P^T \cdot \Omega^{-1} \cdot P\right]^{-1} \times \left[(\tau\Sigma)^{-1} \cdot \Pi_{eq} + P^T \cdot \Omega^{-1} \cdot Q\right] \tag{6.13}$$

6.4 An application for market timing purposes

The B–L model is commonly adopted for strategic asset allocation purposes. However, this methodology can be applied in order to identify short-term changes to the strategic portfolio. In fact, this approach shows a remarkable efficiency in translating the opinions of Tactical Investment Committees in numerical estimates to be used as inputs in an optimization model.

However, if the Black–Litterman model is employed for tactical asset allocation, some changes are required. When applied to generate a tactical portfolio, the Bayesian *prior* is that expected returns (μ) are random variables normally distributed, centred around the strategic expected returns (Π_{STR})[2] that if used as inputs in a mean–variance optimization (given a targeted parameter of risk aversion) return an efficient portfolio having the strategic composition. These expected returns can be named *strategic neutral*. In doing so, the asset manager's purpose is to diverge from the strategic asset allocation (not from the *market neutral* portfolio). Without short-term views, tactical expected returns equal the strategic ones and the asset allocation does not change.

The *prior* (Π_{STR}) is always estimated via the *reverse optimization*, but inputs change:

- the *market neutral* portfolio (W_{MN}) is replaced by the *strategic portfolio* (W_{STR});
- the risk aversion parameter must be calculated using the strategic inputs $\left(\lambda = \frac{E(R)_{STR} - r_f}{\sigma^2_{STR}}\right)$.

The equilibrium (or strategic neutral) expected returns are given by:

$$\Pi_{STR} = r_f \cdot I + (\lambda\Sigma) \cdot W_{STR} \tag{6.14}$$

The process continues with the quantification of tactical views.

Asset managers do not like to define exact estimates about short-term trends of asset classes. In other words, it is difficult to estimate with accuracy the numerical values of the Q vector. In fact, asset managers feel much more comfortable with qualitative (*the market will perform very well*) rather than quantitative views (*the market performance will be 5 per cent*). For this reason, a successful application of the Black–Litterman model requires:

- to work with qualitative views;
- to transform qualitative views in point estimates.

For this purpose, a simple and effective way to move from qualitative to quantitative estimates is the following:

1. the analyst communicates its qualitative expectation (*strong positive, positive, neutral, negative, strong negative*) about the short-term performance of an asset class (or a portfolio of asset classes);

2. a percentage (*Perc*) is associated with each qualitative expectation:
   $Perc_{strong\ negative} = 20\%$
   $Perc_{negative} = 40\%$
   $Perc_{neutral} = 50\%$
   $Perc_{positive} = 60\%$
   $Perc_{strong\ positive} = 80\%$
3. the numerical view is then determined as follows:

$$Tact_{View} = E(R)_{Str} + \text{stnorminv}(Perc) \times \sigma_{Str} \tag{6.15}$$

where:

$E(R)_{Str}$ = strategic expected return of the asset class (or the portfolio);
stnorminv(*Perc*) = the inverse of the standardized normal at the corresponding probability in *Perc*;
σ_{Str} = strategic standard deviation of the asset class (or the portfolio).

When the qualitative view is positive (negative), the confidence level is higher (lower) than 50 per cent and the tactical view is better (worse) than the strategic expected return. The rationale underlying this *modus operandi* is the following: point estimates are not necessary, what is needed is a signal to be compared to the strategic data.

If the Ω matrix is calculated as suggested in the previous paragraph, the parameters $c_1, c_2, \ldots, c_K$ can be calculated avoiding a direct estimation:

1. the asset manager communicates a qualitative confidence (for example, *very high, high, medium, low, very low*) in every view;
2. then a confidence level (that will act as c parameter) is associated with each qualitative confidence:
   Very low = 4%
   Low = 8%
   Medium = 12%
   High = 16%
   Very high = 20%

The *instability* of the mean-variance optimization is well known (Jorion, 1985; Best and Grauer, 1991a, 1991b): small changes in inputs cause large changes in portfolio composition. For this reason, the values associated to the qualitative confidence should not be high.

The use of a numerical example will be useful both to clarify the characteristics of the model and to appreciate its consistency with the business of asset management. In this regard, the numerical exercise reproduces the behaviour of an equity fund manager involved with a problem of tactical asset allocation. He has selected five asset classes, and each of them is associated with a market index (Table 6.1).

Table 6.1 Asset classes and market indexes

Asset classes	Market indexes
Equity Europe	MSCI Europe – Gross index
Equity North America	MSCI North America – Gross index
Equity Japan	MSCI Japan – Gross index
Equity Pacific excluding Japan	MSCI Pacific free ex Japan – Gross index
Equity Emerging Market	MSCI EM (Emerging Markets) – Gross index

Table 6.2 The strategic portfolio composition

Asset classes	Weights
Equity Europe	31.20%
Equity North America	47.90%
Equity Japan	9.00%
Equity Pacific excluding Japan	3.80%
Equity Emerging Market	8.10%

Table 6.3 The covariance matrix

	Asset class 1	Asset class 2	Asset class 3	Asset class 4	Asset class 5
Asset class 1	0.03948	0.03824	0.03765	0.03792	0.04713
Asset class 2	0.03824	0.04607	0.03478	0.03040	0.04386
Asset class 3	0.03765	0.03478	0.09444	0.06984	0.09136
Asset class 4	0.03792	0.03040	0.06984	0.09455	0.10289
Asset class 5	0.04713	0.04386	0.09136	0.10289	0.14207

The asset manager has already set the strategic weights (W_{STR}) that the fund will keep (on average) in the long run (Table 6.2). In order to develop the tactical changes, he relies on the B–L model.

The first stage concerns the estimation of the equilibrium expected returns (Π_{STR}). Π_{STR} is estimated by a *reverse optimization*. The inputs required are:

- the strategic weights (W_{STR}) in Table 6.2;
- the covariance matrix (Σ) in Table 6.3;
- the risk aversion parameter (λ).

The *risk-free* rate is 2.5 per cent. Given the column vector with the strategic weights (W_{STR}) and the covariance matrix (Σ) of returns, the variance of the strategic portfolio is:

$$\sigma^2_{STR} = W^T_{STR} \cdot \Sigma \cdot W_{STR} = 0.04302 \tag{6.16}$$

The strategic *risk premium* $[E(R)_{STR} - r_f]$ is expected to be 5.117 per cent.

The risk aversion parameter is computed as follows:

$$\lambda_{Str} = \frac{E(R)_{STR} - r_f}{\sigma^2_{STR}} = \frac{5.117\%}{0.04302} = 1.189 \tag{6.17}$$

The equilibrium (strategic neutral) expected returns are calculated from the expression:

$$\Pi_{Str} = r_f \cdot I + (\lambda \Sigma) \cdot W_{STR} = \begin{bmatrix} E(R)_{Eq.Europe} \\ E(R)_{Eq.\,North\,America} \\ E(R)_{Eq.Japan} \\ E(R)_{Eq.Pacific\,ex\,Japan} \\ E(R)_{Eq.Emerging\,Markets} \end{bmatrix} = \begin{bmatrix} 7.17\% \\ 7.48\% \\ 8.09\% \\ 7.81\% \\ 9.56\% \end{bmatrix} \tag{6.18}$$

The first stage ends with the τ estimation:

$$\tau = 0.0526 \tag{6.19}$$

The next step is the tactical prediction (short-term view). To forecast the views distribution we need to know P, Q and Ω.

Assume that the fund manager has formulated the following tactical opinions:

1. Equity Europe will perform better than Equity North America; the confidence is low;
2. Equity Emerging Market will perform better than Equity Japan; the confidence is low.

It is obvious that the analyst pursues a reallocation favourable to European and Emerging Countries against North America and Japan. In order to move from qualitative opinions to quantitative views, a percentage equal to 60 per cent is associated with the hypothesis that a market performs BETTER than another. Moreover, a LOW confidence means a confidence level equal to 8 per cent.

P, Q and Ω are:

$$P = \begin{bmatrix} +1 & -1 & 0 & 0 & 0 \\ 0 & 0 & -1 & 0 & +1 \end{bmatrix} \tag{6.20}$$

$$Q = \begin{bmatrix} \dfrac{\begin{bmatrix} +1 & -1 & 0 & 0 & 0 \end{bmatrix} \times \begin{bmatrix} 7.17\% \\ 7.48\% \\ 8.09\% \\ 7.81\% \\ 9.56\% \end{bmatrix} + \text{stnorminv}(60\%) \times}{\sqrt{\begin{bmatrix} +1 & -1 & 0 & 0 & 0 \end{bmatrix} \times \Sigma_{STR} \times \begin{bmatrix} +1 \\ -1 \\ 0 \\ 0 \\ 0 \end{bmatrix}}} \\ \dfrac{\begin{bmatrix} 0 & 0 & -1 & 0 & +1 \end{bmatrix} \times \begin{bmatrix} 7.17\% \\ 7.48\% \\ 8.09\% \\ 7.81\% \\ 9.56\% \end{bmatrix} + \text{stnorminv}(60\%) \times}{\sqrt{\begin{bmatrix} 0 & 0 & -1 & 0 & +1 \end{bmatrix} \times \Sigma_{STR} \times \begin{bmatrix} 0 \\ 0 \\ -1 \\ 0 \\ +1 \end{bmatrix}}} \end{bmatrix} = \begin{bmatrix} 2.11\% \\ 7.35\% \end{bmatrix} \tag{6.21}$$

$$\Omega = \begin{bmatrix} \left(\frac{1}{8\%} - 1\right) \cdot \begin{bmatrix} +1 & -1 & 0 & 0 & 0 \end{bmatrix} \cdot (\tau\Sigma) \cdot \begin{bmatrix} +1 \\ -1 \\ 0 \\ 0 \\ 0 \end{bmatrix} & 0 \\ 0 & \left(\frac{1}{8\%} - 1\right) \cdot \begin{bmatrix} 0 & 0 & -1 & 0 & +1 \end{bmatrix} \cdot (\tau\Sigma) \cdot \begin{bmatrix} 0 \\ 0 \\ -1 \\ 0 \\ +1 \end{bmatrix} \end{bmatrix}$$

$$= \begin{bmatrix} 0.00549 & 0 \\ 0 & 0.03255 \end{bmatrix} \tag{6.22}$$

Table 6.4 Strategic versus tactical expected returns

	Strategic equilibrium	**Views**	**Tactical expected returns**
$E(R)_{Eq\,Europe}$-$E(R)_{Eq\,N.Amer.}$	−0.31%	2.11%	−0.11%
$E(R)_{Eq\,Em.Mkts}$-$E(R)_{Eq\,Japan}$	1.47%	7.35%	1.95%

The tactical expected returns are calculated as follows:

$$\Pi_{TACT} = \left[(\tau\Sigma)^{-1} + P^T \cdot \Omega^{-1} \cdot P\right]^{-1} \times \left[(\tau\Sigma)^{-1} \cdot \Pi_{Str} + P^T \cdot \Omega^{-1} \cdot Q\right]$$
$$= \begin{bmatrix} 7.28\% \\ 7.39\% \\ 8.12\% \\ 8.25\% \\ 10.07\% \end{bmatrix} \tag{6.23}$$

Table 6.4 shows the gap between strategic (*prior distribution*) and tactical (*posterior distribution*) expected returns. Given a low confidence level, the tactical expected returns are close to the strategic ones.

In order to capture the tactical weights, the following constrained optimization is solved:

$$\begin{aligned} & W_{TACT}^{Max}\left(W_{TACT}^T \cdot \Pi_{TACT}\right) \\ & \text{s.t.} \\ & \textstyle\sum_{i=1}^{5} w_i = 1 \\ & w_i \geq 0 \quad \text{with } i = 1,\ 2,\ 3, 4,\ 5. \\ & \lambda = \frac{W_{TACT}^T \cdot \Pi_{TACT} - r_f}{W_{TACT}^T \cdot \Sigma \cdot W_{TACT}^T} = \lambda_{Str} = 1.189 \end{aligned} \tag{6.24}$$

The short-term asset allocation is optimal if it maximizes the tactical expected returns and has a coefficient of risk aversion equal to the strategic one (λ_{Str}).

The output is:

$$W_{Tact} = \begin{bmatrix} 49.08\% \\ 30.03\% \\ 1.66\% \\ 3.79\% \\ 15.44\% \end{bmatrix} \tag{6.25}$$

Figure 6.1 shows short-term changes. They fully confirm the asset manager's expectation: asset classes with a positive (negative) view have increased (decreased) their tactical weights. Because of low confidence, tactical changes are not very large.

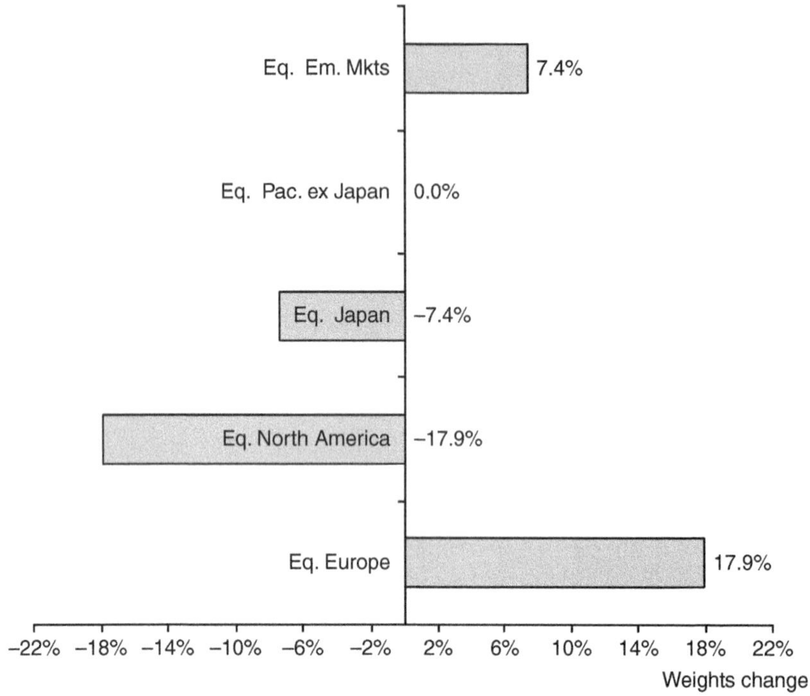

Figure 6.1 Tactical changes

In addition, Relative VaR (Re-VaR) or Tracking Error Volatility (TEV) constraints may be useful to avoid extreme short-term changes.

6.5 Conclusion

Too often, tactical asset allocation techniques are naïve. Mathematical procedures are carefully ignored to avoid point estimates. The Black–Litterman model is ideal to remove the analysts' aversion to mathematical models. However its use requires appropriate skills: errors can lead to ambiguous or unreasonable solutions. A good quantitative expertise and a period of training/calibration are therefore necessary to build a good Bayesian *market timing* tool.

Notes

1. The investment committees often produce forecasts involving two markets.
2. When applied for strategic asset allocation purposes, expected returns (μ) are centred around the equilibrium expected returns (Π_{eq}).

References

Best, M. J. and R. R. Grauer (1991a) 'Sensitivity analysis for mean-variance portfolio problems', *Management Science*, 37, 980–99.

——(1991b) 'On the sensitivity of mean-variance-efficient portfolios to changes in asset means: Some analytical and computationals results', *Review of Financial Studies*, 4, 315–42.

Black, F. and R. Litterman (1991) 'Asset allocation: Combining investor views with market equilibrium', *Journal of Fixed Income*, 1, 7–18.

——(1992) 'Global portfolio optimization', *Financial Analysts Journal*, 48, 28–43.

Frankfurter, G. M., H. E. Phillips and J. P. Siegle (1971) 'Portfolio selection: The effects of uncertain mean, variances, and covariances', *The Journal of Financial and Quantitative Analysis*, 6, 1251–62.

Jobson, J. D. and B. Korkie (1980) 'Estimation for Markowitz efficient portfolios', *Journal of the American Statistical Association*, 75, 544–54.

——(1981) 'Potential performance and tests of portfolio efficiency', *Journal of Financial Economics*, 10, 433–66.

Jorion, P. (1985) 'International portfolio diversification with estimation risk', *Journal of Business*, 58, 259–78.

Lintner, J. (1965) 'The valuation of risk assets and the selection of risky investments in stock portfolios and capital budgets', *Review of Economics and Statistics*, 47, 13–37.

Markowitz, H. M. (1952) 'Portfolio selection', *Journal of Finance*, 7, 77–91.

——(1959) *Portfolio Selection. Efficient Diversification of Investments* (New York: John Wiley & Sons).

Meucci, A. (2005) *Risk and Asset Allocation* (Berlin Heidelberg: Springer).

Mossin, J. (1966) 'Equilibrium in a capital asset market', *Econometrica*, 34, 768–83.

Sharpe, W. F. (1964) 'Capital asset prices: A theory of market equilibrium under conditions of risk', *Journal of Finance*, 19, 425–42.

7
Performance and Governance in Investment Management Companies

Maria Cristina Arcuri

7.1 Introduction

Asset management is a crucial sector for the Italian financial system, which continues to receive attention from scholars, market participants and the legislature.

National and international regulatory framework highlights the importance of identifying and managing potential conflicts of interest in the provision of investment services and collective management; in this perspective, it is essential to increase the decisional autonomy of the Investment Management Companies (IMCs, the Italian *Società di Gestione del Risparmio - SGR*).

Many contributions, among which Lener (2005), as well as frequent actions by the market operators, have pointed out the importance of investigating the possible consequences generated by the ownership structures of the IMCs. The present research is ranked amongst this trend of literature: it purposes to direct the analysis on the governance system of IMCs, paying attention to their profitability and, in particular, to the receivable and payable commissions structure (Linciano and Marrocco, 2002; Otten and Schweitzer, 2002).

The purpose of the research is to understand whether the presence of financial brokers (banks and insurance companies), as shareholders of the IMCs, could generate some consequences in terms of the different commissions system implemented. The research has been conducted on the four-year period 2006 to 2009.

Based on the previous studies, we expect differences between the banking/insurance and independent IMCs, especially in reference to the payable commissions. Moreover, the analysis could supply useful information in reference to the subjects of fund governance and conflict of interests.

7.2 Literature review

Asset management is a very important sector for the Italian financial system, so that numerous studies (Stoughton et al., 2011) have highlighted the need to foster its growth and development.

Much more so following the recent financial crisis defined by many studies (Kirkpatrick, 2009; Randall Wray, 2009) as the most serious recession since the years after World War II.

Also asset management, in Italy and abroad, suffered from this tricky period, so it appears important to study this sector, paying attention to the investment management companies and, in particular, to their governance structure.

We will focus the analysis on the governance system of the IMCs, also in the light of the particular structure of the Italian asset management sector. Messori (2008) defines *distortions* from the supply side, with the two following aspects:

- IMCs generally belong to a banking or insurance group;
- a *vertical integration* exists between production and distribution.

In Italy, the supply model of asset management products is essentially based on the banking networks of the same group of IMCs. This means that the same distribution channel often offers the asset management products to customers as an alternative to other more opaque and risky financial instruments: it follows a potential conflict of interest.

Asset management continues to receive attention, not only from scholars and market participants, but also from the legislature. The new national[1] and international[2] regulatory framework highlights the importance of identifying and managing potential conflicts of interest in the provision of investment services and to strengthen the decisional autonomy of the IMCs.

Many contributions (Lener, 2005; La Porta et al., 1997, 1998) have stressed the importance of investigating the possible consequences of ownership of asset managers. Moreover, a wide literature (Walter, 1999; Burkart et al., 2003; Boot et al., 2006) describes the costs and benefits of the governance system and other studies (Weisbach, 1988; Borokhovich et al., 1996; Khorana et al., 2009) deal with the characteristics of different governance mechanisms and their implications.

Many researches (Klapper and Love, 2004; Himmelberg et al., 1999) suggest that better corporate governance (CG) would affect the level of investor protection. The analysis of the governance characteristics is even more significant if we consider that IMCs are exposed to agency problems (Jensen and Meckling, 1976) and, also, to the so-called *fund governance*, that is the potential conflict of interest between their members and the participants to the funds they manage.

Such conviction is reinforced by many researches (Faccio and Lang, 2002; La Porta et al., 1999), which prove how the existence of little-efficient governance systems is associated with a lower level of protection for investors.

One of the major distortions caused by the Italian distribution system of asset management products, based mainly on the banking group networks holding the IMCs, consists of the structure of costs (commissions) charged to the investor (Chordia, 1996; Knuutila et al., 2007; Otten and Schweitzer, 2002).

In Italy the asset management products are designed to secure very large *commissions* to the distributors and to bear substantial costs for ancillary services offered by the banking group.

Linciano and Marrocco (2002) maintain that the presence of *commissions* agreements represents a critical area for the efficiency of the asset management sector in Italy, because it promotes potential conflicts of interests.

This results in a high incidence of distribution and accessories costs with respect to the production costs, so that the buyers of asset management products are charged with high total costs and the IMCs retain an inadequate share of their revenues (Elton et al., 2003; Sirri and Tufano, 1999). In light of this situation, it is important to study the profitability of the IMCs.

Some studies (Cable, 1985; Gorton and Schmid, 2000) show a significant positive impact on the profitability by the banking participation to the companies; instead, other researches (Chirinko and Elston, 2006) stress the absence of significant differences between independent companies or companies owned by banks.

So, it appears fundamental to analyse the commissions systems of these intermediaries. Many studies (Ferris and Chance, 1987; LaPlante, 2001; Malhotra and McLeod, 1997) have expanded the subject, pointing out that some factors, like the dimensions, the age and the product management style, affect the level of commissions.

De Rossi et al. (2008) believe that the predominance of the bank distribution channels could generate rigidity conditions in pricing of asset management, by reducing the possibility for investors to benefit from economies of scale generated by the managing activities.

7.3 Sampling and methodology

The empirical analysis concerns the Italian asset managers: the mentioned IMCs (SGR).

Our study aims to analyse any connection between the IMCs' ownership structure and the driving factors of their profitability.

To this end, we created a sample of IMCs for all associated with Assogestioni.[3] All useful information has been obtained from the following sources of information: the balance sheet and profit and loss of IMCs, their official websites and the Assogestioni website. The analysed sample was built, firstly, by creating two sub-samples for each year we have analysed. Then, the eight sub-samples were grouped into two systems of equations.

Table 7.1 IMCs: sample and sub-samples composition

Year	Total	Independent IMCs	Not independent
2006	74	15	59
2007	74	15	59
2008	72	13	59
2009	62	13	49

As shown in Table 7.1 for each sub-sample the number of IMCs changes over the time as well as the proportion of independent and not independent IMCs. The study is conducted with particular reference to the independence of those entities from the banking or insurance group.

The concept of *independence* we have considered for the analysis is borrowed from article 2359 of the Italian Civil Code, which identifies two types of relations between companies: the control and the association.

The article in question reads exactly:

> *Are considered controlled companies:*
> *1) companies in which another company holds the majority of votes exercisable in the general assembly; 2) companies in which another company holds sufficient votes for exercising a dominating influence in general assemblies; 3) companies which are subjected to a dominating influence of another company based on special contractual constraints.*
>
> *For the purpose of applying number 1) and 2) of the first paragraph, the voting rights due to a subsidiary (controlled) company, trust company and to a third party are also calculated; are not calculated instead the votes due on behalf of third parties. Are considered associated, companies on which another company exercises a considerable influence. Influence is presumed when in the general assemblies at least one fifth of the votes or one tenth if the company has shares traded on the stock market, can be exercised.*

In particular, starting from the definition of *considerable influence*, the following criteria were noted: the IMC is not independent if the banking-insurance overall holding is at least 20 per cent (a fifth of the votes in general assembly). In other words, if the shareholding of the IMC is held at least for 20 per cent by banking-insurance players, the investment management company is considered *associated* to the distribution network.

The results of the research are achieved through the use of a particular statistical methodology, the *seemingly unrelated regression* (*SUR*), that is a multi equational method formulated by Zellner (1962, 1963). The *SUR* technique is applied to economic models that may have multiple equations apparently independent of each other and it enables us to estimate the equations jointly and makes the estimators of the coefficients more efficient than least squares estimators of the single-equation. One of the potential benefits of the *SUR* methodology is that it incorporates the cross-section estimates of the residues in the estimated coefficients and statistical tests. The regression coefficients in all equations are estimated simultaneously by applying the Aitken's generalized least squares (GLS) to the whole system of equations. The Aitken's estimators are constructed thanks to an estimate of variances and covariances of the disturbance terms, based on the residues resulting from application of least squares according to a logic equation by equation.

Mathematically:

$$y\mu = X\mu\beta\mu + u\mu \tag{7.1}$$

we suppose that the (7.1) is the μ-th equation of an M equation regression system with y_μ (Tx1) vector of observations on the μ-th *dependent* variable, X_μ (Txl$_\mu$) matrix with rank l_μ of observations on l_μ *independent* non-stochastic variables, β_μ (l_μx1) vector of the regression coefficients and u_μ (Tx1) vector of random error terms, each with mean zero. The system, of which (7.1) is an equation may be written as:

$$\begin{bmatrix} y_1 \\ y_2 \\ \cdot \\ \cdot \\ \cdot \\ y_M \end{bmatrix} = \begin{bmatrix} X_1 & 0 & . & . & . & 0 \\ 0 & X_2 & . & . & . & 0 \\ \cdot & \cdot & \cdot & \cdot & \cdot & \cdot \\ \cdot & \cdot & \cdot & \cdot & \cdot & \cdot \\ \cdot & \cdot & \cdot & \cdot & \cdot & \cdot \\ 0 & 0 & . & . & . & X_M \end{bmatrix} \cdot \begin{bmatrix} \beta_1 \\ \beta_2 \\ \cdot \\ \cdot \\ \cdot \\ \beta_M \end{bmatrix} + \begin{bmatrix} u_1 \\ u_2 \\ \cdot \\ \cdot \\ \cdot \\ u_M \end{bmatrix} \tag{7.2}$$

$$y = X\beta + u \tag{7.3}$$

where y = [y'1y'2 .... y'M], β = [β'1β'2 .... β'M], u = [u'1u'2 .... u'M] and X represents the block diagonal matrix on the right side of (7.2). It is assumed that the M (Tx1) disturbance vector in (7.2) and (7.3) is assumed to have the following variance–covariance matrix:

$$\Sigma = V(u) = \begin{bmatrix} \sigma_{11}I & \sigma_{12}I & . & . & . & \sigma_{1M}I \\ \sigma_{21}I & \sigma_{22}I & . & . & . & \sigma_{2M}I \\ \cdot & \cdot & \cdot & \cdot & \cdot & \cdot \\ \cdot & \cdot & \cdot & \cdot & \cdot & \cdot \\ \cdot & \cdot & \cdot & \cdot & \cdot & \cdot \\ \sigma_{M1}I & \sigma_{M2}I & . & . & . & \sigma_{MM}I \end{bmatrix} .$$

$$= \begin{bmatrix} \sigma_{11} & \sigma_{12} & . & . & . & \sigma_{1M} \\ \sigma_{21} & \sigma_{22} & . & . & . & \sigma_{2M} \\ \cdot & \cdot & \cdot & \cdot & \cdot & \cdot \\ \cdot & \cdot & \cdot & \cdot & \cdot & \cdot \\ \cdot & \cdot & \cdot & \cdot & \cdot & \cdot \\ \sigma_{M1} & \sigma_{M2} & . & . & . & \sigma_{MM} \end{bmatrix} \otimes I = \Sigma_c \otimes I \tag{7.4}$$

where I is a matrix of order T × T and $\sigma_{\mu\mu'} = E(u_{\mu t} u_{\mu' t})$ for t = 1, 2, ... , T and μ, μ′ = 1, 2, ..., M.

In temporal cross-sectional regressions, t is the time and (7.3) implies constant variances and covariances from period to period, as well as the absence of any autocorrelation or serial correlation of the disturbance terms. Formally, we regard at (7.2) or (7.3) as a single-equation regression model and apply Aitken's generalized least squares. That is, we pre-multiply both sides of (7.3) by a matrix H which is such that E (Huu 'H') = HΣH '= I. In terms of transformed variables (the original variables pre-multiplied by H), the system satisfies the assumptions of the least squares model. The application of least squares will yield a best linear unbiased estimator (the estimator of Aitken's generalized least squares),[4] which is:

$$b^* = (X'H'HX)^{-1} X'H'Hy = \left(X'\Sigma^{-1}X\right)^{-1} X'\Sigma^{-1}y \tag{7.5}$$

In constructing this estimator, we need the inverse of Σ, which is given by:

$$\Sigma^{-1} = V^{-1}(u) = \begin{bmatrix} \sigma_{11}I & . & . & . & \sigma_{1M}I \\ . & . & . & . & . \\ . & . & . & . & . \\ . & . & . & . & . \\ \sigma_{M1}I & . & . & . & \sigma_{MM}I \end{bmatrix} = \Sigma_c^{-1} \otimes I \tag{7.6}$$

The Aitken estimator of the coefficient vector is:

$$b^* = \begin{bmatrix} b_1^* \\ b_2^* \\ . \\ . \\ . \\ b_M^* \end{bmatrix}$$

$$= \begin{bmatrix} \sigma_{11}X_1'X_1 & \sigma_{12}X_1'X_2 & . & . & . & \sigma_{1M}X_1'X_M \\ \sigma_{21}X_2'X_1 & \sigma_{22}X_2'X_2 & . & . & . & \sigma_{2M}X_2'X_M \\ . & . & . & . & . & . \\ . & . & . & . & . & . \\ . & . & . & . & . & . \\ \sigma_{M1}X_M'X_1 & \sigma_{M2}X_M'X_2 & . & . & . & \sigma_{MM}X_M'X_M \end{bmatrix}^{-1} \begin{bmatrix} \sum_{\mu=1}^{M} \sigma_{1\mu}X_1'y_\mu \\ . \\ . \\ . \\ \sum_{\mu=1}^{M} \sigma_{M\mu}X_M'y_\mu \end{bmatrix} \tag{7.7}$$

We conducted two different analyses, whose objectives are the following:

- to try to understand if a link exists between the ownership and the profitability;
- to try to understand if a link exists between the ownership and the commissions structure.

Our research refers to the four-year period 2006 to 2009 and the variables we considered are the following:

- The independent variables are the ownership and the market share of IMCs. Ownership is represented by a dummy variable with value '1' if the IMC belongs to a banking or insurance group and "0" if the IMC is independent. Market share was added in order to keep in mind the size of the individual IMC; it is calculated by placing in relation the individual IMC's annual managed asset with the sector's gross total managed assets.
- The profitability, which is the dependent variable of the first analysis, was determined, for any year, by the following financial ratios: Return on Equity (ROE) and Return on Assets (ROA).
  The decision to measure the profitability not only by calculating the ROE, but also considering the ROA, was carried out in order to facilitate comparison of the IMCs, taking into account any distortion effect arising from differences in the use of leverage and cost of capital (Lehmann and Weigand, 2000).
- The dependent variables of the second study are represented by receivable and payable commissions (operating, incentive, subscription/redemption, switch and other commissions), meaning, in general, from revenues and related charges on the services supplied and received by the broker, based on specific contractual provisions (guaranties, collections and payments, management and brokerage and so on).

Every kind of commission represents the normalized annual amount of payable or receivable commissions each time analysed. All annual amounts of commissions, gathered from the financial statements, are normalized based on the value of management pertaining to the specific product analysed. As such, for example, the amount of annual management commissions pertaining to own management of mutual investment funds has been normalized for the total amount of own managed CIUs (Collective Investment Undertakings), while the amount of annual management commissions pertaining to own individual management has been normalized for the total amount of own individual managing activities for that year, and so on.

7.4 Results

The results of our analysis were obtained by studying the influence of ownership of the IMCs on their profitability.

First of all we calculated the average values of ROE and ROA indicators for the two groups of IMCs (Table 7.2).

Table 7.2 Profitability of AMCs

	2006		2007		2008		2009	
	Indep. AMCs	**Bank./Ins. AMCs**	**Indep. AMCs**	**Bank./Ins. AMCs**	**Indep. AMCs**	**Bank./Ins. AMCs**	**Indep. AMCs**	**Bank./Ins. AMCs**
ROE	0.31	0.24	0.35	0.24	0.25	0.03	0.22	0.12
ROA	0.31	0.22	0.37	0.22	0.34	0.60	0.23	0.11

Table 7.3 Relation between ownership and profitability

Year	**ROE and ROA**	**Ownership**	**p-value**	
2006	ROE	−0.15	0.03	**
	ROA	−0.16	0.02	**
2007	ROE	−0.18	0.01	***
	ROA	−0.24	0.00	***
2008	ROE	-0.33	0.12	
	ROA	0.57	0.65	
2009	ROE	−0.15	0.03	**
	ROA	−0.18	0.02	**
F test (relation between ownership and profitability)				
	Value	Probability		Value
F(8,472)	2.81	[0.00]	F(8,472)	2.81

Notes:
ROE = Return on Equity
ROA = Return on Assets

Table 7.2 shows the average values of ROE and ROA indicators for the two groups of IMCs, showing a higher profitability of independent investment management companies for any year, except 2008.

Given the described results, the application of the *SUR* methodology (Table 7.3) allows us to demonstrate the significance of the IMCs' ownership in influencing the profitability.

Table 7.3 shows the estimated coefficients, by using the *SUR* method, of the ownership (independent variable), indicating the significance at 1 per cent (***) and 5 per cent (**), the profitability indicators, ROE and ROA (dependent variables), and the year. The F test and the p-value have confirmed the significance of the results. In particular, we test the hypothesis that the coefficients of the significant variables are zero against the alternative hypothesis that at least one of them is different from zero.

Table 7.3 confirms the results of Table 7.2: it shows a higher profitability of independent asset management companies for the following years: 2006, 2007 and 2009. This could be due to the practice of banking IMCs to recognize high commissions to the distributor, which creates greater costs for non-independent management companies and, consequently, penalizes their profitability.

In 2008 we have not statistical significance of ownership of IMCs. This might lead one to believe that the profitability of that year may have been influenced by other factors, primarily the recent financial crisis, which has culminated in 2008. In particular, one might think that the banking IMCs have managed to maintain the highest overall profitability by using their distribution channels.

Given the important results regarding the profitability of the investment management companies, the following analysis aims to examine its determinants: receivable and payable commissions.

7.4.1 Receivable commissions

The analysis of the receivable commissions has pointed out some interesting results summarized in Table 7.4.

Based on the *SUR* method, Table 7.4 shows the estimated coefficients of the independent variables ownership and market share, indicating the significance at 1 per cent (***) or at 5 per cent (**), the receivable commission (dependent variable) and the year. As shown in Table 7.4, we subjected the

Table 7.4 Relation between ownership, market share and receivable commissions

Year	Commissions	Ownership	p-value	Market share	p-value
				2.46	1.87e-01 ***
				0.25	7.58e-09 ***
2006					
	Mgt comm. Mutual funds				
	Inc. comm. Mutual funds	−0.00	0.03 **		
	Sub./Red. comm. Individual mgt			0.00	0.00 ***
2008	Sub./Red. comm. open pens. funds			0.01	0.00 ***
	Inc. comm. mgt by mand	−0.00	0.04 **		

F test (relation between ownership, market share and receivable commissions)

	Value	Probability
F(55,3025)	501.92	[0.00]

Notes:
Inc. Comm. Mutual funds = Incentive commissions of mutual investment funds
Mgt comm. Mutual funds = Management commissions of mutual funds
Sub./Red. comm. Individual mgt = Subscription/redemption commissions related to individual management
Sub./Red. comm. open pens. funds = Subscription/redemption commissions related to open pension funds.
Inc. comm mgt by mand. = Incentive commissions of management by mandates

empirical analysis to an F test, which have confirmed the significance of the results.

In 2006, incentive commissions of the mutual investment funds are significant. In particular, the analysis proves that when IMCs belong to a banking or insurance group, the amounts of these commissions are lower.

In 2008, incentive commissions of management by mandates are significant: their value is greater for the banking (or insurance) IMCs.

In the years 2007 and 2009 there are not significant differences concerning the IMCs' ownership and their market share. The latter seems to affect, in 2006, the mutual funds management and incentive commissions: increasing market share of the IMCs, also increases the incidence of these commissions. Moreover, in 2008, the market share positively affects the amount of subscription/redemption commissions related to individual management and opened pension funds.

In light of the described results, we could affirm that there is not a specific type of commission income able to differentiate banking (or insurance) and independent IMCs.

7.4.2 Payable commissions

Table 7.5 reports significant coefficient in the analysis of the payable commissions.

Table 7.5 shows the estimated coefficients of the independent variables (ownership and market share), indicating the significance at 1 per cent (***), at 5 per cent (**) or at 10 per cent (*), the payable commission (dependent variable) and the year. As shown in Table 7.5, in 2006 the ownership of IMCs affected the payable management commissions, incentive commissions and other commissions on mutual investment funds. In details, these commissions tend to be higher for banking (or insurance) IMCs. The F test and the p-value confirm the significance of the results.

The analysis of 2007 confirms these results: payable management, incentive and other commissions continue to be higher for not independent IMCs.

In 2008 the significance of payable management commissions on mutual funds is confirmed: banking IMCs show higher payment management commissions, as compared to the independents. In addition, we can note that banking IMCs show higher subscription/redemption on mutual funds and other commission concerning opened pension funds.

Finally, also the market share positively affects payable commissions. In particular, in 2006, it seems to affect the mutual funds management commissions, in 2007, the other commissions on opened pension funds and, in 2008, the subscription/redemption on mutual funds and other commission on opened pension funds. We can note that increasing market share of the IMCs, also increases the incidence of these commissions.

In 2009 there are not significant results concerning payable commissions.

Table 7.5 Relation between ownership, market share and payable commissions

Year	Commissions	Ownership	p-value		Market share	p-value	
2006	Mgt comm. Mutual funds	0.00	0.01	***	0.14	5.75e-06	***
	Inc. Comm. Mutual funds	0.00	0.02	**			
	Other Comm. Mutual funds	−0.00	7.89e-05	***			
2007	Mgt comm. Mutual funds	0.00	0.01	***			
	Inc. Comm. Mutual funds	0.00	0.09	*			
	Sub./Red. comm. Mutual funds	0.00	0.03	**			
	Other Comm. Mutual funds	−0.00	0.03	**			
	Other Comm. open pens. funds				0.00	0.01	**
2008	Mgt comm. Mutual funds	0.00	0.05	*			
	Sub./Red. comm. Mutual funds	0.00	0.02	**			
	Sub./Red. comm. Individual mgt				0.01	0.00	**
	Other Comm. open pens. funds	4.33e-06	0.03	**	5.99e-05	0.09	*
F test (relation between ownership, market share and receivable commissions)							
	Value	Probability					
F(60,3540)	333,86	[0.00]					

Notes:
Inc. Comm. Mutual funds = Incentive commissions of mutual investment funds
Mgt comm. Mutual funds = Management commissions of mutual investment funds
Other Comm. open pens. funds = Other commissions related to open pension funds
Other Comm. Mutual funds = Other commissions of mutual investment funds
Sub./Red. comm. Mutual funds = Subscription/redemption commissions related to mutual investment funds
Sub./Red. comm. Individual mgt = Subscription/redemption commissions related individual management.

In summarising the analysis, we notice how the items of greater interest throughout the considered years are, first of all management commissions on mutual funds and, then, incentive and other commissions.

This evidence could demonstrate how the *commissions* policy is probably a developed practice among banking (or insurance) IMCs. These results are consistent with the literature and the observations in the operating world. We believe it is important to consider the potential problem of profitability loss deriving from the high commissions paid to distributors of the IMCs group.

7.5 Conclusion

The asset management industry is undergoing a profound transformation, also following the recent financial crisis. The turbulent environment enforces academics and practitioners to generate insight for doing business, so it appears important to study the asset management protagonists.

The aim of this study is to investigate the existence of differences between banking/insurance and independent investment management companies with regard to profitability and their commissions' structure.

Our results concern, first of all, that the average value of ROE and ROA indicators for the two groups of IMCs (banking/insurance and independent). Profitability of independent investment management companies is higher than banking or insurance IMCs for any year, except 2008. This could be due to the practice of banking IMCs of paying commissions to the distributors. Since the *commissions* policy seems to penalize the profitability of non-independent management companies, we decided to analyse the commission structure of IMCs. With regard to the receivable commissions, there are not decisive differences between banking (or insurance) and independent IMCs. Instead, the analysis of payable commissions shows more interesting results. The main differences between banking (or insurance) IMCs and independent IMCs concern the following kinds of commissions: the management commissions on mutual funds and the incentive and other commissions. In the light of these results we conclude that the *commissions* policy could penalize the profitability of IMCs belonging to a banking or insurance group, so there might be negative consequences in terms of higher costs charged to investors.

The study provides, therefore, a possible contribution to the debate, in the academic and operational context, about the distinctive features of the investment management companies characterized by a connection between production and distribution. This is even more interesting, in the light of the Italian context of asset management, where there are the prevalence of non-independent IMCs. The variety of distribution channels is, however, considered essential to increase the efficiency of asset management industry. The study of Stoughton et al. (2011) shows, for example, that a positive relationship exists between the variety of distribution channels through which a fund is located and its performance.

Future research will be targeted to delve into the subject of *commissions* (the Italian *retrocessioni*), expanding the time horizon of the analysis. Finally, it could be interesting for the future, to try to understand whether the ownership of the IMCs is able to influence also the performance of the products they offer to their clients.

Notes

1. Savings Act (Law No. 262 of 28 December 2005).
2. MiFID (Directive No. 2004/39/EC on Markets in Financial Instruments) and UCITS III (Directives 2001/107/EC and 2001/108/EC) and UCITS IV (Directive 2009/65/EC).
3. Assogestioni is the professional association of the Italian asset managers.

4. The quadratic form that we have minimized in the Aitken's approach is not the sum of the squares of the originating disturbances terms, but the processed noises. This makes the Aitken's estimator more efficient than classical least squares estimator based on the original variables.

References

Boot, A. W., R. Gopalan and A. V. Thakor (2006) 'The entrepreneur's choice between private and public ownership', *Journal of Finance,* 61, 801–36.

Borokhovich, K., R. Parrino and T. Trapini (1996) 'Outside directors and CEO selection', *Journal of Financial and Quantitative Analysis,* 31, 337–55.

Burkart, B., F. Panunziand and A. Shleifer (2003) 'Family firms', *Journal of Finance,* 58, 2176–202.

Cable, J. (1985) 'Capital market information and industrial performance: The role of West German banks', *Economic Journal*, 95, 118–32.

Chirinko, R. and J. Elston (2006) 'Finance, control and profitability: The influence of German banks', *Journal of Economic Behavior & Organization*, 59, 69–88.

Chordia, T. (1996) 'The structure of mutual fund charges', *Journal of Financial Economics,* 41, 3–39.

De Rossi, F. M., D. Gariboldi, G. Leggieri and A. Russo (2008) 'Il marketing dei fondi comuni italiani. Modelli organizzativi, costi, andamento e nuove prospettive conseguenti all'introduzione della MIFID nell'ottica della vigilanza', www.consob.it (homepage), date accessed 01 July 2012.

Elton, E., M. Gruber and C. Blake (2003) 'Incentive fee and mutual funds', *Journal of Finance*, 58, 779–804.

Faccio, M. and L. Lang (2002) 'The ultimate ownership of western European corporations', *Journal of Financial Economics,* 65, 365–95.

Ferris, S. P. and D. M. Chance (1987) 'An empirical analysis of mutual funds expense ratios: A note', *Journal of Finance*, 42, 1077–82.

Gorton, G. and F. Schmid (2000) 'Universal banking and the performance of German firms', *Journal of Financial Economics*, 58, 29–80.

Himmelberg, C., R. G. Hubbard and D. Palia (1999) 'Understanding the determinants of managerial ownership and the link between ownership and performance', *Journal of Financial Economics*, 53, 353–84.

Jensen, M. and W. Meckling (1976) 'Theory of the firm: Managerial behavior, agency costs and ownership structure', *Journal of Financial Economics*, 3, 305–60.

Khorana, A., H. Servaes and P. Tufano (2009) 'Mutual fund fees around the world', *Review of Financial Studies*, 22, 1279–310.

Kirkpatrick, G. (2009) 'The corporate governance lessons from the financial crisis', www.oecd.org (homepage), date accessed 01 July 2012.

Klapper, L. F. and I. Love (2004) 'Corporate governance, investor protection, and performance in emerging markets', *Journal of Corporate Finance*, 10, 703–28.

Knuutila, M., V. Puttonen and T. Smythe (2007) 'The effect of distribution channels on mutual fund flows', *Journal of Financial Services Marketing*, 12, 88–96.

LaPlante, M. (2001) 'Influences and trends in mutual fund expense ratios', *Journal of Financial Research*, 24, 45–63.

La Porta, R., F. Lopez de Silanes and A. Shleifer (1999) 'Corporate ownership around the world', *Journal of Finance*, 54, 471–517.

La Porta, R., F. Lopez de Silanes, A. Shleifer and R. Vishny (1997) 'Legal determinants of external finance', *Journal of Finance*, 52, 1131–50.

——(1998) 'Law and finance', *Journal of Political Economy*, 106, 1113–55.

Lehmann, E. and J. Weigand (2000) 'Does the governed corporation perform better? Governance structures and corporate performance in Germany', *European Finance Review*, 4, 157–95.

Lener, R. (2005) 'Corporate governance rules for investment funds in Italy', *European Business Organization Law Review*, 6, 269–90.

Linciano, N. and E. Marrocco (2002) 'Fondi di fondi e accordi di retrocessione – Analisi degli effetti degli accordi di retrocessione sule scelte di investimento e sui costi a carico dei patrimoni gestiti', www.consob.it (homepage), date accessed 01 July 2012.

Malhotra, D. and R. McLeod (1997) 'An empirical analysis of mutual fund expenses', *Journal of Financial Research*, 20, 175–90.

Messori, M. (2008) 'I problemi del settore italiano del risparmio gestito', www.assogestioni.it (homepage), date accessed 01 July 2012.

Otten, R. and M. Schweitzer (2002) 'A comparison between the European and the U.S. mutual fund industry', *Managerial Finance*, 28, 14–35.

Randall Wray, L. (2009) 'Money manager capitalism and the global financial crisis', *Real-world Economics Review*, 51, 55–69.

Sirri, E. and P. Tufano (1999) 'Costly search and mutual fund flows', *Journal of Finance*, 53, 1589–622.

Stoughton, N. M., W. Youchang and J. Zechner (2011) 'Intermediated investment management', *Journal of Finance*, 66, 947–80.

Walter, I. (1999) 'The global asset management industry: Competitive structure, conduct and performance', *Journal of Financial Markets, Institutions and Instruments*, 8, 1–78.

Weisbach, M. (1988) 'Outside directors and CEO turnover', *Journal of Financial Economics*, 20, 431–60.

Zellner, A. (1962) 'An efficient method of estimating seemingly unrelated regressions and tests for aggregation bias', *Journal of the American Statistical Association*, 57, 348–68.

——(1963) 'Estimators for seemingly unrelated regression equations: Some exact finite sample results', *Journal of the American Statistical Association*, 58, 977–92.

Part II

Real Estate Investment Vehicles and Markets during the Crisis

8

The Quality of Real Estate Data: The Italian Case

Francesca Battaglia, Claudio Porzio and Gabriele Sampagnaro

8.1 Introduction

The chapter[1] discusses issues concerning the quality of property data from different sources and resulting implications for market participants. It is divided into two sections. In the first section, we discuss the nature and availability of property data for the Italian market. Our initial exploration of the quality and accessibility of some domestic data documents the presence of many property data sources, each of which uses different methods of data collection. The high number of data sources and their methodological heterogeneity produce excessive data discrepancies, hardly compatible with efficient research and professional investment processes. Using a set of longitudinal aggregated property values, we proceed to estimate the level of uniformity of data using correlation and cointegration analysis.

The second section provides an examination of the potential effects of data non-uniformity on the decision-making process. To this end, we describe three simulations which deal with the implications of the lack of uniformity of data for mortgage loan lenders, real estate investment vehicles, and asset allocation planners.

8.2 Conceptual framework

In general, the nature of the real estate asset makes a convincing comparison with the other traditional asset classes difficult. Stephan (2005) examines the criteria behind collecting and evaluating real estate data, focusing on the difficulties encountered in compiling them as well as the various limitations of the data themselves. Some factors, such as the heterogeneity of property, the low frequency of transactions, and the high fragmentation (urbanization) of the markets, seriously limit the possibility of estimating real estate relationships accurately. These features lead the research team to prefer secondary data rather than primary data. While primary data are gathered by researchers, secondary data are collected from other sources: universities, government agencies, real estate appraisals, and market research firms. Secondary data are certainly less expensive and less time consuming than primary data, but they are seldom expressed appropriately for the intended purpose. Moreover, transaction records frequently contain empty data fields, and class definitions seldom fit analysts' needs exactly (Greer and Kolbe, 2006).

Because of the indisputable link between economic forecasting and the reliability of data, many governments have taken on the task of gathering data, and their involvement plays a vital role in providing reliable and valid information for property market performance. In many cases, however, data is often inaccurate or incomplete at the time of collection, rendering adjustment procedures necessary to ensure the validity and reliability of the dataset available (Ge and Harfield, 2007).

A large number of agencies, and limited government involvement in data collection, represent two factors able to reduce greatly the efficiency of the real estate market. In those countries where these characteristics are found, there is also a noticeable lack of coordination and centralization between data-collectors, which negatively affects the possibility to calculate homogeneous estimates. As for implications for the market, the inefficiency of data collection systems undoubtedly affects the operation of financial institutions involved in the real estate sector, including performance measurement of real estate funds, mortgage loan management by banks, and the identification of the real estate weight in a mixed-asset portfolio of pension or mutual funds.

In general, two types of indices have been proposed as measures for real estate values: appraisal-based and transaction-based indices. Appraisal-based indices are based on appraisal estimates but transaction-based indices on actual transactions. The low frequency of transactions experienced by the direct real market results in greater reliance on appraisal-based indices.

However, appraisal-based indices have various drawbacks, such as a methodological bias produced by the smoothing effect of the returns, which have been well documented in the literature.[2] The main issues deriving from returns smoothing include the overestimation of real estate in mixed portfolios, because of its unnaturally low correlation with the other asset classes, and methodological problems connected with the availability of real estate indices. These drawbacks give rise to the need for revision of the construction and measurement of real estate appraisal-based indices; indeed, the NCREIF Property Index itself, being an appraisal-based benchmark, is affected by the same kind of issues.

The autocorrelation of appraisal indices return is still under discussion in the literature, and there are contrasting opinions about its level of intensity. The relevance of appraisal smoothing is supported by a broad stream of studies; it is worth mentioning those by Geltner (1989), Geltner (1991), Ross and Zisler (1991), Quan and Quigley (1991), Geltner and Goetzmann

(2000), Geltner and Ling (2007), Lin and Vandell (2007);[3] a lower number of contributions attribute a smaller role to the smoothing phenomenon.[4]

Finally, a third stream of studies, although more limited, is worth mentioning; this stream denies the existence of any autocorrelation between returns. Of these, the study by Lai and Wang (1998) can be quoted, in which the authors underline how some observations referring to the real estate market are justified by causes different from the serial correlation between real estate returns (for example the investor risk premium). In order to neutralize the return smoothing or to reset volatilities artificially lower than the real ones, several methodologies (originating from Geltner's studies) of return unsmoothing have been proposed.[5]

When focusing on the real-estate fund case, one of the more sensitive activities involved in its management is certainly the planning and monitoring of the expected financial results. From this point of view, the determination of an *interim* internal rate of return (IRR) represents an indisputably useful tool of measurement. The estimation of an expected internal rate of return must take into account multiple factors regarding the size and time of the in-coming and out-going cash flows. Concentrating on the incoming cash flows only, fund performance is typically attributable to the following three categories: (a) ground rent; (b) property sale values; (c) returns from liquid management. Consistent with this consideration, the availability of reliable data for each of these sources of return (ground rent, property sale values, liquidity returns) constitutes an indispensable requisite from which to construct a financial plan endowed with objectivity and, in terms of its usability by third parties (investors, analysts, etc.), an adequate level of transparency. As a consequence, the unreliability of real estate data produces instability in IRR calculation (because it can change depending on the data source), thus hindering the making of appropriate investment choices.

Moving on to the case of the loan mortgage lender, the relationship between data quality and credit management is to some extent observable and measurable. The quality of property data affects the bank's residential mortgage management with regards, for example, to the loss given default (LGD) estimation. In lending, loss given default is the magnitude of likely loss on exposure and is expressed as a percentage of this. It is assumed that LGD may be explained largely by loan characteristics; the nature and the expected value of the underlying property, as well as variables measuring the default, foreclosure and settlement process (see Qi and Yang, 2009). The role of property values as an explanatory variable to predict LGD entails the use of reliable data sources. Despite extensive literature about the requirements for an accurate property appraisal and for high quality control from a management viewpoint, few papers focus on the link between the quality of property data sources and LGD predictions. According to the Italian version of the regulation for prudential supervision of banks, the exposures secured by real estate property have to satisfy certain conditions, including an adequate monitoring of property value used as collateral (Banca d'Italia, 2006).[6] In an attempt to clarify the relationship between the quality of property data and mortgage loan management, we carry out some simulations out in order to submit the regular calculation of LGD to a variety of scenarios related to the set of available time series. The simulation results show the existence of a precise functional relationship between the value of the collateral and the data sources from a regulatory (capital requirements) and management (pricing policy) point of view.

Finally, we turn to the issue of the effect of data divergence on investment portfolio composition in a mean-variance framework. The role of real estate in diversifying mixed-asset portfolios has been well recognized in the literature (*inter alia*, Seiler et al., 1999). The majority of these studies focus on the effects of including real estate investment in a mixed-asset portfolio, revealing results consistent with a diversification benefit. This benefit is typically explained by some attributes of real estate investment, such as low correlation with other traditional asset classes, its suitability for inflation-hedging, and its high level of risk-adjusted performance, and so on (Hudson-Wilson et al., 2003).

After including a subset of comparable property indices (provided by different data sources) in a set of *n* financial asset classes, we launch a series of portfolio optimizations in order to identify the sensitivity of efficient frontier curvature to the property data source employed. In this case too, the results show how the non-uniformity of data constitutes a significant issue in ensuring correctness and validity in investment choices.

8.3 Study of domestic data harmonization

8.3.1 Data description

The set of data is composed of 21 time series, provided by 5 different data sources and containing the historical values of property indices for 2 geographical areas: Italy (10 out of 21) and Milan (11 out of 21). Each data-provider offers coverage of all or part of the traditional market segments: residential, commercial, office, and industrial.[7] The time interval of the data varies from a minimum of 5 to a maximum of 42 years as shown in Table 8.1.

A preliminary analysis of the data reveals the presence of a different frequency of time observations, since in some cases the index values are monthly while in others they are six-monthly or yearly. To ensure the uniformity of the comparisons between data, we standardize the data frequency on a common quarterly basis, using linear interpolation.

The adoption of a linear interpolation raises legitimate questions about the significance of a comparison between manipulated time series rather than raw time series. However, an interpolation generates a smoothing out of values and, in general, this contributes to the blunting of outliers rather than

Table 8.1 Data description: time intervals and geographical markets

		Real estate market: Italy			
Type	**Source #1**	**Source #2**	**Source #3**	**Source #4**	**Source #5**
Residential	1988–2008	1997–2008	2002–2007	–	–
Commercial	1988–2008	1997–2008	n. a.	–	–
Office	1988–2008	1997–2008	2002–2007	–	–
Industrial	–	1997–2008	2002–2007	–	–
		Real Estate market: Milan			
Type	**Series #1**	**Series #2**	**Series #3**	**Series #4**	**Series #5**
Residential	1965–2008	1993–2007	–	2001–2008	1995–2007
Commercial	1965–2008	1993–2007	–	2001–2008	2001–2007
Office	–	1993–2007	–	–	1997–2007
Industrial	–	1993–2007	–	–	–

to their amplification. In other words, while the use of data interpolation certainly affects the correctness of the results, its most likely effect would be an underestimation of data dissimilarity which, from a prudential point of view, represents a more acceptable effect than an overestimation.

For each region, the data represents average prices over time of housing, commercial, office and industrial properties. Because our raw data for index values is expressed in different units of measurement, we proceed to standardize the time series families in order to allow a straight comparison between them. After converting the data into index numbers (with the base value equal to 100), we use a log transformation to stabilize the variance of series and then we estimate the first log difference. The choice of first log difference rather than log levels is explained in a series of graphs (omitted for brevity): while all the time series of log levels show an overall positive trend as a reflection of the domestic market upturn of the last decade, the scatter plot of the first log difference shows various contrasting movements between data related to the same property category but provided by different sources. This preliminary evidence reveals a substantial discrepancy in the rates of change of the indices, reflecting the lack of homogeneity in data collection methods.

The data were gathered adopting both transaction-based and appraisal-based methods, but we are unable to identify the prevalent approach used by each data source due to limited transparency and the incompleteness of the methodology descriptions available. While one of the five time-series families, named Source#5, certainly follows a transaction-based approach to gathering data, the other sources' data-collection methods of the other data sources appear indistinguishable.

8.3.2 Methodology

To investigate the discrepancies between data, we adopt a three-step analysis consisting of (1) a dissimilarity test, (2) correlation and (3) cointegration analysis. Thus, first of all in order to detect dissimilarities between the data, we implement a simple test based on the ratio between property index values. For each pair of comparable time series, we calculate the value of a ratio R_{XY}. The ratio R_{XY} is the simple average of the quotients between the values of two comparable time series (X and Y) with a time interval length of m:

$$R_{XY} = \frac{1}{m} \sum_{i=1}^{m} \frac{X_i}{Y_i} \tag{8.1}$$

More precisely, two time series are comparable if they are related to a common time interval and to a homogeneous class of property. The interpretation of the ratio is straightforward: the closer the ratio gets to one, the more the two series analysed will be statistically equal; conversely, the further the ratio moves away from one, the less homogeneous the series will be. To assess the significance of the relationship between the two series, we test the null hypothesis H_0: ratio $= 1$ by using the F statistic.

The second step is the calculation of the correlation matrix of property indices both for log levels and for first differences. The aim of the correlation analysis is to validate the previous graph (omitted) according to which the log-level time series appears to be characterized by a quasi-similar trend, while the change rate (first log difference) is not. The lack of a single data-gathering approach, and the consequent low level of standardization of information, make a low positive correlation coefficient probable, while the presence of a negative value would be considered unexpected and symptomatic of a more significant phenomenon of data divergence.

The cointegration analysis represents our third step towards reaching a definitive assessment on the issue of data uncertainty. The lack of homogeneity potentially observed in the two previous steps does not appear to be final since it does not take into consideration the possibility that despite the divergence between the returns in the interval observed, two or more series can show a long-term equilibrium relationship. For this purpose, one can proceed to verify the existence of a common trend between the time series, whose presence would moderate the opinion expressed about the dissimilarity between sources of property data, and the consequent inefficiency of market information processes.

Generally speaking, two variables are cointegrated if they have a common stochastic trend, that is, if they move together for a long period of time despite the trend not always being (visually) observable. More formally, two variables that are stationary in their first differences but non-stationary in their levels, are said to be cointegrated if there is a stationary linear combination between them. In order for the two historical series to be considered as cointegrated, it is necessary for both to be (i) integrated by the same n level, and (ii) their linear combination (that is *cointegration relationship*) to be integrated by a level less than n. The general relationship from which the identification of a cointegration phenomenon proceeds is:

$$y_t = \beta_0 + \beta_1 x_t + \xi_t \tag{8.2}$$

The model illustrated by equation (8.2) represents the so-called cointegration regression, and can be interpreted as the stochastic representation of the relationship that connects the variables to each other (it is also worth mentioning that $y_t = \beta_1 x_t$). The error term ξ_t is representative of the deviations from the equilibrium relationship. To test for cointegration it is therefore necessary to investigate the stationarity of the error term; in the case of stationarity of the residuals ξ_t there is cointegration between X and Y. When there is cointegration between the variables, and therefore a long-term relationship between them, assuming certain conditions, it would be possible to establish an ECM (*Error Correction Mechanism*) able to estimate the velocity of convergence of the dependent variable (Y) with the equilibrium relationship corresponding to each variation of the independent variable (X).

The considerations expressed above thus make it necessary to consider the issue of cointegration by means of an investigation into the level of stationarity present in the residuals from the cointegration regression (1). The stationarity of the residuals can be assessed in two ways: graphically or descriptively. A graphic assessment involves the observation of both the residuals (*Y-axis*) plotted against time (X-axis), and the residuals at time *t* (*Y-axis*) plotted against those at time *t–1*. If in either of these cases a stationary dynamic is evident, it is possible to plausibly hypothesize the presence of cointegration. The use of a statistical-descriptive method for identifying the presence of cointegration requires, on the other hand, that the regression of cointegration be submitted to a series of tests. The first is the Durbin Watson test (*DW test*) which, to summarize briefly, estimates the presence of autocorrelation between the residuals; a value of the DW statistic near to zero is indicative of the presence of autocorrelation in the residuals and, therefore, of their non-stationarity. Vice versa, a higher value of the DW statistic is indicative of stationarity in the residuals (the absence of autocorrelation) and, therefore, the presence of cointegration. A second investigative test (consistent with the approach adopted by Engle and Granger, 1987) consists in putting the residuals from cointegration regression through the ADF test (Augmented Dickey Fuller); when the residuals are stationary, there will be cointegration, while otherwise it is not possible to establish the presence of an equilibrium relationship in the long-term between the two variables (the variables are not cointegrated).[8] A third investigation method for testing for the presence of the cointegration phenomenon is represented by the Phillips–Perron test (PP test); its mechanism can be approximated to that of the ADF test in so far as it offers the advantage of offering greater robustness

Table 8.2 Dissimilarity ratio analysis

	1st Panel – dissimilarity ratio between national time series											
	Retail			**Commercial**			**Industrial**			**Office**		
	#1	**#2**	**#3**	**#1**	**#2**	**#3**	**#1**	**#2**	**#3**	**#1**	**#2**	**#3**
#1	1.00			1.00			–			1.00		
#2	0.60*	1.00		1.15	–		–	1.00		1.11	1.00	
#3	2.05*	1.89	1.00	–	–	1.00	-	1.51	1.00	0.04*	2.02*	1.00

	2nd Panel – Dissimilarity ratio analysis between Milan time series											
	Retail				**Commercial**				**Office**			
	#1	**#2**	**#4**	**#5**	**#1**	**#2**	**#4**	**#5**	**#1**	**#2**	**#4**	**#5**
#1	1.00				1.00				–			
#2	1.16	1.00			0.74	1.00			–	1.00		
#4	1.37	0.96	1.00		0.98	1.23	1.00		–	1.37	–	
#5	1.11	0.88	0.85	1.00	2.07	1.15	0.88	1.00	–	-	-	1.00

Notes: * Statistically significant at 95% (H_0: ratio=1; H_A: ratio $\neq$ 1); (–) indicate time series pairs which are not comparable for analysis purposes

to the heteroschedasticity of the error terms and does not require the choice of a lag optimal for the lags in its base regression.

8.3.3 Empirical results

The main results of the three-step process are reported in Table 8.2 (dissimilarity ratio, R_{XY}), Table 8.3 (correlation analysis), and Tables 8.4 and 8.5 (ADF-t and cointegration analysis) respectively.

We extended the R_{XY} ratio analysis (step one) to the 21 couples of comparable time series in terms of time interval and class of property extracted from the original dataset. Achieving results with values close to one would be indicative of a convergence between data, while the results reported in Table 8.2 are consistent with a preliminary indication of the lack of harmonization between data.

The average value of R_{XY} for all the 21 cases is 1.196, with a standard deviation equal to 0.51 (max = 2.05, min = 0.04). If we distinguish between the two geographical areas, we note a slight increase in divergence for the indices relating to Italy: in this case the R_{XY} average value is 1.297 (with a standard deviation of 0.72, approx. 55 per cent) while for the indices related to Milan, the R_{XY} average value is 1.13 (with a standard deviation of 0.35, approx. 30 per cent).

The results of the correlation analysis seem to confirm the hypothesis of discrepancy in the data, especially for those relating to the national indices rather than a single urban area (Milan). The correlation matrix shown in

Table 8.3 Correlation matrix

		1st Panel – correlation coefficients between national time series									
		Retail			Commercial		Industrial		Office		
		#1	#2	#3	#1	#2	#2	#3	#1	#2	#3
Retail	#1	1.00									
	#2	0.27	1.00								
	#3	–0.67*	–0.70*	1.00							
Commercial	#1	0.88*	0.04	–0.70*	1.00						
	#2	0.25	0.22	–0.47*	–0.09	1.00					
Industrial	#2	0.17	0.02	0.76*	0.07	0.13	1.00				
	#3	–0.42	–0.68*	0.58*	–0.41	–0.21	0.44	1.00			
Office	#1	0.92*	0.04	–0.66*	0.84*	0.08	0.21	–0.50*	1.00		
	#2	0.64*	0.26	–0.45*	0.49*	0.48*	0.42*	–0.27	0.62*	1.00	
	#3	0.31	0.62*	–0.51	0.29	–0.01	–0.22	0.55*	0.55*	0.72*	1.00

		2nd Panel – correlation coefficients between time series for Milan city										
		Retail				Commercial				Office		Industrial
		#1	#2	#4	#5	#1	#2	#4	#5	#2	#4	#2
Retail	#1	1.00										
	#2	0.45*	1.00									
	#4	0.58*	0.89*	1.00								
	#5	0.23	0.26	0.50*	1.00							
Commercial	#1	0.47*	0.44*	0.35*	0.26	1.00						
	#2	0.47*	0.69*	0.71*	0.66*	0.35*	1.00					
	#4	0.42*	0.75*	0.83*	0.36*	0.64*	0.41*	1.00				
	#5	0.15	–0.19	–0.29	–0.21	–0.02	–0.16	–0.21	1.00			
Office	#2	0.47*	0.93*	0.83*	0.18*	0.51*	0.68*	0.77*	–0.08	1.00		
	#4	0.39*	0.71*	0.74*	0.31	0.69*	0.33*	0.98*	–0.18	0.79*	1.00	
Industrial	#2	0.49*	0.78*	0.75*	0.35*	0.41*	0.83*	0.53*	0.16	0.81*	0.40*	1.00

Notes: * Statistically significant at 95 % (H0: $\rho = 0$; HA: $\rho \neq 0$). The time intervals for each correlation coefficient are shown in Table 8.1.

Table 8.4 ADF unit root test (time interval: June 1997 to June 2008)

Time Series	R.E. category	Levels	*p* value	1st/2nd difference	*p* value	Order of integration
Source#1	Residential	−1.29 (4) (−3.54)	0.89	−4.56 (4) (−3.54)	0.00	I(2)
Source#2	Residential	−1.36 (4) (−3.54)	0.87	−6.58 (2) (−3.54)	0.00	I(2)
Source#1	Commercial	−2.18 (1) (−3.52)	0.50	−4.08 (1) (−3.54)	0.01	I(1)
Source#2	Commercial	−2.57 (1) (−3.52)	0.30	−3.74 (1) (−3.53)	0.02	I(1)
Source#1	Office	−2.73 (1) (−3.52)	0.22	−4.86 (4) (−3.54)	0.00	I(1)
Source#2	Office	−3.15 (1) (−3.52)	0.09	−4.39 (4) (−3.54)	0.00	I(1)

Notes: Augmented Dickey Fuller (ADF) test to check the stationarity of a series under the null hypothesis that series is non-stationary. We present a model with trend and constant. The ADF statistics are obtained from:

$\Delta x_t = a_0 + b_0 u_{t-1} + \sum_{j=1}^{p} c_{0j} \Delta x_{t-j} + \varepsilon_t$

where Δ is the difference operator, a0, b0 and c0 are the coefficients to be estimated, x is the variable whose time series are examined and w is the white-noise error term. Values in parentheses show the lag length of the ADF test. Values in square brackets indicate 5% critical value adopted from MacKinnon (1991). Details of the ADF regression (trend and constant) are not included to save space but are available on request.

Table 8.3 reveals a wide range of correlation coefficients, most of which are statistically significant.

With regard to the national indices, the range of correlations is $-0.698 \leq \rho \leq 0.721$ (with a standard deviation equal to 0.568), while for the city of Milan, we observe a smaller interval of $-0.2349 \leq \rho \leq 0.7484$ (st. dev. = 0.374). The presence of some negative signs in the correlation matrix is surprising since it reveals an outcome more compatible with a comparison between (different) asset classes rather than within a (similar) asset class. Although we cannot exclude some bias in the data, as we shall discuss shortly, these findings clearly demonstrate the existence of significant data divergence and raise some legitimate doubts about the informational efficiency of the domestic real estate market and the accuracy of information provided on it.

In both cases (ratio and correlation analysis), the incongruity of data-base systems appears stronger for the national index data (11 out of 21 indices). This result could be explained by the adoption of an advanced data collection procedure in the urban area of Milan (provided by the local board of trade) not yet widespread in the rest of the market.

Table 8.5 Cointegration analysis between two real estate data sources

RE category		***Residential***		***Commercial***		***Office***	
dep. variable		**log (Source#2)**	**Δlog (Source#2)**	**log (Source#2)**	**Δlog (Source#2)**	**log (Source#2)**	**Δlog (Source#2)**
ind. variable		**Log (Source#1)**	**Δlog (Source#1)**	**Log (Source#1)**	**Δlog (Source#1)**	**Log (Source#1)**	**Δlog (Source#1)**
Cointegration regression							
β		1.59	0.63	0.82	−0.12	0.92	0.75
(t value)		(28.47)	(1.83)	(29.88)	(−0.57)	(56.32)	(5.23)
[p –value]		[0.00]	[0.07]	[0.00]	[0.57]	[0.00]	[0.37]
R^2		0.95	0.07	0.95	0.08	0.99	0.39
(adjR^2)		(0.95)	(0.07)	(0.95)	(−0.02)	(0.99)	(0.38)
Test statistic		Residual- based test					
CRDW[a]	DW	0.05 *(1.03)*	0.50 1.03	0.10 1.03	0.65 1.03	0.13 1.03	0.88 1.03
ADF[b]	ADF-t	−0.74 (lag 1) *(−3.51)*	−2.55 (lag 1) *(−3.51)*	−2.95 (lag 1) *(−3.51)*	−2.91 (lag 4) *(−4.77)*	−3.26 (lag 3) *(−4.40)*	−3.20 (lag 1) *(−3.51)*
PP[c]	Z_p	−2.33 *(−19.42)*	−18.2 *(−19.34)*	−5.03 *(−19.42)*	−16.1 *(−19.34)*	−5.91 *(−19.42)*	−18.1 *(−19.34)*
	Z_t	−1.56 *(−3.52)*	−3.47 *(−3.52)*	−1.53 *(−3.52)*	−3.13 *(−3.52)*	−1.72 *(−3.52)*	−3.306 *(−3.52)*

[a] The critical values of the cointegrating regression Durbin Watson test are reported in Engle and Yoo (1987).
[b] The critical values for the ADF test are from MacKinnon (1991). The lag length was chosen according to the Schwartz criterion.
[c] The critical values of the Phillips-Perron test are taken from Philips and Ouliaris (1990).
The numbers in italics in parentheses are critical values.

		Source #2-Italy		
		Res.	*Off.*	*Comm.*
Source #1 -Italy	*Res.*	not cointegrated*		
	Off.		not cointegrated*	
	Comm.mercial			not cointegrated*

Note: *The absence of cointegration is observed for both the levels and first differences.

Figure 8.1 Summary of cointegration analysis results

Our interest in this issue invites a further level of investigation aimed at investigating the existence of a long-term relationship able to moderate or refine the assessment of dishomogeneity shown above. To this end, we proceed to run a cointegration test for the time series of national indices.

In order to enhance the statistical significance of the results, we select the time-series pairs with an adequate time interval, excluding from the cointegration analysis any data with a time-interval of less than ten years. Imposing this selection criterion, we obtain three pairs of time series provided by two data property sources (Source #1-Italy and Source #2-Italy), covering the residential, commercial and office sectors respectively. Each time series pair is then submitted to an ADF test (Augmented Dickey Fuller) to estimate its order of integration (see Table 8.4). The resulting cointegration outcomes are reported in summarized form in Figure 8.1, while the detailed presentation of the residual test results of the cointegration regression are given in Table 8.5.

The results are consistent with the absence of cointegration for each of the cases analysed, revealing non-negligible independence among data structures. Moreover, data show that the absence of cointegration is observed both for the historical series of absolute values (logarithmic levels) as well as for the returns series (first differences). Consequently, the lack of cointegration is an obstacle to achieving an ECM in order to approximate the convergence velocity to an equilibrium relationship between variables.

To summarize, the lack of a long-term relationship between data gathered from distinct sources, as well as the aforementioned characteristic of nonconformity, lead us to believe that the real-estate information systems are not at all adequate. However, some possible explanations of the empirical findings need to be explored. For example, the poor traceability of the valuation dates for the real estate portfolio to which the indices are linked impedes the correct synchronization of time series which, incidentally, may render the results of a comparison between information sources inefficient or implausible. Further, in spite of the traditional asset class markets (for example stocks and bonds), where the indices reflect the performance of a group of a similar type, real estate indices are based on portfolios that differ in terms of urban location and other hedonic variables (green areas, proximity to transport infrastructures, car parkings, and so on).

8.4 Implications for the market

The accuracy of real estate data is a topic of interest to many market participants. In this section we develop three simulations to show how the level of data homogeneity impacts on some of the operations carried out by financial institutions involved in real estate investment management. The simulations refer respectively to: (1) the impact of disharmonized data on IRR calculation of real estate funds; (2) the sensitivity of LGD (loss given default) values to the pricing of the collateral for bank mortgage management processes; (3) the relationship between the weights of an optimal mixed-asset portfolio and the source of property data, in a mean–variance optimisation framework.

8.4.1 A Simulation on the IRR funds

To assess the impact of data divergence on the valuation of a real estate fund, we conduct a sequence of back-tests for the internal rate of return (IRR) calculation, adopting a different real estate data source for each iteration. As is well known, the IRR calculation of a real estate investment is a function of three parameters: (1) rental cash flow, (2) cash management, and (3) the end value of properties. Assuming a real estate fund with an extremely simplified structure of assets, we design a procedure of IRR backtesting consisting in an IRR sensitivity analysis, setting different values for the third of the above parameters (the end value of the properties in the portfolio), keeping the other two constant. The back-testing procedure is iterated n times, where n represents the number of sub-periods selected and related to the different property end values.

The modulation of end values follows a mechanism defined as follows: given the $i_{th}(i=1..n)$ subperiod of m years, and given the availability of property index data provided by the j_{th} source ($j=1..h$), the i_{th} property end value is set as equal to the (hypothetical) initial value of the property compounded at m annual yields intrinsic to the corresponding time series interval. Following this mechanism, we select six five-year subperiods ($n=6$, and $m=5$) and three commercial property indices related to the city of Milan and provided by three different data-sources ($h=3$). The six subperiods started from January 1998 and each is separated from the previous one by a year; thus we obtain the following sequence of subperiods: 1st) January 1998 - December 2002; 2nd) January 1999 – December 2003; 3rd) January 2000 – December 2004; 4th) January 2001 – December 2005; 5th) January 2002 – December 2006; 6th) January 2003 – December 2007.

We then assume a five-year investment in a real estate fund invested in only two properties (A and B) whose financial characteristics are illustrated in the upper part of Table 8.6. With these established conditions, for each of the three data sources selected, we calculate six property portfolio end values and, consequently, six IRR values (keeping the other cash flow constant). The results are shown in Table 8.6, where some sensitivity measures are used.

The last row and last column of Table 8.6 show the standard deviation of the IRR 'within' subperiods and 'between' data-sources respectively. While analysis of the 'within subperiod' indicator is not so important for our aim, an inspection of the results of the second indicator appears indispensable. By looking at the results of 'between data-source' standard deviation, it becomes clear how the choice of data sources may affect the evaluation of the IRR in each subperiod; this influence is also significant in some cases, and varies between 2.5 per cent and 25.6 per cent.

These findings are consistent with the previous remarks about the existence of scarcely negligible data divergence for the Italian real estate market. In general, the results of this IRR simulation confirm how important it is to have access to comprehensive, reliable and timely evidence of property transactions in order to make informed predictions, and how this represents an issue of great concern to both market participants and policymakers who rely on price signals for decision-making (Lum, 2004).

8.4.2 Reliability of the time series and LGD evaluation

Recent turbulence in international financial systems originating in the mortgage markets highlights the close relationship between developments in real estate prices and the soundness of the financial sector (Koetter and Poghosyan, 2008). The exposure of a bank to the real estate market has implications for the sensitivity of property-collateralized loan value to housing price changes. We address this issue through a simulated loss given default calculation. According to the risk management terminology adopted in the Basel II framework, loss given default (LGD) denotes the fraction of exposure that will not be recovered following default. The purpose of the simulation described here is to analyse how the real estate data source affects LGD prediction for a property-secured loan. In general, the regulatory formula for a collateralized loan can be approximated as follows:

$$LGD = 1 - \frac{\sum_{t=1}^{n} \frac{E(RV)_t}{(1+i)^t} - \sum_{t=1}^{n} \frac{Exp_t}{(1+i)^t}}{EAD} \tag{8.3}$$

The term *E(RV)* denotes the expected recovery value of the collateral (property or properties). While cash recoveries are easy to evaluate, the evaluation of non-cash recovery, such as the repossession of properties, is complex, and can be tackled on an ad-hoc basis using reliable property market information. *Exp* indicates post-default administrative expenses and can be split into

Table 8.6 Simulating IRR calculation: main results

Assumptions:					
Portfolio composition	**Date of investment**	**Date of liquidation**	**Initial price**	**Annual rental**	**Costs**
Property A	t_0	t_5	100	1	0
Property B	t_0	t_5	200	2	0

End values of the fund							
Subperiod	Jan 1998–Dec 2002	Jan1999–Dec 2003	Jan 2000–Dec 2004	Jan 2001–Dec 2005	Jan 2002–Dec 2006	Jan 2003–Dec2007	SDWSP*
Data Source #1	413.3	409.1	409.3	414.2	399.2	388.9	2.41%
Data Source #2	433.3	691.7	565.2	453.1	433.3	339.8	25.47%
Data Source #3	416.6	444.4	413.3	389.9	364.5	345.8	9.19%
*SDDS***	2.5%	29.9%	19.2%	7.6%	8.6%	7.5%	
Internal Rate of Return (IRR) of the fund							
Subperiod	Jan 1998–Dec 2002	Jan1999–Dec 2003	Jan 2000–Dec 2004	Jan 2001–Dec 2005	Jan 2002–Dec 2006	Jan 2003–Dec2007	SDWSP
Data Source #1	18.1%	17.9%	17.9%	18.1%	17.5%	17.0%	2.49%
Data Source #2	19.0%	28.3%	24.1%	19.8%	19.0%	14.6%	22.87%
Data Source #3	18.2%	19.4%	18.1%	17.0%	15.8%	14.9%	9.67%
SDBDS**	2.5%	25.6%	17.6%	7.6%	9.0%	8.3%	

Notes:
*SDWSP: standard deviation within sub-periods.
**SDBDS: standard deviation between data sources.
SDWSP and SDBDS are expressed as percentages of the IRR average value.

direct costs (court costs, attorney and bailiff fees, cost of appraisal, and so on), and indirect costs (for example the operating costs of the lender's recovery department). The discount rate i can be inferred by following an appropriate risk-based hypothesis, while t is the time at which the lender obtains recoveries or pays the costs. Finally, EAD is the exposure at the time of default, that is the sum of the flows relating to the position outstanding, and discounted at the date of default.

For the purpose of our analysis, we use a simplified back-testing technique, which analyses the sensitivity of LGD predictions to the different expected recovery values estimated using a set of properly-selected property data sources. In particular, we select six time-series Milan housing prices from four sources of data split into two groups: three indices of new housing prices and three indices of previously-occupied housing prices. We then assume default by the debtor three years from the starting date (November 1997) on a secured loan repayment, the structure of which is illustrated in the upper part of Table 8.7. By setting a predetermined purchase price (housing market value at t_0), we simulate six probable property recovery values at time t_{rec} subsequent to the time of the debtor's default t_{def} ($t_{def} > t_{rec}$). Each recovery value is calculated as the property market value at t_0 compounded at the annual growth rate extracted over the period $t_0 - t_{def}$ in one of the six time series employed.

Table 8.7 Simulation of loss given default prediction

Simulation assumptions			
Loan amount	€600,000	Date of default	$t_{def} = t_4$ (2001)
Predetermined property purchase price (€)	€300,000	Date of recovery*	t_5 (2002)
Loan start date	t_0 (Nov 1997)	Exp*	1.8% of outstanding
Date of first instalment payment	t_1 (December 1998)	Discount rate	3%
Annual instalment (€)	€44,149.05	EAD**(€)	€598,709.77

Previously occupied housing prices (Milan)		***New housing prices (Milan)***	
Time series	**Estimated LGD**	**Time series**	**Estimated LGD**
Source#1	42.00%	*Source#1*	38.48%
Source#2	35.98%	*Source#3*	36.45%
Source#3	31.33%	*Source#4*	33.30%

*Notes:** Exp indicates the default administrative expenses; its value (1.8%) is consistent with the results of a central bank survey (see Supervisory Bulletin of the Bank of Italy n.12, 2001).

** Assuming default occurred in 2001, the exposure at default, EAD, is equal to the sum of the annual instalment for that year and the one following, discounted at the default time. The LGD values assume property repossession one year after the default.

The results of the LGD-data sensitivity relationship are shown in Table 8.7, where different LGD values are given. The confirmation of LGD sensitivity to the property data source is consistent with the results which emerged from the previous analytical test, and raise some issues about the risk management processes of lenders (principally banks).

The IRB method (internal rating method) introduced by the Basel Committee on Banking Supervision, requires banks, under certain conditions, to carry out stress tests on their portfolio of loans in order to measure overall exposure to credit risk and, consequently, to adapt their capital adequacy. The available data on which the stress tests are based are typically obtained from both internal and external sources. Internal data consist of loan information, default outcomes and internal payment records. Data obtained externally instead consist of accounts, external payment records and property data. This confirms the fact that banks are interested in using accurate estate databases, since there is a correlation (albeit slight) between the quality of external data sources and the assessment of portfolio risk (and therefore a prudent capital requirement). Moreover, this is a further argument for the involvement of financial authorities, such as central banks, in the collection and dissemination of reliable real estate data.

8.4.3 Data divergence and the investment choices

Finally, we come to the last issue discussed in this paper: the relationship between data property divergence and the quality of investment choices. The basic idea is to select a set of asset class indices, including domestic real estate, and to create a sequence of portfolio optimizations, varying the property data at each iteration. By changing the property index at each optimization, we analyse the sensitivity of portfolio weights to the data source switch, measuring the consequent implications for the investment choices with an appropriate variable (DARaP, see below).

The tenet of portfolio theory is diversification within a mix of asset classes with an appropriate risk-return profile and a low correlation, to mitigate risk to the whole portfolio. In spite of its limitations (Chopra and Ziemba, 1993), the Markowitz Mean–Variance approach is widely used and represents the most suitable model for achieving optimal portfolio selection.

Using the classical principles of efficient frontier construction, we select five asset classes and estimate their expected returns, as well as their covariance matrix. The set of asset classes is made up of equity, bond, and real estate indices listed as follows: (1) S&P500 (US stock market); (2) MIBTEL (Italian stock market); (3) MTS BTP 10Y (long-term domestic government bonds); (4) domestic risk free-rate (MTS BOT); (5) a property index selected from the available set (Table 8.1).

The estimation of efficient frontier input represents an issue widely discussed in the literature. However, the merely descriptive purpose of this paragraph leads us to choose a simplified approach rather than more refined models (for example the Black and Litterman model and the Bayes-Stein approach). Thus, the expected returns are expressed as the annualized average of historical quarterly returns; the historical approach is then extended to the estimation of the covariance matrix.

From the available set of property indices, we recognize three triplets of comparable time series belonging to three data sources and related to both geographical area and the three main real estate segments (residential, commercial, office). For each triplet (that is for each data source) we can potentially proceed to the construction of three efficient frontiers, by changing the property index at each optimization iterate. However, to improve the significance of optimization outcomes, we exclude from the subset of (nine) series those with less than ten years of data. Imposing this criterion, we identify two time series triplets (six series), provided by two different sources and related respectively to the residential, commercial and office segments of the city of Milan. We then carry out six portfolio optimizations (one for each time series), obtaining three pairs of comparable efficient frontiers as shown in Figure 8.2. The expected returns and risks are estimated on an annual basis and are equal to the historical average and the standard deviation for the period June 1997 to June 2008 respectively.[9]

To determine the sensitivity of portfolio composition to each data change, we use a proxy of return/risk ratio for each frontier, which we call DARaP (Decile Average Risk adjusted Performance). In detail, the mean DARaP variable may be explained as follows: for each efficient frontier it represents the average value of the return-to-risk ratio of ten 'decile portfolio', where this term describes the portfolio with a risk equal to a decile of the volatility interval (max σ - min σ). Formally, we write:

$$DARaP = \frac{1}{10}\sum_{i=1}^{10}\frac{R_i}{\sigma_i} \tag{8.4}$$

where with R_i and σ_i we denote the return and risk (σ_i) respectively of the optimal portfolio corresponding to the ith decile of the volatility interval of the frontier.

In general, if we calculate the DARaP for two efficient frontiers (A and B) differing in terms of the source of data of one (or more) asset classes, a proxy of the sensitivity of portfolio composition to the data change would be shown by the value $\Delta DAR3_{A,B}$, where:

$$\Delta DARaP = \left| \frac{\max\{DARaP_A, DARaP_B\} - \min\{DARaP_A, DARaP_B\}}{\min\{DARaP_A, DARaP_B\}} \right| \tag{8.5}$$

The $\Delta DARaP_{A,B}$ variable captures the geometric translation of the efficient frontier when a data change occurs. Thus, a high (low) value of $\Delta DARaP_{A,B}$

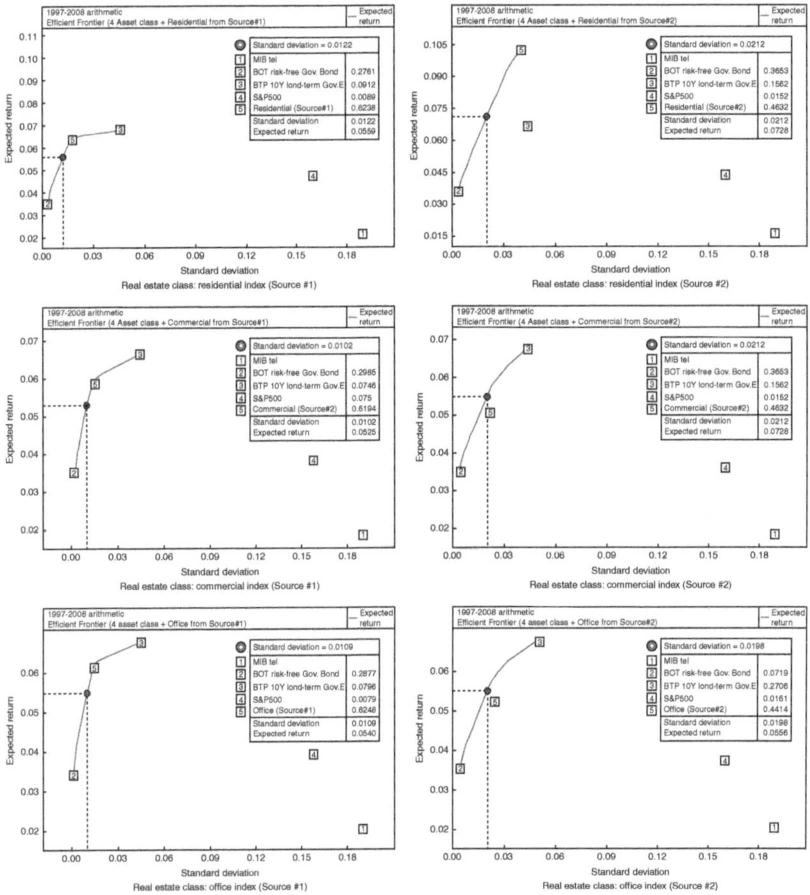

Figure 8.2 Comparable efficient frontiers (input is historical values, June 1997 to June 2008)

is consistent with discrepancies (convergence) between sources of data. The results of efficient frontier comparison are summarized in Table 8.8, where rows indicate the data source of the property index inserted in the portfolio optimization and the $\Delta DARaP_{A,B}$ values, while the columns are indicative of the category of real estate indices.

The ΔDARaP value is between 29.22 per cent and 46.27 per cent, revealing a significant change in portfolio weights due to the substitution of the property data source. These findings are consistent with those of the previous simulations, and suggest much caution is needed in the selection of the property benchmark to include in portfolio optimization tests, especially for

Table 8.8 Map of Decile Average Risk adjusted Performance (DARaP) values

		Type	
	Residential	*Commercial*	*Office*
Source #1 (A)	3.668	4.727	5.349
Source #2 (B)	4.747	3.527	3.657
$\Delta DARaP_{A,B}$ *(%)*	29.22	34.02	46.27

Notes: For each efficient frontier DARaP denotes the average value of the return to risk ratio of ten *'decile portfolio'*, that is a portfolio with a risk equal to one decile of the frontier volatility interval (max σ – min σ).

those which are mean-variance based. The most serious practical limitations of the mean-variance approach are, in fact, the ambiguity and instability of portfolios. Small changes in input assumption often lead to large changes in the composition of optimized portfolios (Michaud, 1998). Therefore, optimal weights will change significantly over time as a direct result of making estimation errors (Kallberg and Ziemba, 1984; Adler, 1987). Thus, in the case of a high level of divergence between property indices (for example the office sector in Table 8.8), and to impede the amplification of estimation errors, it would be appropriate to adopt a procedure at least able to mitigate the discrepancy of the data (that is the calculation of average index values).

8.5 Conclusion

Data quality plays a vital role in providing reliable and valid information for property market performance. Its relationship with the assessment of financial stability and monetary policy is much debated among academics and policymakers alike. The complexity of the market itself and differences in its functioning impede the adoption of standardized data collection procedures in different countries. Thus, gathering reliable and comparable data on property markets has proved very difficult (Zhu, 2005). Furthermore, it is not uncommon to find markets where multiple, very different data collection methods coexist.

By focusing on the Italian real estate market, we have discussed the reliability of domestic property data sources, taking into account variables such as the frequency of collection, data-gathering methodology, and the area covered. Furthermore, we have conducted three simulations in order to measure the impact of data divergence for, respectively, real estate investment vehicles, loan mortgage lenders, and the asset allocation of optimized portfolios. Our results show a poor level of homogeneity between data both for national time series and for urban data time series. These findings raise the issue of how important it is to have quick access to comprehensive and reliable evidence of property transactions in order to make informed predictions, and how this represents a critical question for both policymakers and market participants who rely on price signals for decision-making. Looking forward, there is the need for action aimed at improving the quality of property data and enhancing the comparability of across-data sources.

Notes

1. Author's contribution: GS conceived the study, designed and implemented the cointegration analysis, the IRR and mean-variance simulations and wrote the manuscript. FB assembled the input data, conducted the correlation/ratio analysis and carried out the LGD simulation, and helped GS to write paragraph 8.4.2. CP participated in the design and coordination of the study and gave conceptual advice. All authors have read and approved the final manuscript.
2. The smoothing effect is related to the tendency of a time series of returns to show a link between the return t with the previous t-1; smoothed returns leading to the following effects: (1) return autocorrelation; (2) low standard deviation of returns; (3) low correlation with the returns of other asset classes not characterized by smoothing.
3. For a more detailed review of the appraisal bias literature see Yiu et al. (2006).
4. See Edelstein and Quan (2006) and Webb et al. (1992).
5. See, for example, Geltner and Goetzmann (2000), Galtzaff and Geltner (2000), Bond et al. (2006).
6. 'Accordingly: (i) the value of the property shall be verified at least once every three years for residential property and once every year for commercial real estate, or more frequently where the market is subject to significant changes in conditions. Statistical methods may also be used to monitor the value of the property and to identify property that requires verification; (ii) where the verifications under point (i) reveal a material decline in the value of the property, a valuation shall be made by an independent valuer, based on a value that shall not exceed the market value', Banca d'Italia, 2006, pp. 21–2.
7. The privacy disclaimers of some sources of data do not authorize the use of data for external research. For this reason, the historical series available are identified by code (data source 1, data source 2 and so on).
8. Other investigation methods also exist for verifying the phenomenon of cointegration, including: the restricted vector autoregression test, RVAR; augmented restriction vector autoregression, ARVAR; the unrestricted vector autoregression test, UVAR; and the augmented restriction autoregression vector, AUVAR. For a review see Engle and Granger (1991).
9. For reasons of brevity, the covariance matrix and expected return are not shown here, but are available from the author on request.

References

Adler, M. (1987) 'Global asset allocation: Some uneasy questions', *Investment Management Review*, 1, 13–18.

Banca d'Italia (2006) 'New regulations for the prudential supervision of banks', www.bancaditalia.it (homepage), date accessed 01 July 2012.

Bank for International Settlements (2005) 'Real estate indicators and financial stability', www.bis.org (homepage), date accessed 01 July 2012.

Bond, S., S. Hwang and G. Marcato (2006) 'Evaluating unsmoothing procedures for appraisal data, http://www.areuea.org/ (homepage), date accessed 01 July 2012.

Chopra, V. K. and W. T. Ziemba (1993) 'The effects of errors in means, variances, and covariances on optimal portfolio choice', *Journal of Portfolio Management*, 20, 6–11.

Edelstein, R. and D. Quan (2006) 'How does appraisal smoothing bias real estate returns measurement?' *Journal of Real Estate Finance and Economic*, 32, 41–60.

Engle, R. F. and C. W. J. Granger (1987) 'Cointegration and error correction: Representation, estimation and testing', *Econometrica*, 55, 251–76.

——(1991) *Long Run Economic Relationships* (Oxford: Oxford University Press).

Engle, R. F. and B. S. Yoo (1987) 'Forecasting and testing in co-integrated systems', *Journal of Econometrics*, 35, 143–59.

Ge, X. and T. Harfield (2007) 'The quality of data and data availability for property research', http://hdl.handle.net/10453/7375 (homepage), date accessed 01 July 2012.

Geltner, D. (1989) 'Bias in appraisal-based returns', *AREUEA Journal*, 17, 338–52.

——(1991) 'Smoothing in appraisal-based returns', *Journal of Real Estate Finance and Economics*, 4, 327–45.

Geltner, D. and W. Goetzman (2000) 'Two decades of commercial property returns: A repeated measure regression-based version of the NCREIF index', *Journal of Real Estate Finance and Economics*, 21, 5–21.

Geltner, D. and D. Ling (2007) 'Indices for investment benchmarking and return performance analysis in private real estate', *International Real Estate Review*, 10, 17–36.

Greer, G. and P. T. Kolbe (2006) *Investment Analysis for Real Estate Decisions* (Chicago: Deaborn Real estate Education).

Hudson-Wilson, S., F. J. Fabozzi and J. N. Gordon (2003) 'Why real estate? – An expanding role for Institutional investors', *Journal of Portfolio Management*, 29, 12–25.

Kallberg, J. G. and W. T. Ziemba (1984) 'Mis-specification in portfolio selection problems' in G. Bamberg and A. Spremann (eds), *Risk and Capital* (New York: Springer-Verlag).

Koetter, M. and T. Poghosyan (2008) 'Real estate markets and bank distress', http://www.bundesbank.de/ (homepage), date accessed 01 July 2012.

Lai, T. and K. Wang (1998) 'Appraisal smoothing: The other side of the story', *Real Estate Economics*, 26, 511–35.

Lin, Z. and K. Vandell (2007) 'Illiquidity and pricing biases in the real estate markets', *Real Estate Economics*, 35, 291–330.

Lum, S. K. (2004) 'Property price indices in the Commonwealth – construction methodologies and problems', *Journal of Property Investment & Finance*, 22, 25–54.

Michaud, R. (1998) *Efficient Asset Management* (New York: Oxford University Press).

Phillips, P. C. B. and S. Ouliaris (1990) 'Asymptotic properties of residual based tests for cointegration', *Econometrica*, 58, 165–93.

Qi, M. and X. Yang (2009) 'Loss given default of high loan-to-value residential mortgages', *Journal of Banking & Finance*, 33, 788–99.

Quan, D. and J. Quigley, (1991) 'Price formation and the appraisal function in real estate', *Journal of Real Estate Finance and Economics*, 4, 127–46.

Ross, S. and R. Zisler (1991) 'Risk and return in real estate', *Journal of Real Estate Finance and Economics*, 4, 175–90.

Seiler, M. J., J. R. Webb and F. C. N. Meyer (1999) 'Diversification issues in real estate investment', *Journal of Real Estate Literature*, 7, 163–79.

Stephan, V. A. (2005) 'Obtaining real estate data: Criteria, difficulties and limitations', www.bis.org (homepage), date accessed 01 July 2012.

Webb, R. B., M. Miles and D. Guilkey (1992) 'Transactions-driven commercial real estate returns: The panacea to asset allocation models?' *AREUEA Journal*, 20, 325–57.

Yiu, C. Y., B.S. Tang and L. H. T. Choy (2006) 'Alternative theories of appraisal bias', *Journal of Real Estate Literature*, 14, 321–44.

Zhu, H. B. (2005) 'The importance of property markets for monetary policy and financial stability', www.bis.org (homepage), date accessed 01 July 2012.

9
Real Estate Trends and Portfolio Rebalancing: Evidence from Main European Markets

Gianluca Mattarocci and Georgios Siligardos

9.1 Introduction

There has been much academic debate on the effectiveness of intra-asset diversification and on how to optimally apply it. Sectorial provenience and the location of real estate assets were initially the most valid segments for an efficient diversification (Miles and McCue, 1982). By this time, more sophisticated methods had been elaborated to provide a better segmentation, expanding the possibilities of intra-asset diversification. In particular, concerning the geographical segmentation, it had been proposed that regions – or urban areas – classified according to economic function might form a basis for a more effective risk management strategy (Lee and Byrne, 1998).

Key issues in implementing the diversification are timing and the frequency of re-balances. Many studies focus on decoding the asset management strategies of real estate funds. The passive management that distinguished the real estate sector during the previous decades is giving way to more active strategies and to a short-term perspective for investments (Pyhrr et al., 2003).

Diversification issues and portfolio rebalancing on a short time horizon make necessary to develop more efficient and specific market indices as they could better capture the trends of the sector. Those innovations and the highest quality of indices available created the proper requisite to research effective strategies for real estate funds.

The aim of this chapter is to compare the optimal portfolio asset allocation (based on different sector performance indices) with the real strategy adopted by fund managers in order to evaluate the impact and the interdependence of the indices on fund management. We conduct the analysis on major European countries (France, Germany, Italy and UK) to better frame the tendencies and dynamics of the market.

The analysis has two main focuses. The first aim is to examine whether or not the fund management followed market trends in reallocating its assets, under the terms of sectorial diversification. The second approach assesses the statistical significance of the improvement in performance for portfolios in which a diversification policy had a positive relation with the optimal portfolios, constructed with respect to the market indices.

The results show that the managers' choices were not always optimized – or not aligned to the theoretical allocation – and that fund managers do not significantly modify the strategy on the basis of the real estate market trends during the life of their investments. The empirical evidences show that portfolio managers could achieve better trade-offs if they modify their strategy on the basis of real estate asset dynamics.

9.2 Literature review

Markowitz (1952) was the first to discuss the concept of diversification through the formal development of modern portfolio theory (MPT). Although Markowitz used stocks for his illustration, his theories can be applied to bonds, government treasury securities, real estate, and other financial assets. However, MPT has only been recently applied to real estate investment strategies.

The idea behind the within-asset diversification is to recognize as many distinct groups of sub-asset classifications as possible and to maximize within-group homogeneity while maximizing the heterogeneity between groups. This strategy will lower the correlations between the groups, which in turn will increase the diversification of the portfolio. This growth in diversification causes a decrease in unsystematic risk and a corresponding increase or upward and leftward shift in the efficient frontier. Therefore, the greater the intra-asset diversification, the greater the reduction in overall unsystematic risk and the more likely the portfolio will reach a new and higher optimum (Seiler et al., 1999).

While, in the securitized portfolios, assets vary primarily by size (capitalization) and industry, in real estate, assets vary by size (square footage and value), property type, and geographic/economic region. Therefore, diversification within the real estate sector should require the purchase of many more different properties (Young and Graff, 1995). Empirical evidence has shown the possibility of portfolio risk reduction by increasing the number of real assets that are characterized by having a low correlation and being connected to different factors (Lee and Stevenson, 2005).

Real estate portfolio diversification has been documented in the literature by different authors and with different approaches. The exploration of an optimal diversification factor is still an open research subject that continuously encounters new and better developments. Under this area of research, Grissom and Walther (1987) used data from Houston and Austin (USA), from the years 1975 to 1983 to investigate the benefits of diversification within a real estate portfolio. They found that diversifying across markets and property type reduced unsystematic risk more than across markets or property types alone. Miles and McCue (1984), used a sample of real estate investment trusts (REITs) and regressed their return-to-risk ratios against variables representing the extent of diversification by real estate type and geographic region. They found evidence that diversification by real estate type produces higher risk-adjusted cash yields than geographic diversification.

With a different approach, Cullen (1993) concluded that industrial property was relatively homogeneous and that retail property is partitioned largely in terms of ownership and lease terms rather than location or function. Only the office markets showed a clear geographical substructure, with the City of London offices being distinctive.

Lee and Byrne (1998) discussed the importance of property type in constructing property-only portfolios. They compared a range of efficient frontiers based on sectors, super regions, administrative regions, and functional groups to indicate the most efficient diversification factor. They found that super regions outperformed almost all other diversification strategies, but they also suggested that there should be a more accurate and sophisticated method to define the functional groups. The same authors in 2003 explained that portfolio size is negatively related to specific risk but positively related to systematic risk. This result indeed contradicts MPT, as it specifies that only specific risk is affected by portfolio size, thus explaining the lack of association between size and portfolio variance. Larger funds are more likely to diversify internationally to reduce the market risk (MacCowan, 2008). A recent study performed by Heydenreich (2010) pointed out that economic strategies based on economic diversification show superior risk-adjusted returns than those of the traditional, strictly geographical segmentation.

The literature notes that, generally, the holding period in real estate funds tends to be long, which is especially apparent when comparing real estate assets with other assets classes; however, it is different from the outlook of property unit trusts, opportunity funds and property companies, which aim to trade profitably by moving assets and repeating the process (MacCowan, 2008). Despite the long average holding period, he concluded that the pressure to perform well encourages fund managers to increase their activity in managing funds and to take a short-term perspective in their investments. Earlier, De Witt (1996) conducted a survey in pension funds and found that most real estate fund managers diversify their real estate portfolios consciously and rigorously. Furthermore, managers employ a strategic top–down approach rather than letting their portfolios evolve as more buildings are acquired.

The existing literature also provides explanations of the possible reasons why a rebalancing of real estate portfolios does not occur when there is a change in the expected returns, risk, or correlation in any of the assets in the market. Besides the practical difficulties that the direct properties present in negotiating them, some researchers identify the disproportional transaction costs as the main reason why reallocation does not occur. Optimal portfolios, in theory, should be rebalanced continuously to reflect continuous changes in risk, return, and inter-asset correlations. However, rebalancing could not occur continuously because of the positive transaction costs associated with rebalancing. The greater the cost is to rebalance, the less often the portfolio will be rebalanced and the greater the amount of time the portfolio will not be optimal (Seiler et al., 1999).

9.3 Methodology

Using the FTSE–NAREIT indices for the countries, the methodology adopted different tests that consider more than one aspect to better understand the interrelations between the indices and the fund allocation.

As a preliminary test, we investigated if changes to the portfolio composition of each fund occur yearly. Variation through the different years has been measured by comparing the composition of portfolios at time t and t+1.

In a second step, we consider the correlation of the annual weight variation assigned to each type of asset (office, retail, industrial, residential and other) with the real estate annual variation index in each sector.

The analysis was conducted using a standard pairwise correlation measure and an F-test to measure the significance of the relationship.

$$\rho = \frac{\mathrm{cov}(\Delta index_t^F, \Delta weight_t^F)}{\sigma(\Delta index_t^F)\sigma(\Delta weight_t^F)} \tag{9.1}$$

Where F represents the sector, t the time, Δindex is the annual change of performance indices for the sector F and Δweight is the annual change of the weight assigned to the type of assets in portfolio F by the fund manager. A high value of the index indicates a high sensitivity of the asset management allocation to any change in the market dynamics while low or negative values indicates that the investment selection process is not significantly affected by the market dynamics. In order to test the statistical significance of the correlation measure, we adopt a standard parametric significance test on the pairwise correlation coefficient.

Once having identified the existence or the absence of the correlation between the market dynamics and the portfolio allocation, we consider the difference between an efficient market portfolio and the real asset allocation adopted by the managers. The usefulness of the Markowitz approach for constructing a diversified portfolio in the real estate industry is supported by many studies in the literature (e.g., Chen and Liang (2000) and Lee and Stevenson (2005)). Using Markowitz diversification principles, we constructed a set of efficient portfolios (100) for each country and for each year using the market indexes provided by EPRA[1] and we analyse both differences in the asset allocation and the differences in performance and risk exposure.

Looking at the portfolio composition, a standard Euclidean distance measure is computed comparing each fund with all of the efficient ones (100). In formulas:

$$min\begin{bmatrix} d=\sqrt{\sum_{i=1}^{5}(weight_{it}^{1*}-weight_{it})^2} \\ \dots \\ d=\sqrt{\sum_{i=1}^{5}(weight_{it}^{j*}-weight_{it})^2} \\ \dots \\ d=\sqrt{\sum_{i=1}^{5}(weight_{it}^{100*}-weight_{it})^2} \end{bmatrix} min\begin{bmatrix} d_1=\sqrt{\sum_{i=1}^{5}(weight_{it}^{1*}-weight_{it})^2} \\ \dots \\ d_j=\sqrt{\sum_{i=1}^{5}(weight_{it}^{j*}-weight_{it})^2} \\ \dots \\ d_{100}=\sqrt{\sum_{i=1}^{5}(weight_{it}^{100*}-weight_{it})^2} \end{bmatrix} \tag{9.2}$$

Where i represents the sector (from 1 to 5) and t identifies the year. We summarize the distance measures results considering the minimum distance respective to any portfolio on the frontier assuming that the minimization procedure is a good technical procedure for identifying the efficient portfolio with the more coherent return/risk profile respect to the real portfolio analysed.

To test whether or not the portfolios near the frontier achieve a better performance, a methodological approach used by Gibbon et al. (1989) and improved by Lee and Stevenson (2005) was utilized. To compare real estate funds with the nearest portfolios in the efficient frontiers, a Sharpe ratio has been computed for both the real and the theoretical portfolios:

$$Sharpe_{it}=\frac{r_{it}-r_{ft}}{\sigma_{it}} \tag{9.3}$$

$$Sharpe_{it}^{*}=\frac{r_{it}^{*}-r_{ft}}{\sigma_{it}^{*}} \tag{9.4}$$

where r_i is the ex-post fund performance, r_i^* is the return achieved by the optimal portfolio more similar to the real one analysed, r_f is the risk free rate, σ_i the standard deviation of the fund performance and σ_i^* is the standard deviation of the optimal portfolio more similar to the real one analysed. All the measures are computed on a yearly time horizon using monthly frequency data.

In order to compare the value of the Sharpe ratios computed for each fund, we use an F-statistics test:

$$F_{it}=\frac{\frac{(T-N_2)(\text{Sharpe}_{it}^{*2}-\text{Sharpe}_{it}^2)}{N}}{(1+\text{Sharpe}_{it}^2)} \tag{9.5}$$

Where T is the number of observations available for each fund in each year (12), N_1 represent the number of the sectors in which the fund invests (from 1 to 5), N_2 the number of the sectors in which the optimized portfolio invests (from 1 to 5), N is defined as the difference between N_2 and N_1, $Sharpe_{it}$ represents the Sharpe Ratio for the real estate fund and $Sharpe^*_{it}$ the Sharpe ratio for the theoretical optimal portfolios.

9.4 Sample

The sample that the research is based on is from four different markets, United Kingdom, France, Germany, Italy, which comprises the majority of European real estate investment promoted by funds (Table 9.1).

The sample comprises data on the yearly portfolio composition for an extended number of funds for each country, their performances from 2007 to 2010 and the trends in each sector of the real estate market. The choice of the time horizon is constrained by the data available on the market as being the only one that reduces significantly the variability over time of the sample size.

For the first category, we attempted to gather information on the property funds from year 2007 until 2010 for each country. Our aim was to investigate the asset allocation by property type, and as a consequence, we gathered data describing this feature and its evolution for the period 2007 to 2010.

For the Italian market, the sample for 2010 comprised 20 funds compared to the almost 180 operating funds (listed and non-listed) in the same year. The total assets owned by the funds under consideration amounted to nearly €15 billion for the latest year of our interval.

With respect to the French market, a number of almost 80 funds were investigated out of the 140 funds operating in 2010. The sample totalled assets of approximately 16 billion euros, which is almost 90 per cent of the total property fund market in France. In this case, the primary source was the 'Institut de l'Epargne Immobilière et Foncière' (IEIF). For the British Market, a mean number of 20 property funds per year were investigated, and the data was mostly collected in a singular way by the information promoted for each fund; the property funds operating in year 2010 totalled to nearly 65 collecting assets of 32 billion pounds. Finally, for Germany, almost 30 open-ended property funds comprised the sample. In that case, the same collection method as that for the Britain market was followed. In Germany, almost 45 open-ended funds were operating, managing assets of approximately 83 billion euros.

Financial data concerning the performance of each fund were collected from Datastream®for the overall time horizon (2007 to 2010) with a monthly frequency.

To measure the real estate market trends, we used the sector indices included in the FTSE EPRA-NAREIT Global Real Estate Index that the

Table 9.1 Sample composition (number of funds)

Year	France	Germany	Italy	UK
2007	78	26	19	19
2008	77	26	19	19
2009	77	26	19	19
2010	77	26	18	19

Table 9.2 Indexes of summary statistics

		Eurozone	UK		
Year	**Sector**	**mean**	**σ**	**Mean**	**σ**
	Office	–3.63%	1.14%	–6.46%	2.64%
	Retail	–2.04%	2.18%	–5.57%	4.46%
2007	Industrial	–3.35%	2.08%	–5.64%	3.25%
	Residential	–5.40%	2.40%	–5.62%	7.95%
	Other	10.46%	15.54%	16.28%	42.52%
	Office	–3.32%	7.89%	–8.48%	10.51%
	Retail	–3.93%	8.06%	–8.82%	18.62%
2008	Industrial	–6.85%	41.02%	–8.01%	18.38%
	Residential	–9.68%	40.37%	–10.17%	97.92%
	Other	18.75%	210.11%	27.66%	261.66%
	Office	5.33%	8.94%	4.68%	10.11%
	Retail	6.67%	7.55%	0.96%	12.96%
2009	Industrial	5.68%	19.34%	0.57%	71.99%
	Residential	11.07%	18.33%	9.69%	57.20%
	Other	–14.29%	88.59%	–10.99%	314.20%
	Office	1.57%	3.74%	3.44%	1.98%
	Retail	1.68%	7.71%	2.18%	1.99%
2010	Industrial	0.73%	3.72%	–0.39%	3.24%
	Residential	3.43%	4.37%	–0.17%	9.44%
	Other	–2.56%	29.64%	–1.33%	21.90%

literature identifies as a better proxy for active investment strategies (Serrano and Hoesli, 2009). Summary statistics on the reference indexes for each market are presented in Table 9.2.

For France, Germany and Italy we use as real estate market indices the Eurozone EPRA–NAREIT index while for the UK we were able to identify the country specific index. Information available distinguishes among different real estate investment types and, coherently with the information available for the asset allocation of each real estate fund, we consider separately the following investment categories: office, retail, industrial, residential and the residual category of other type of buildings. The time horizon (2007 to 2010)

Table 9.3 Portfolio rebalancing over a one-year time horizon

	France	Germany	Italy	UK
N° funds				
2007–2008	43.67%	100.00%	92.86%	94.12%
2008–2009	44.94%	87.50%	100.00%	88.24%
2009–2010	46.20%	100.00%	90.91%	94.12%
Average	44.94%	95.83%	94.59%	92.16%
Mean percentage change				
2007–2008	3.83%	4.32%	2.19%	16.15%
2008–2009	4.53%	0.93%	8.32%	4.16%
2009–2010	5.23%	1.48%	3.45%	4.14%
Average	4.53%	2.24%	4.65%	8.15%

and the frequency (monthly) of the indices data are coherent with the asset allocation data.

9.5 Results

A preliminary analysis was made to determine whether the rebalancing actions of the portfolios occurred at least yearly. In order to identify the role of portfolio rebalancing we compare year by year the sector asset allocation of all the funds in the sample (Table 9.3).

Excluding France every year at least 87 per cent of the funds considered, effectuate changes in their portfolio composition, selling existing assets or acquiring new ones. The analysis of the relevance of the changes demonstrate that the portfolio rebalancing affects the portfolio allocation and the mean yearly weight modification varies from 2.24 per cent (Germany) to 8.15 per cent (UK).

Once we have shown the existence of portfolio rebalancing also for the real estate funds selected, we tested for the existence of a statistical correlation between the asset allocation change and the sector trend variation in the real estate industry. We use a standard pairwise correlation test for each country in order to measure the reaction of the asset allocation weights to a change in the performance trend of a real estate sector (Table 9.4).

The correlation analysis demonstrates that the asset allocation choices are not affected by the sector trend and frequently the asset managers adopt a contrarian strategy with respect to the market trend (negative correlation). The UK market is the only one that on average presents a positive correlation between asset manager choices and market trend for more than one of the sectors considered (office and retail). In France only the weight assigned to the industrial sector is positively related to the sector trend in the current year while for Germany and Italy no positive correlation could be identified.[2] All

Table 9.4 Pairwise correlation results

		Office	Retail	Industrial	Residential	Other
France	Mean	7.25%	−10.58%	41.97%	−27.21%	−22.85%
	Min	−62.42%	−66.56%	14.79%	−34.25%	−66.63%
	Max	66.66%	66.62%	54.80%	−20.16%	27.50%
Germany	Mean	22.82%	−2.97%	−0.39%	−2.29%	27.68%
	Min	−27.71%	−64.22%	−63.31%	−63.36%	−50.83%
	Max	65.60%	65.42%	65.97%	49.64%	66.29%
Italy	Mean	−11.93%	1.34%	22.40%	0.00%	−22.40%
	Min	−66.21%	−66.58%	−48.21%	0.00%	−66.67%
	Max	64.27%	61.64%	66.25%	0.00%	54.20%
UK	Mean	50.68%	18.47%	−49.04%	0.00%	−44.30%
	Min	42.73%	−9.57%	−66.49%	0.00%	−58.02%
	Max	66.58%	54.27%	−26.75%	0.00%	−30.57%

Notes: * t statistics significant at 90%; ** t statistics significant at 95%; *** t statistics significant at 99%.

results obtained are not statistically significant, so we can suppose that the portfolio composition is not strictly driven by real estate market trends.

In order to measure the degree of misalignment between fund managers' choices and optimal asset allocation, we constructed efficient portfolios for the four markets, and we tried to measure the distance of the real estate portfolios from a theoretical optimal portfolio composition. The results showed that the real estate portfolio is always inefficient (Table 9.4).

Distributing the portfolios in percentiles according to their distance from the efficient frontier, the UK market shows a better alignment with respect to theoretical optimal portfolios. German and Italian fund managers define their investment strategy without considering the sector trend and so their portfolios are the more different with respect to the optimal ones (Table 9.5).

In order to evaluate the effect of the misalignment on the performance achieved by the real estate funds, we compare the Sharpe ratio for the theoretical and real portfolio for all the markets analysed on the overall time horizon (Table 9.6).

The analysis of the mean results demonstrates that the optimal portfolio allocation does not always achieve the best performance. The UK funds are the funds that achieved a higher improvement in the mean risk-return trade-off following Markowitz's principles, while for the other countries, the mean-variance approach creates value only in 2008.

Following the methodology proposed by Gibbons et al. (1989), we tested the statistical relevance of the mean-variance diversification approach for the sample analysed (Table 9.7).

Negative values for the F-test indicate an outperformance of the theoretical portfolios over the real ones. The test for the UK market presented an average

Table 9.5 Minimum distance from the efficient frontier in percentiles

Percentile	France				Germany			
	2007	2008	2009	2010	2007	2008	2009	2010
0.10	0.35	0.42	0.32	0.41	0.44	0.42	0.40	0.41
0.20	0.37	0.59	0.42	0.51	0.44	0.46	0.41	0.41
0.30	0.39	0.67	0.59	0.68	0.44	0.47	0.42	0.41
0.40	0.41	0.69	0.61	0.69	0.44	0.47	0.42	0.41
0.50	0.41	0.76	0.64	0.73	0.44	0.50	0.42	0.41
0.60	0.42	0.87	0.72	0.81	0.44	0.53	0.42	0.59
0.70	0.58	0.88	0.72	0.81	0.44	0.55	0.42	0.63
0.80	0.71	0.93	0.81	0.90	0.45	0.60	0.42	0.66
0.90	0.87	0.94	0.86	0.95	0.60	0.63	0.45	0.76
1.00	0.95	0.95	0.87	0.96	0.72	0.77	0.53	0.88
Percentile	**Italy**				**UK**			
	2007	2008	2009	2010	2007	2008	2009	2010
0.10	0.31	0.46	0.24	0.50	0.39	0.21	0.36	0.10
0.20	0.39	0.46	0.47	0.50	0.39	0.23	0.44	0.14
0.30	0.43	0.47	0.52	0.50	0.39	0.26	0.59	0.17
0.40	0.44	0.47	0.58	0.60	0.39	0.29	0.61	0.19
0.50	0.48	0.51	0.61	0.75	0.39	0.32	0.72	0.19
0.60	0.53	0.58	0.63	0.77	0.39	0.34	0.72	0.21
0.70	0.58	0.60	0.74	0.81	0.39	0.37	0.73	0.23
0.80	0.64	0.71	0.79	0.87	0.39	0.38	0.86	0.26
0.90	0.72	0.82	0.87	0.93	0.45	0.40	0.87	0.28
1.00	0.78	0.97	0.98	1.03	0.47	0.41	0.87	0.41

Table 9.6 A comparison of Sharpe ratio real and optimal portfolios (mean value)

	France	Germany	Italy	UK
Real Sharpe				
2007	3.58	0.91	2.28	–4.08
2008	–15.88	–4.50	–5.61	–12.54
2009	1.63	14.33	1.66	–1.92
2010	15.84	6.38	0.02	6.03
Optimal Sharpe				
2007	–0.25	–0.70	–0.44	–0.81
2008	–0.46	–0.61	–0.49	–0.49
2009	–0.04	–0.08	–0.05	–0.32
2010	–0.02	–0.02	–0.16	0.64

Table 9.7 F-test results

		France	Germany	Italy	UK
2007	F	−3.17	−1.36	−1.95	−5.09
	p-value	0.118	0.341	0.046	0.058
2008	F	−3.03	−2.17	−3.2	−6.41
	p-value	0.125	0.184	0,064	0.039
2009	F	−3.47	−3.15	−2.49	−5.36
	p-value	0.104	0.105	0,068	0.053
2010	F	−4.60	0.03	−2.76	−6.08
	p-value	0.069	0.969	0.066	0.043

of 95 per cent of significance, a result that confirms the hypothesis that portfolios optimized on the basis of the past trends could perform better for this country. Also the Italian real estate market is characterized by a positive and significant relation (around 95 per cent) that demonstrates the usefulness of the Markowitz approach for maximizing the return for unit of risk assumed.

For the French and German market, the results demonstrate that, in most of the years considered, the historical performance of real estate indices is not a useful tool for constructing the best investment portfolio and other criteria are normally adopted by the fund managers in order to select their investment opportunities.

9.6 Conclusions

The real estate sector is no longer considered as only an additional component in a mixed portfolio and the relevance of 'only property portfolio' diversification is increasing over time. The techniques which migrated from the classic financial instruments are constantly evaluated by many researchers in order to understand their potential utility.

The information quality in the real estate indices is increasing over time and nowadays sector indices measure in better ways the performance of the market segment.

The analysis proposed on the European real estate asset managers demonstrates that their investment strategies are normally not related to the sector trends. Only for few funds, there is a correlation between the asset allocation choices and sector trends and the differences between real portfolio and optimal ones are not residual. The choice to define a different asset allocation than the optimal one can imply also a worse return-risk trade-off for the fund manager and this result is more frequent in some markets (Italy and UK) than others.

Results presented support the hypothesis that standard diversification criteria can work also for an only-property portfolio and historical data about performance and indices could be used in order to improve the efficacy of the diversification strategy. Worldwide statistics on portfolio rebalancing demonstrate that the portfolio rebalancing choice is significantly affected by transaction costs that could disincentive the asset manager to adopt his/her optimal diversification strategy (Collett et al., 2003). A more detailed analysis of the transaction costs could demonstrate that results achieved are also useful for modifying the investment strategies adopted by fund managers independently with respect to the liquidity of the market.

Notes

The authors are members of the Laboratory of Real Estate Finance promoted by the Ph.D. in Banking and Finance of University of Rome 'Tor Vergata'. The chapter is the result of the authors' common efforts and continuous exchange of ideas. The individual sections of the chapter can be acknowledged as follows: Sections 9.3, 9.4 and 9.5 to Gianluca Mattarocci and others to Georgios Siligardos.

1. The optimal portfolios were developed based on the performance of the EPRA-NAREIT indices for Eurozone and the UK market, separately.
2. Results on lagged relationships are coherent with the ones proposed in the table and the authors will provide to interested readers the full details about the lagged correlation.

References

Chen, P. and Y. Liang (2000) 'Optimal diversification: Is it really worthwhile?' *Journal of Real Estate Portfolio Management*, 6, 7–16.

Collett, D., C. Lizieri and C. Ward (2003) 'Timing and the holding periods of institutional real estate', *Real Estate Economics*, 3, 205–22.

Cullen, I. (1993) 'Cluster analysis and property risk', www.rics.org (homepage), date accessed 01 July 2012.

De Witt, D. P. M. (1996) 'Real estate portfolio management practices of pension funds and insurance companies in the Netherlands: A survey', *Journal of Real Estate Research*, 11, 131–48.

Gibbons, M. R., S. A. Ross and J. Shanken (1989) 'A test of the efficiency of a given portfolio', *Econometrica*, 57, 1121–52.

Grissom, T. K. J. and C. Walther (1987) 'Diversification works in real estate too', *Journal of Portfolio Management*, 13, 66–71.

Heydenreich, F. (2010) 'Economic diversification: Evidence for the United Kingdom', *Journal of Real Estate Portfolio Management*, 16, 71–86.

Lee, S. and P. Byrne (1998) 'Diversification by sector, region or function? A mean absolute deviation optimization', *Journal of Property Valuation & Investment*, 16, 38–56.

Lee, S. and S. Stevenson (2005) 'Testing the statistical significance of sector and regional diversification', *Journal of Property Investment & Finance*, 23, 394–411.

MacCowan, R. (2008) 'A behavioural study of the decision processes underpinning disposals by property fund managers', *Journal of Property Investment & Finance*, 26, 342–61.

Markowitz, H. (1952) 'Portfolio selection', *Journal of Finance*, 7, 77–91.

Miles, M. and T. McCue (1982) 'Historic returns and institutional real estate portfolios', *AREUEA Journal*, 10, 184–99.

——(1984) 'Commercial real estate returns', *AREUEA Journal*, 12, 355–77.

Pyhrr, S. A., W. Born, C. A. Manning and S. E. Roulac (2003) 'Project and portfolio management decisions: A framework and body of knowledge model for cycle research', *Journal of Real Estate Portfolio Management*, 9, 1–16.

Seiler, M. J., J.R. Webb and F. C. Neil Myer (1999) 'Diversification issues in real estate investment', *Journal of Real Estate Literature*, 7, 163–79.

Serrano, C. and M. Hoesli (2009) 'Global securitized real estate benchmarks and performance', *Journal of Real Estate Portfolio Management*, 15, 1–19.

Young, M. S. and R.A. Graff (1995) 'Real estate is not normal: a fresh look at real estate return distributions', Journal of Real Estate Finance and Economics, 10, 225–59.

10 The Role of Risk Measures Choices in Ranking Real Estate Funds: Evidence from the Italian Market

Claudio Giannotti and Gianluca Mattarocci

10.1 Introduction

Return distribution of some financial instruments (like hedge funds) does not fit with the hypothesis of normality of returns and so, for those instruments, new and more complex Risk Adjusted Performance measures (hereinafter RAP) are proposed. The rankings based on these new measures are not always coherent with those defined using more simple ones and could show qualities (like a higher time persistence) that are desirable for an investor (Carretta and Mattarocci, 2008).

Italian real estate investment vehicles are characterized by a high heterogeneity of the risk drivers (i.a. Giannotti and Mattarocci, 2009) and by the absence of a unique criterion for constructing a diversified portfolio of investments (i.a. Giannotti and Mattarocci, 2008). Empirical analyses proposed in literature demonstrate that return distribution of real estate investment vehicles is asymmetric (Hutson and Stevenson, 2008) and skewed (Lizieri et al., 2007). On the basis of this evidence, the new and more complex RAP studied for the hedge fund industry could be considered useful also for evaluating Italian real estate funds.

This chapter measures the risk related to misspecified risk measure for the evaluation of real estate funds looking at the Italian market for the period 2001 to 2009. The chapter demonstrates the lack of normality for almost all Italian real estate funds and so the choice of the risk measure that considers or not this feature could significantly affect the rankings of investment opportunities. The risk measure choice affects not only the ranking but also the time persistence of the results and more complex measures are those that ensure an higher stability of the rankings. In order to evaluate the usefulness of the new RAPs in constructing a portfolio, we compare the performance achieved by portfolios constructed using the past values of different RAPs and we point out some differences in performance achieved by portfolios constructed using different RAPs.

The chapter presents a literature review about the studies on RAP measures applied to the real estate industry (Section 10.2) and conducts an empirical analysis on the Italian market (Section 10.3). After a brief description of the sample (Section 10.3.1), the chapter summarizes the main approaches proposed in literature in order to evaluate the risk-return profile of an investment vehicle with not normal returns (Section 10.3.2) and points out the impact of the risk measure choice on the ranking of investment opportunities (Section 10.3.3). The last section summarizes conclusions and implications of the results achieved.

10.2 Literature review

The analysis of the risk return profile of Real Estate Investment Vehicles is normally performed looking at RAP measures, indexes constructed considering both the historical return and a measure of the risk exposure assumed in the yearly time horizon (Brueggman et al., 1984).

The more widespread measure used in order to evaluate the risk-return trade-off is the Sharpe ratio, a measure of excess return with respect to the risk free rate for unit of risk assumed (Brueggman et al., 1984). Empirical analysis on ranking constructed on the past value of the Sharpe index demonstrates that the RAP allows better discriminating among REITs only if they are significantly diversified (Benefield et al., 2009).

The role of diversifiable and non-diversifiable risk for a real estate investment vehicle is normally analysed using the Treynor index that measures the return per unit of non-systemic risk assumed (Ooi and Liow, 2004). Results obtained show that the exposure related to real estate investment vehicles is prevalently caused by a diversifiable risk and so rankings based on the Treynor index distinguish better among REITs (Radcliffe et al., 1974).

The Jensen alpha measure is used in order to evaluate the capability of the manager to outperform the market achieving a performance higher than the expected return defined using a CAPM or APT model (Kallberg et al., 2000). Results obtained in the REIT industry demonstrate good capabilities of funds managers to construct the optimal portfolio achieving the highest returns from the market mispricing of real estate assets (Gallo et al., 2000) and, especially if performance fees ensured to the manager are high, there is an high incentive in creating value for the investors due to direct impact on the managers' wealth (Philpot and Peterson 2006). Using the Jensen alpha approach for identifying the best managers who are able to beat the market using an active portfolio strategy, an investor can maximize profits especially for a short-term horizon investment strategy (Hendricks et al., 1993).

Analysis of the performance achieved by listed real estate property companies and REITS demonstrates a lack of normality in the return distribution

(Lizieri and Ward, 2000). Real estate investment vehicles show frequently a returns' distribution with higher skewness and kurtosis with respect to other financial instruments (Myer and Webb, 1993).

The choice to remove the assumption of normality implies the definition of different and more complex approaches for evaluating the risk-return profile of the REITs and it causes also a change in the portfolio construction process (Byrne and Lee, 2004). Models constructed using more than the second moment of the distribution (like kurtosis) explain better the performance achieved by real estate investment vehicles especially if the analysis is released using high frequency data (Lizieri et al., 2007).

Despite the findings related to the non-normality of performance achieved by real estate investment vehicles, literature about the risk adjusted performance measurement of this type of investment is based essentially on the standard mean-variance approach (Young and Graff, 1995). In fact standard RAP measures used in order to evaluate the REIT industry look only at the first and second moment of the return distribution and studies on the asset management industry demonstrate that if we remove the normality assumption the risk-return profile of an investment vehicle could significantly change (Bird and Gallagher, 2002).

10.3 Empirical analysis

10.3.1 Sample

The sample considers all real estate funds listed in the Italian market and traded in 2009 and includes 23 Italian real estate funds. On the basis of overall Italian market statistics (source Assogestioni), the sample selected could be considered representative of the market analysed (Table 10.1).

Even if the number of funds considered is small with respect to the overall market (only 23 of the 154 funds existing at 2009), on the basis of the asset under management, the sample stands for more the 21.89 per cent of the overall market and so the bigger funds are considered in the analysis.

Only one Italian real estate fund is listed before the 2000 and so, in order not to have a too small sample for each year, the choice of the horizon is constrained to the time period 2001 to 2009. Data collected attains the closing price for each trading day for all listed funds and the amount of dividends paid in each trading day.

For each real estate fund we collect daily data and we measure the performance for each trading day as the logarithm of the ratio between the current closing price plus dividends eventually paid and the closing price in the previous trading day. In formulas:

$$ {}_{t-1}R_t = \ln\left(\frac{P_t + D_t}{P_{t-1}}\right) \qquad (10.1) $$

Table 10.1 Sample description

Fund name	Listing date	Asset under management 31 December 2009
Alpha immobiliare	4 July 2002	537,833,183 €
Atlantic 1	7 June 2006	742,495,349 €
Atlantic 2 – Berenice	19 July 2005	637,476,570 €
Beta immobiliare	24 October 2005	230,287,272 €
BNL portfolio immobiliare	2 January 2002	437,315,443 €
CAAM RE Europa	17 November 2003	221,227,779 €
CAAM RE Italia	3 June 2006	275,583,711 €
Caravaggio	16 May 2005	334,375,253 €
Delta Immobiliare	11 March 2009	328,204,487 €
Estense Grande Distribuzione	3 August 2004	409,789,091 €
Europa Immobiliare 1	4 December 2004	411,237,566 €
Immobilium 2001	29 October 2003	148,979,669 €
Invest Real Security	1 January 2005	183,286,908 €
Investietico	1 November 2004	249,844,486 €
Obelisco	14 June 2006	243,707,118 €
Olinda	09 December 2004	649,305,787 €
Piramide Globale	26 November 2002	55,430,399 €
Polis	20 April 2001	361,633,481 €
Risparmio immobiliare uno	4 June 2001	193,088,699 €
Securfondo	2 October 2001	196,575,750 €
Tecla fondo uffici	4 March 2004	734,515,749 €
Unicredit Immobiliare uno	4 June 2001	599,349,929 €
Valore Immobiliare globale	29 November 1999	207,644,612 €
N°of Italian real estate funds (listed and unlisted)		154
AUM of the overall Italian Market (listed and unlisted)		38,316,900,000 €

where P_t is the closing price a time t, D_t is the dividend eventually paid at time t and ln is the natural logarithm. Defined as the measure of daily returns, the Shapiro–Wilk normality test is released in order to identify the funds for which this assumption could be considered reasonable (Shapiro and Wilk, 1965).

The analysis of the return distribution dynamics show that almost always real estate funds show a daily performance that could not be considered normally distributed (Table 10.2).

The Shapiro–Wilk test confirms that in almost all years and for almost all funds the hypothesis of normality could be rejected with a confidence level of 99% because in only one case (Olinda in 2004) the assumption of normality could be considered reasonable.

On the basis of these findings, RAP measures studied for investment vehicles with non-normal performance could be suitable also for the Italian real estate mutual funds.

Table 10.2 Shapiro–Wilk test of normality for Italian real estate performance

	Code	2001	2002	2003	2004	2005	2006	2007	2008	2009
Alpha immobiliare	01	–	6.96***	10.33***	9.04***	7.84***	9.32***	7.58***	6.35***	5.30***
Atlantic 1	02	–	–	–	–	–	7.39***	5.70***	6.75***	7.75***
Atlantinc 2 – Berenice	03	–	–	–	–	4.39***	7.26***	10.32***	7.20***	10.28***
Beta immobiliare	04	–	–	–	–	4.82***	8.97***	6.73***	10.81***	8.95***
BNL portfolio immobiliare	05	–	8.03***	5.91***	5.24***	8.35***	8.83***	8.19***	5.90***	3.12***
CAAM RE Europa	06	–	–	5.01***	3.86***	5.34***	4.59***	6.38***	6.61***	3.18***
CAAM RE Italia	07	–	7.87***	5.69***	4.26***	8.70***	10.64***	8.54***	7.31***	6.36***
Caravaggio	08	–	–	–	–	6.58***	8.46***	8.27***	7.83***	10.31***
Delta Immobiliare	09	–	–	–	–	–	–	–	–	9.13***
Estense Grande Distribuzione	10	–	–	–	2.75***	5.84***	7.90***	6.97***	7.41***	7.19***
Europa Immobiliare 1	11	–	–	–	–	–	2.15**	8.36***	9.05***	7.93***
Immobilium 2001	12	–	–	3.62***	7.29***	8.26***	9.44***	7.22***	8.50***	7.50***
Invest real security	13	–	–	–	–	8.65***	8.38***	8.76***	9.44***	9.08***
Investietico	14	–	–	–	2.11**	5.56***	7.07***	8.43***	6.91***	6.73***
Obelisco	15	–	–	–	–	–	6.89***	8.48***	8.99***	8.49***
Olinda	16	–	–	–	−1.13	9.93***	9.43***	5.96***	7.08***	4.19***
Piramide Globale	17	–	2.40***	5.28***	8.30***	7.58***	6.49***	11.38***	11.60***	10.13***
Polis	18	2.13**	6.35***	4.95***	5.87***	8.72***	7.90***	5.10***	6.56***	6.76***
Risparmio immobiliare uno	19	–	–	–	–	–	–	–	–	7.34***
Securfondo	20	4.65***	8.33***	7.33***	7.76***	8.63***	9.052***	7.68***	8.49***	8.03***
Tecla fondo uffici	21	–	–	–	9.08***	7.53***	9.861***	8.99***	6.44***	3.78***
Unicredit Immobiliare uno	22	2.56***	6.46***	6.53***	6.46***	5.64***	8.236***	6.48***	6.75***	4.31***
Valore Immobiliare globale	23	3.29***	7.83***	8.01***	6.95***	5.99***	7.52***	7.59***	7.61***	8.37***

Notes: *** Significant at 99% level ** Significant at 95% level * Significant at 90% level – Fund not available

10.3.2 Methodology

Looking at studies available about the performance evaluation of financial instruments (hedge funds), we identify a set of RAP measures that use the same definition of performance but are characterized by a different assumption on the measure of risk.[1] We start from the more widespread RAP measure for the asset management industry, the Sharpe ratio. In formula:

$$ {}_{t_1}Sharpe_{t_2} = \frac{{}_{t_1}R_{t_2} - {}_{t_1}R_{t_2}^{Rf}}{\sigma\left(R_t\right)} \tag{10.2} $$

where, looking at the time horizon t_1-t_2 (one year), the numerator represents the extra-return of the real estate fund with respect to the risk free rate (an Italian Treasury Bills with a coherent time horizon) while the denominator is the standard deviation of returns. The formula (10.2) is a measure of the excess return compared to the risk free rate for each unit of risk assumed (Sharpe, 1994) and it looks at the overall distribution of results assuming the normality of returns summarizing the risk profile of the investment in the first and the second moment of the return distribution.

We consider a set of RAP measures constructed on lower partial moment that look only at the distribution of results lower than a given threshold (the risk free rate). In detail:

$$ {}_{t_1}ROPS_{t_2} = \frac{{}_{t_1}R_{t_2} - {}_{t_1}R_{t_2}^{Rf}}{\frac{1}{t_2\text{-}t_1}\sum_{t=t_1}^{t_2}\max\left(Rf - R_t, 0\right)^0} \tag{10.3} $$

$$ {}_{t_1}ROAS_{t_2} = \frac{{}_{t_1}R_{t_2} - {}_{t_1}R_{t_2}^{Rf}}{\frac{1}{t_2\text{-}t_1}\sum_{t=t_1}^{t_2}\max\left(Rf - R_t, 0\right)^1} \tag{10.4} $$

$$ {}_{t_1}Sortino_{t_2} = \frac{{}_{t_1}R_{t_2} - {}_{t_1}R_{t_2}^{Rf}}{\sqrt[2]{\frac{1}{t_2\text{-}t_1}\sum_{t=t_1}^{t_2}\max\left(Rf - R_t, 0\right)^2}} \tag{10.5} $$

$$ {}_{t_1}Kappa_{t_2}^{n=3} = \frac{{}_{t_1}R_{t_2} - {}_{t_1}R_{t_2}^{Rf}}{\sqrt[3]{\frac{1}{t_2\text{-}t_1}\sum_{t=t_1}^{t_2}\max\left(Rf - R_t, 0\right)^3}} \tag{10.6} $$

$$ {}_{t_1}Kappa_{t_2}^{n=4} = \frac{{}_{t_1}R_{t_2} - {}_{t_1}R_{t_2}^{Rf}}{\sqrt[4]{\frac{1}{t_2\text{-}t_1}\sum_{t=t_1}^{t_2}\max\left(Rf - R_t, 0\right)^4}} \tag{10.7} $$

Formula 3 defines a measure (ROPS) constructed using the lower partial moment of order 0 and it represents the excess return with respect to the probability of losses (Pedersen and Rudholm-Alfvin, 2003). Formula 4 constructs an index (ROAS) using the lower partial moment of order 1 and measures the excess return with respect to the mean expected losses (Pedersen and Rudholm-Alfvin, 2003). Formula 5 proposes a measure (Sortino) that uses the lower partial moment of order 2 and computes the excess return with respect to the downside risk (Sortino and Forsey, 1996). Formulas 6 and 7 consider respectively the lower partial moment of order 3 and 4 in order to define a return-risk profile of the investment (Kappa) that considers also respectively the skewness and the kurtosis of the distribution (Kaplan and Knowles, 2004).[2]

The alternative specification of the risk measures considered are those based on maximum drawdown risk measurement approaches. Formulas are the following:

$$ {}_{t_1}Calmar_{t_2} = \frac{{}_{t_1}R_{t_2} - {}_{t_1}R_{t_2}^{Rf}}{\left|{}_{t_1}MDD_{t_2}\right|} \tag{10.8} $$

$$ {}_{t_1}Sterling_{t_2} = \frac{{}_{t_1}R_{t_2} - {}_{t_1}R_{t_2}^{Rf}}{\sum_{t=1}^{n} \frac{1}{n} \left|{}_{t_1}MDD_{t_2}^{i}\right|} \tag{10.9} $$

$$ {}_{t_1}Burke_{t_2} = \frac{{}_{t_1}R_{t_2} - {}_{t_1}R_{t_2}^{Rf}}{\sum_{t=1}^{n} \frac{1}{n} \left({}_{t_1}MDD_{t_2}^{i}\right)^2} \tag{10.10} $$

Formula 8 considers only the maximum loss and defines a measure (Calmar) that computes the excess return respective to the worst performance (Young, 1991). Formula 9 looks at the n worst performances achieved by the fund and defines an index (Sterling) as a ratio between excess return and the arithmetic mean of these n losses (Kestner, 1996).[3] Formula 10 considers the square root of the sum of the squares of n drawdowns and defines a measure (Burke) of the excess return respective to this measure of risk (Burke, 1994).[4]

Other risk proxies considered uses the Value at Risk (hereinafter VaR) as a measure of risk exposure with a level of confidence of α percentage[5] (coherently with the literature, we assume an α equal to 95 per cent). We construct the following RAP measures based on VaR:

$$ {}_{t_1}VaR\,Ratio_{t_2} = \frac{R_t - R_{rf}}{{}_{t_1}VaR_{t_2}} \tag{10.11} $$

$$ {}_{t_1}CVaR\,Ratio_{t_2} = \frac{{}_{t_1}R_{t_2} - {}_{t_1}R_{t_2}^{Rf}}{{}_{t_1}CVaR_{t_2}} \tag{10.12} $$

$$_{t_1}MVaRRatio_{t_2} = \frac{_{t_1}R_{t_2} - _{t_1}R^{Rf}_{t_2}}{_{t_1}MVaR_{t_2}} \tag{10.13}$$

Formula 11 computes the ratio between the VaR and the investment at time 0 and defines a measure (VaR Ratio) as a ratio between excess return and this risk measure (Dowd, 2000). Formula 12 considers the average loss at a given threshold, the so-called conditional VaR, and computes an index (CVaR ratio) as the ratio between excess return and the mean loss (Agarwal and Naik, 2004). Formula 13 takes into account the non-normality of distribution for extreme losses using the Cornish-Fisher expansion to modify the VAR estimates and defines a measure (MVaR ratio) as the ratio between excess return and the maximum corrected exposure (Gregoriou and Gueyie, 2003).

The last RAP measure derives from the omega measure, a ratio between the area of gains and losses related to the investment (Shadwick and Keating, 2002) and uses the put-call parity proposed by Black and Scholes for deriving the Sharpe Omega (Kazemi et al., 2004). In formula:

$$_{t_1}Sharpe\ Omega_{t_2} = \frac{_{t_1}R_{t_2} - _{t_1}R^{Rf}_{t_2}}{e^{-rf}\,_{t_1}E\left[\max(_tR_t - _tR^{Rf}_t, 0\right]_{t_2}} \tag{10.14}$$

where the denominator represents the value of a put option with strike price equal to R_f and a time horizon coherent with the evaluation period.

Following approaches presented in literature in order to test the relevance of the choices in the construction of a risk adjusted performance measure (Eling and Schuhmacher, 2006), we perform for each year a correlation between rankings based on different performance measures using Spearman's rank correlation coefficient. The analysis of correlation is released considering all funds listed at time t independently to their starting listing date. This type of analysis allows us to test the sensitivity of RAP rankings to the choice of the risk measure and repeating the analysis for some years we obtain results that are not strictly affected by events that occurs in only one year.

RAP measures are frequently used by investors in order to select the best investment for the future and they have to define rankings stable over time in order to discriminate between lucky and skilled fund managers. Following approaches presented in the literature (i.e. Carhart, 1997), we construct a one-year contingency table in order to compare ranking position at time t-1 and t for all funds listed at time t-1. Results are summarized through some statistics about the number of funds characterized by timely persistence performance in the yearly time horizon.

Following available literature (Lin and Young, 2007) we use the past performance in order to identify the best real estate investment vehicle at time t (the top 25 per cent) and the worst ones (the worst 25 per cent) but we differ from other studies in that we identify the winners and losers not looking only at the returns but categorize best and worst investments on the basis of their past RAPs' values. In order to evaluate the usefulness of the strategy compared to other solutions available, we compare the performance of these strategies with a benchmark: the naïve diversification strategy equally weighted and naïve diversification strategy value weighted. In detail we consider the following strategies:

1. Benchmark – Equally weighted

We consider all the funds available at time t-1 and we invest the same amount of money in each of them ($i_t = j_t = \frac{1}{N_t}$). Every year we update the portfolio composition on the basis of the number of the new real estate funds available.

2. Best performers at time t-1 – Equally weighted

We consider for each RAP the ranking defined at time t-1 and we select only the funds that are classified in the first quartile (number of funds $n_t = \frac{N_t}{4}$). We invest the same amount of money in all the n funds classified in the first quartile by the RAP measure ($i_t = j_t = \frac{1}{n_t}$) and every year we update the portfolio composition on the basis of the past year's RAP values.

3. Worst performers at time t-1 – Equally weighted

We consider for each RAP the ranking defined at time t-1 and we select only the funds that are classified in the fourth quartile (number of funds $n_t = \frac{N_t}{4}$). We invest the same amount of money in all the n funds classified in the first quartile by the RAP measure ($i_t = j_t = \frac{1}{n_t}$) and every year we update the portfolio composition on the basis of the past year's RAP values.

4. Benchmark – Value weighted

We consider all the funds available at time t-1 and we invest in each fund an amount of money defined on the basis of its market value compared to those of all N funds available ($i_t = \frac{MV_{i,t}}{\sum_{k=1}^{N_t} MV_{t,k}}$). Every year we update the portfolio composition on the basis of the number and size of real estate funds available.

5. Best performers at time t-1 – Value weighted

We consider for each RAP the ranking defined at time t-1 and we select only the funds that are classified in the first quartile (number of funds $n_t = \frac{N_t}{4}$). The amount invested in each fund is defined on the basis of its market value compared to those of the n funds classified in the first quartile ($i_t = \frac{MV_{i,t}}{\sum_{k=1}^{n_t} MV_{t,k}}$). Every year we update the portfolio composition on the basis of the past year's RAP values.

6. Worst performers at time t-1 – Value weighted

We consider for each RAP the ranking defined at time t-1 and we select only the funds that are classified in the fourth quartile (number of funds $n_t = \frac{N_t}{4}$). The amount invested in each fund is defined on the basis of its market value compared to those of the n funds classified in the fourth quartile ($i_t \frac{MV_{i,t}}{\sum_{k=1}^{n_t} MV_{t,k}}$). Every year we update the portfolio composition on the basis of the past year's RAP values.

For all the strategies we compute the annual performance achieved by each strategy and we compare year by year results achieved. In order to summarize results obtained on the overall time horizon, we compute the the mean return achieved on the whole time horizon and the number of rebalances during the overall time period in order to evaluate the performance of a long-term strategy and the frequency of the rebalances. RAP measures that minimize the number of rebalances for a given return will be preferred by the investor due to the lower transaction costs related to the investment strategy.

10.3.3 Results

An analysis of summary statistics on the ranking position assigned using different RAP measure to each real estate funds shows that difference attains not only the mean position assigned but also the variability of the ranking over time (Table 10.3).

The comparison of the ranking assigned to each fund using different RAP measures shows that funds listed for only a few months (09 – Delta immobiliare and 19 – Risparmio Immobiliare) are those for which the choice of the risk measure affects the ranking position more.

For all other funds, differences in the mean ranking position are less relevant if we exclude RAPs constructed using the maximum drawdown and the Value at Risk. For these types of measure the choice to consider only the maximum drawdowns or the losses higher with respect to an established threshold could affect the significance of the mean ranking because the risk exposure is too affected by the presence (in some or all years) of any outlier (Wu and Xiao, 2002).

The variability over time of the rankings is also significant because on the basis of the year selected there could be a change in the ranking position assigned of more than two ranking positions. Excluding funds that are listed for one year, measures like ROAS, Sortino, Kappa (N = 4) and Sterling show a high variability over time of the ranking assigned for more than 57 per cent of funds considered. This high variability of the ranking assigned could be a result of the higher sensitivity of these measures with respect to a change of the risk–return profile of the investment or an excessive concern to some outliers in the return distribution.

Table 10.3 Summary statistics on ranking constructed on different RAPs (time horizon: 2001 to 2009)

Fund code		Sharpe	ROPS	ROAS	Sortino	Kappa (n=3)	Kappa (n=4)	Calmar	Sterling	Burke	VaR Ratio	CVaR ratio	MVaR ratio	Sharpe Omega
01	M	5	6	6	5	6	6	10	6	6	6	6	10	5
	σ	5.81	4.63	4.81	6.19	6.48	6.14	7.82	6.12	6.80	3.20	3.20	4.00	5.06
02	M	12	10	12	13	15	13	10	13	14	15	15	15	11
	σ	6.75	6.48	7.54	6.85	6.38	6.29	6.98	6.14	6.85	9.22	9.34	8.39	6.25
03	M	9	9	9	9	9	9	13	9	9	11	10	10	10
	σ	5.83	7.79	6.72	6.31	6.06	6.31	7.25	6.38	6.07	9.34	8.64	7.64	5.90
04	M	10	14	12	9	9	9	13	9	10	11	10	10	11
	σ	4.10	6.99	3.81	4.49	6.40	4.62	3.65	3.85	4.32	7.92	6.86	7.47	4.69
05	M	8	8	7	8	8	8	11	8	7	7	8	7	8
	σ	3.87	3.44	3.20	3.93	5.90	4.14	6.09	4.06	4.41	3.24	3.42	4.04	3.12
06	M	12	11	11	12	13	12	8	12	12	12	12	12	12
	σ	4.97	4.65	4.20	4.54	4.78	4.51	6.10	4.22	4.16	4.02	4.89	3.77	3.95
07	M	9	8	8	9	10	9	9	9	9	8	8	10	8
	σ	4.11	3.48	4.17	4.46	5.59	4.46	5.26	4.37	5.06	3.02	3.65	4.58	4.44
08	M	8	10	9	9	7	9	13	8	8	9	9	8	10
	σ	6.98	8.07	7.78	7.70	6.12	7.43	6.40	7.35	6.56	6.80	6.80	4.36	8.19
09	M	23	23	22	23	16	23	2	23	19	23	23	1	23
	σ	–	–	–	–	–	–	–	–	–	–	–	–	–
10	M	10	10	10	10	10	10	11	10	10	10	10	11	10
	σ	8.52	7.92	7.63	8.52	7.47	8.52	7.03	8.13	8.31	6.98	7.87	7.17	7.87
11	M	18	17	20	19	19	19	3	20	20	17	18	18	17
	σ	2.75	4.73	1.89	3.00	3.11	2.06	2.63	1.89	2.38	4.92	5.35	5.74	5.00
12	M	10	9	9	10	11	9	10	9	10	9	9	8	10
	σ	7.29	6.58	6.88	6.95	6.65	7.11	7.10	6.19	6.92	4.08	4.08	5.99	7.35

(*Continued*)

Table 10.3 (Continued)

Fund code		Sharpe	ROPS	ROAS	Sortino	Kappa (n=3)	Kappa (n=4)	Calmar	Sterling	Burke	VaR Ratio	CVaR ratio	MVaR ratio	Sharpe Omega
13	M	14	12	14	13	11	13	10	13	12	13	12	11	13
	σ	5.86	4.30	5.59	5.17	6.88	5.86	7.16	4.97	6.89	5	5.12	6.84	7.07
14	M	10	8	9	10	12	10	12	10	10	9	10	10	9
	σ	4.68	4.15	4.83	4.68	6.02	5.01	6.88	4.96	6.10	4.12	3.99	3.02	4.46
15	M	16	15	16	16	13	16	7	16	15	15	15	16	15
	σ	6.18	5.25	6.40	5.94	5.32	6.18	7.35	5.94	4.97	6.55	5.32	4.97	6.95
16	M	11	11	12	12	10	11	9	12	12	9	9	9	11
	σ	3.14	4.17	2.88	3.83	3.88	3.67	6.45	3.62	3.51	7.76	8.12	8.04	4.18
17	M	12	14	13	11	9	11	8	11	10	13	12	9	14
	σ	6.64	7.76	7.15	6.27	5.90	6.20	3.62	6.65	6.76	6.82	7.07	6.02	7.34
18	M	8	9	8	8	8	8	8	8	8	8	9	9	8
	σ	6.00	6.58	5.55	5.80	5.71	5.85	6.08	5.95	5.87	6.09	6.17	6.22	5.72
19	M	20	14	23	21	23	20	4	22	23	14	14	19	14
	σ	–	–	–	–	–	–	–	–	–	–	–	–	–
20	M	8	8	8	8	8	8	9	8	8	9	9	8	8
	σ	5.77	5.44	5.59	5.77	6.36	5.80	5.91	5.77	5.85	5.52	5.43	6.62	5.77
21	M	8	8	8	8	9	8	13	8	9	8	8	11	8
	σ	2.43	2.66	2.88	3.10	3.78	2.66	3.58	3.19	2.34	5.57	5.69	7.66	2.59
22	M	5	5	5	5	5	5	12	5	5	5	5	6	5
	σ	4.40	3.88	3.54	4.42	4.12	3.60	6.50	4.14	4.11	3.17	3.50	4.76	3.54
23	M	8	9	7	9	8	9	8	8	8	8	9	8	8
	σ	6.71	6.67	5.85	6.31	5.30	6.46	5.36	6.51	5.50	5.22	5.32	4.85	6.74

Notes: M = Mean ranking position σ = Standard deviation of ranking positions in the time period 2001–2009
– = Standard deviation could not be computed because the fund is listed only for one year

Comparing rankings on a one-year time horizon (Table 10.4), we analyse the time persistence of the rankings constructed using different RAP measures for the time horizon 2001 to 2009.

There are some periods in which the performance achieved by the real estate vehicles is so stable over time (2002–3, 2006–7 and 2007–8) that, independently of the RAP measure selected, it presents a ranking persistence equal to 100 per cent. For all the other years normally the persistence is higher for the last years (2005–6 and 2008–9) with respect to the oldest years considered in the sample (like 2001–2, 2003–4 and 2004–5).

The Calmar ratio shows the lower time persistence of the rankings over time and frequently on funds could be affected by a change of more than two ranking classes due to the RAP high sensitivity to any negative performance. The low persistence of the Calmar measure is clearer in the last years of the time horizon compared to the older ones.

In order to compare the time persistence achieved by different RAP measures we compute an overall measure of persistence considering the weighted mean of the results achieved in each one-year time horizon using as weights the number of funds considered in each ranking. Results show that, even if the Sharpe index constructs rankings that are quite persistent over time, some more complex RAPs achieve better results. In fact, the ROAS, Kappa (4), Sterling, Burke and Sortino show a mean higher persistence of the results achieved and this results is achieved by ensuring (except for the Burke ratio) a higher or at least equal persistence of the result with regard to the Sharpe ratio for all the years analyzed.

In order to study the relationship between the trends of rankings based on different RAP measures, we compute a standard yearly correlation analysis. Summary statistics of yearly correlation (mean, maximum and minimum) are presented in Table 10.5.

The analysis of results achieved by the correlation analysis demonstrates that rankings constructed using different risk measures are comparable because, except for the Calmar ratio, the correlation is almost always positive and the mean value for the time horizon considered is higher than 60 per cent. The anomaly of the Calmar ratio could be explained on the basis of the sensitivity of the formula to any change in the maximum loss achieved by the investment and it misrepresents the overall risk of an investment (Rogers and Dyke, 2006).

Excluding Calmar ratio and measures constructed on Value at Risk (VaR ratio, CVAR ratio and MVaR ratio), for at least one year rankings defined with RAP that do not assume the normality of returns is perfectly coherent with the ranking defined by Sharpe ratio. The minimum correlation identified between ranking constructed on these measures and the one defined by the Sharpe ratio is never less than 60 per cent.

The yearly correlation is significantly variable over time especially for RAP measure constructed on Maximum Drawdown (Calmar ratio) and Value at

Table 10.4 Contingency persistence matrix (time horizon: 2001 to 2009)

Time period	Positions changed	Sharpe	ROPS	ROAS	Sortino	Kappa (n = 3)	Kappa (n=4)	Calmar	Sterling	Burke	VaR Ratio	CVaR ratio	MVaR ratio	Sharpe Omega
2001–2002	± 0	0.00%	0.00%	0.00%	0.00%	0.00%	0.00%	25.00%	0.00%	0.00%	0.00%	0.00%	0.00%	0.00%
	± 1	25.00%	75.00%	75.00%	25.00%	25.00%	50.00%	25.00%	75.00%	25.00%	50.00%	50.00%	50.00%	50.00%
	± 2	50.00%	0.00%	25.00%	50.00%	25.00%	25.00%	50.00%	0.00%	0.00%	25.00%	25.00%	25.00%	25.00%
	More	25.00%	25.00%	0.00%	25.00%	50.00%	25.00%	0.00%	25.00%	75.00%	25.00%	25.00%	25.00%	25.00%
2002–2003	± 0	100.00%	100.00%	100.00%	100.00%	87.50%	100.00%	0.00%	100.00%	100.00%	100.00%	100.00%	100.00%	100.00%
	± 1	0.00%	0.00%	0.00%	0.00%	12.50%	0.00%	0.00%	0.00%	0.00%	0.00%	0.00%	0.00%	0.00%
	± 2	0.00%	0.00%	0.00%	0.00%	0.00%	0.00%	100.00%	0.00%	0.00%	0.00%	0.00%	0.00%	0.00%
	More	0.00%	0.00%	0.00%	0.00%	0.00%	0.00%	0.00%	0.00%	0.00%	0.00%	0.00%	0.00%	0.00%
2003–2004	± 0	50.00%	50.00%	70.00%	50.00%	50.00%	50.00%	0.00%	50.00%	50.00%	30.00%	10.00%	20.00%	50.00%
	± 1	0.00%	10.00%	0.00%	0.00%	0.00%	0.00%	0.00%	10.00%	10.00%	20.00%	40.00%	40.00%	0.00%
	± 2	30.00%	20.00%	30.00%	40.00%	50.00%	40.00%	40.00%	40.00%	40.00%	20.00%	20.00%	30.00%	20.00%
	More	20.00%	20.00%	0.00%	10.00%	0.00%	10.00%	60.00%	0.00%	0.00%	30.00%	30.00%	10.00%	30.00%
2004–2005	± 0	42.86%	42.86%	71.43%	42.86%	21.43%	57.14%	0.00%	42.86%	42.86%	42.86%	42.86%	57.14%	42.86%
	± 1	7.14%	35.71%	28.57%	7.14%	78.57%	7.14%	0.00%	0.00%	35.71%	7.14%	7.14%	7.14%	21.43%
	± 2	42.86%	7.14%	0.00%	42.86%	0.00%	28.57%	35.71%	50.00%	21.43%	50.00%	50.00%	28.57%	21.43%
	More	7.14%	14.29%	0.00%	7.14%	0.00%	7.14%	64.29%	7.14%	0.00%	0.00%	0.00%	7.14%	14.29%
2005–2006	± 0	77.78%	50.00%	100.00%	77.78%	88.89%	88.89%	0.00%	88.89%	94.44%	50.00%	50.00%	50.00%	50.00%
	± 1	0.00%	11.11%	0.00%	5.56%	11.11%	0.00%	5.56%	11.11%	5.56%	50.00%	50.00%	38.89%	16.67%
	± 2	22.22%	33.33%	0.00%	16.67%	0.00%	11.11%	5.56%	0.00%	0.00%	0.00%	0.00%	0.00%	33.33%
	More	0.00%	5.56%	0.00%	0.00%	0.00%	0.00%	88.89%	0.00%	0.00%	0.00%	0.00%	11.11%	0.00%

2006–2007	± 0	100.00%	100.00%	100.00%	100.00%	100.00%	100.00%	100.00%	100.00%	100.00%	100.00%	100.00%	100.00%	100.00%
	± 1	0.00%	0.00%	0.00%	0.00%	0.00%	0.00%	0.00%	0.00%	0.00%	0.00%	0.00%	0.00%	0.00%
	± 2	0.00%	0.00%	0.00%	0.00%	0.00%	0.00%	0.00%	0.00%	0.00%	0.00%	0.00%	0.00%	0.00%
	More	0.00%	0.00%	0.00%	0.00%	0.00%	0.00%	0.00%	0.00%	0.00%	0.00%	0.00%	0.00%	0.00%
2007–2008	± 0	100.00%	100.00%	100.00%	100.00%	100.00%	100.00%	100.00%	100.00%	100.00%	100.00%	100.00%	100.00%	100.00%
	± 1	0.00%	0.00%	0.00%	0.00%	0.00%	0.00%	0.00%	0.00%	0.00%	0.00%	0.00%	0.00%	0.00%
	± 2	0.00%	0.00%	0.00%	0.00%	0.00%	0.00%	0.00%	0.00%	0.00%	0.00%	0.00%	0.00%	0.00%
	More	0.00%	0.00%	0.00%	0.00%	0.00%	0.00%	0.00%	0.00%	0.00%	0.00%	0.00%	0.00%	0.00%
2008–2009	± 0	90.48%	61.90%	100.00%	95.24%	71.43%	90.48%	4.76%	100.00%	85.71%	61.90%	61.90%	0.00%	61.90%
	± 1	9.52%	38.10%	0.00%	4.76%	28.57%	9.52%	4.76%	0.00%	14.29%	38.10%	38.10%	80.95%	38.10%
	± 2	0.00%	0.00%	0.00%	0.00%	0.00%	0.00%	90.48%	0.00%	0.00%	0.00%	0.00%	19.05%	0.00%
	More	0.00%	0.00%	0.00%	0.00%	0.00%	0.00%	0.00%	0.00%	0.00%	0.00%	0.00%	0.00%	0.00%
Weighted Mean	± 0	80.34%	70.94%	90.60%	81.20%	75.21%	83.76%	37.61%	83.76%	82.05%	69.23%	67.52%	58.97%	70.94%
	± 1	3.42%	16.24%	5.98%	3.42%	17.95%	4.27%	2.56%	5.13%	9.40%	18.80%	20.51%	26.50%	13.68%
	± 2	12.82%	7.69%	3.42%	12.82%	5.13%	9.40%	33.33%	9.40%	5.98%	8.55%	8.55%	10.26%	10.26%
	More	3.42%	5.13%	0.00%	2.56%	1.71%	2.56%	26.50%	1.71%	2.56%	3.42%	3.42%	4.27%	5.13%

Table 10.5 Summary statistics of pairwise correlation among rankings defined by different RAP measure (time horizon: 2001 to 2009)

		Sharpe	ROPS	ROAS	Sortino	Kappa (n = 3)	Kappa (n = 4)	Calmar	Sterling	Burke	VaR Ratio	CVaR ratio	MVaR ratio	Sharpe Omega
Sharpe	Mean	1.00												
	Max													
	Min													
ROPS	Mean	0.87	1.00											
	Max	1.00												
	Min	0.60												
ROAS	Mean	0.92	0.84	1.00										
	Max	1.00	0.99											
	Min	0.69	0.60											
Sortino	Mean	0.98	0.86	0.91	1.0000									
	Max	1.00	0.99	1.00										
	Min	0.95	0.60	0.64										
Kappa (n=3)	Mean	0.83	0.66	0.79	0.86	1.0000								
	Max	1.00	0.83	1.00	1.00									
	Min	0.65	0.25	0.43	0.71									
Kappa (n=4)	Mean	0.97	0.86	0.91	0.98	0.88	1.0000							
	Max	1.00	0.99	1.00	1.00	1.00								
	Min	0.93	0.60	0.69	0.93	0.77								
Calmar	Mean	−0.86	−0.73	−0.79	−0.86	−0.74	−0.86	1.0000						
	Max	−0.71	−0.53	−0.38	−0.75	−0.48	−0.75							
	Min	−1.00	−1.00	−1.00	−1.00	−1.00	−1.00							
Sterling	Mean	0.97	0.86	0.94	0.97	0.86	0.98	−0.85	1.00					
	Max	1.00	0.99	1.00	1.00	1.00	1.00	−0.71						
	Min	0.93	0.60	0.85	0.88	0.69	0.95	−1.00						

Burke	Mean	0.91	0.76	0.85	0.93	0.94	0.94	−0.81	0.92	1.0000				
	Max	1.00	0.91	1.00	1.00	1.00	1.00	−0.63	1.00					
	Min	0.74	0.41	0.33	0.76	0.87	0.79	−1.00	0.64					
VaR ratio	Mean	0.83	0.91	0.79	0.83	0.66	0.83	−0.77	0.82	0.73	1.00			
	Max	0.98	1.00	0.98	0.98	0.77	0.98	−0.58	0.98	0.91				
	Min	0.60	0.70	0.60	0.60	0.28	0.60	−0.96	0.60	0.38				
CVaR ratio	Mean	0.83	0.89	0.76	0.84	0.70	0.84	−0.76	0.83	0.76	0.98	1.00		
	Max	0.95	1.00	0.95	0.95	0.83	1.00	−0.51	0.97	0.92	1.00			
	Min	0.60	0.57	0.60	0.60	0.53	0.60	−0.94	0.60	0.60	0.88			
MVaR ratio	Mean	0.64	0.63	0.58	0.65	0.59	0.67	−0.68	0.64	0.61	0.72	0.75	1.00	
	Max	0.98	0.95	0.87	0.90	0.80	0.98	−0.37	0.98	0.80	1.00	0.98		
	Min	0.31	0.25	0.28	0.30	0.35	0.31	−0.85	0.27	0.31	0.34	0.36		
Sharpe Omega	Mean	0.95	0.90	0.93	0.94	0.73	0.92	−0.80	0.92	0.82	0.84	0.82	0.61	1.00
	Max	1.00	1.00	1.00	1.00	1.00	1.00	−0.60	1.00	1.00	0.96	0.94	0.88	
	Min	0.90	0.60	0.82	0.84	0.52	0.80	−1.00	0.82	0.50	0.60	0.60	0.24	

Risk (VaR ratio, CVAR ratio and MVaR ratio) for which the range of variation of correlation between rankings is higher than 60 per cent. For these measures the choice of the year analysed could affect significantly the results due to the relevance assigned to outliers: by definition the first type of measure is affected by every outlier while for the latter the choice of selective threshold (coherently with the literature, we assume an α equal to 95 per cent) expose to the same outliers' risk (Wu and Xiao, 2002).

RAP measures seems to be also suitable in order to select the best investment opportunities because (except for Calmar ratio) the investment released on the past top performers is normally better than the results achieved by a naïve diversification approach for both the equally weighted and the value weighted portfolios (Tables 10.6 and 10.7).

Considering the equally weighted portfolios (Table 10.6), the extra performance achieved selecting investment on the basis of the Sharpe ratio is comparable/equal to the portfolios constructed using the ROAS, the ROPS, the Sterling and the Sharpe Omega past values. Moreover on the overall time horizon ROAS and Sterling make a lower number of portfolio rebalances necessary for achieving the same performance achieved by the Sharpe index. Finally the ROAS and ROPS criteria show also a higher discrimination capability because the spread between best and worst performers is higher than the Sharpe ratio.

Looking at value weighted portfolios (Table 10.7), the choice to construct a value weighted portfolio does not impact significantly on the performance of the best portfolio while it impacts more significantly on the worst performers due to the higher difference in the size of the worst performers portfolio compared to the top ones.

Comparing the performance of the investment strategies constructed using different RAPs, Sharpe, ROAS, ROPS, Sterling ratio and Omega represent always the measures that identify the best investment opportunities available in the market and there is no change in the performance of strategy when we adopt a value weighted approach instead of an equal weighted one. Moreover on the overall time horizon ROAS and Sterling allow to make a lower number of portfolio rebalances necessary for achieving the same performance achieved by the Sharpe index. Finally considering the spread between top and worst performers, only the Sterling ratio allows discriminates better among best and worst investment opportunities with respect to the Sharpe ratio measure.

10.4 Conclusion

The assumption of normality of return distribution for Italian real estate funds is not coherent with the real distribution of results in the last years. The choice of the type of risk measure used in the ranking definition could significantly affect the judgement on the real estate investment vehicles.

Table 10.6 Performance of the investment strategy – equally weighted portfolios

	Top real estate vehicles$_{t-1}$													
	BMK	Sharpe	ROPS	ROAS	Sortino	Kappa (n = 3)	Kappa (n = 4)	Calmar	Sterling	Burke	VaR Ratio	CVaR ratio	MVaR ratio	Sharpe Omega
2001–2002	−0.07	0.02	0.02	0.02	0.02	0.02	0.02	−0.17	0.02	0.02	0.02	0.02	0.02	0.02
2002–2003	−0.04	0.14	0.14	0.14	0.14	0.14	0.14	−0.01	0.14	0.14	0.11	0.11	0.11	0.14
2003–2004	0.03	0.15	0.15	0.15	0.15	0.1	0.15	−0.07	0.15	0.15	0.12	0.12	0.12	0.15
2004–2005	−0.05	0.03	0.03	0.03	0.03	0.03	0.03	−0.10	0.03	0.03	0.03	0.03	−0.01	0.03
2005–2006	−0.01	0.05	0.05	0.05	0.05	0.05	0.05	−0.05	0.05	0.05	0.05	0.05	0.01	0.04
2006–2007	0.07	0.19	0.22	0.22	0.22	0.17	0.20	−0.01	0.22	0.19	0.15	0.15	0.18	0.2
2007–2008	−0.46	−0.07	−0.07	−0.07	−0.16	−0.41	−0.16	−0.64	−0.07	−0.41	−0.07	−0.07	−0.51	−0.07
2008–2009	0.01	0.20	0.21	0.21	0.2	0.17	0.19	−0.03	0.20	0.19	0.17	0.17	0.01	0.21
Overall	−0.07	0.09	0.09	0.09	0.08	0.03	0.08	−0.14	0.09	0.04	0.07	0.07	−0.01	0.09
N° rebalances	–	43	43	41	43	49	43	37	41	47	41	41	31	43

(Continued)

Table 10.6 (Continued)

	Worst real estate vehicles$_{t-1}$													
	BMK	Sharpe	ROPS	ROAS	Sortino	Kappa (n = 3)	Kappa (n = 4)	Calmar	Sterling	Burke	VaR Ratio	CVaR ratio	MVaR ratio	Sharpe Omega
2001–2002	−0.07	−0.12	−0.12	−0.12	−0.12	−0.12	−0.12	−0.02	−0.12	−0.12	−0.12	−0.12	−0.12	−0.12
2002–2003	−0.04	0.00	0.00	0.00	0.00	0.01	0.00	0.11	0.00	0.01	0.00	0.01	0.01	0.00
2003–2004	0.03	−0.05	−0.05	−0.05	−0.05	−0.02	−0.05	0.11	−0.05	−0.05	−0.05	−0.05	0.01	−0.05
2004–2005	−0.05	−0.10	−0.10	−0.10	−0.10	−0.04	−0.10	0.02	−0.10	−0.10	−0.09	−0.10	−0.10	−0.10
2005–2006	−0.01	−0.05	−0.05	−0.05	−0.05	−0.05	−0.05	0.04	−0.05	−0.05	−0.05	−0.05	−0.03	−0.05
2006–2007	0.07	−0.07	−0.07	−0.07	−0.07	−0.07	−0.07	0.20	−0.07	−0.07	−0.07	−0.07	−0.07	−0.07
2007–2008	−0.46	−0.66	−0.81	−0.78	−0.67	−0.57	−0.67	−0.24	−0.64	−0.64	−0.76	−0.61	−0.61	−0.78
2008–2009	0.01	−0.10	−0.11	−0.10	−0.10	−0.03	−0.10	0.18	−0.10	−0.10	−0.11	−0.11	−0.05	−0.10
Overall	−0.07	−0.14	−0.16	−0.16	−0.14	−0.11	−0.14	0.05	−0.14	−0.14	−0.15	−0.14	−0.12	−0.16
N° rebal-ances	-	50	44	48	48	46	46	50	46	50	44	48	48	48

Table 10.7 Performance of the investment strategy – value weighted portfolios

	Top real estate vehicles$_{t-1}$													
	BMK	Sharpe	ROPS	ROAS	Sortino	Kappa (n = 3)	Kappa (n = 4)	Calmar	Sterling	Burke	VaR Ratio	CVaR ratio	MVaR ratio	Sharpe Omega
2001–2002	–	0.02	0.02	0.02	0.02	0.02	0.02	0.00	0.02	0.02	0.02	0.02	0.02	0.02
2002–2003	0.00	0.14	0.14	0.14	0.14	0.14	0.14	0.00	0.14	0.14	0.10	0.10	0.10	0.14
2003–2004	0.04	0.15	0.15	0.15	0.15	0.11	0.15	0.00	0.15	0.15	0.12	0.12	0.12	0.15
2004–2005	–0.04	0.04	0.04	0.04	0.04	0.04	–0.08	0.01	0.04	0.04	0.04	0.04	–0.02	0.04
2005–2006	0.00	0.04	0.04	0.04	0.04	0.04	0.04	0.00	0.04	0.04	0.04	0.04	0.02	0.04
2006–2007	0.07	0.19	0.21	0.21	0.21	0.15	0.20	0.00	0.21	0.19	0.15	0.15	0.16	0.20
2007–2008	–0.44	–0.07	–0.07	–0.07	–0.16	–0.24	–0.16	0.00	–0.07	–0.24	–0.07	–0.07	–0.34	–0.07
2008–2009	0.04	0.21	0.22	0.22	0.21	0.19	0.21	0.00	0.21	0.21	0.18	0.18	0.09	0.22
Overall	–	0.09	0.09	0.09	0.08	0.05	0.07	0.00	0.09	0.07	0.07	0.07	0.02	0.09
N° rebalances	–	43	43	41	43	49	43	37	41	47	41	41	31	43

(Continued)

Table 10.7 (Continued)

	Worst Real Estate Vehicles$_{t-1}$													
	BMK	Sharpe	ROPS	ROAS	Sortino	Kappa (n = 3)	Kappa (n = 4)	Calmar	Sterling	Burke	VaR Ratio	CVaR ratio	MVaR ratio	Sharpe Omega
2001–2002	–	–0.17	–0.17	–0.17	–0.17	0.00	–0.17	0.02	–0.17	–0.17	–0.17	–0.17	–0.17	–0.17
2002–2003	0.00	0.00	0.00	0.00	0.00	0.00	0.00	0.10	0.00	0.01	0.00	0.01	0.01	0.00
2003–2004	0.04	–0.05	–0.05	–0.05	–0.05	–0.02	–0.05	0.12	–0.05	–0.04	–0.05	–0.05	0.05	–0.05
2004–2005	–0.04	–0.10	–0.10	–0.11	–0.11	–0.03	–0.11	0.02	–0.11	–0.09	–0.08	–0.09	–0.10	–0.11
2005–2006	0.00	–0.05	–0.05	–0.05	–0.05	–0.05	–0.05	0.03	–0.05	–0.05	–0.05	–0.05	–0.02	–0.05
2006–2007	0.07	–0.06	–0.06	–0.06	–0.06	–0.06	0.09	0.20	–0.06	–0.06	–0.06	–0.06	–0.06	–0.06
2007–2008	–	–0.66	–0.72	–0.70	–0.65	–0.56	–0.65	–0.30	–0.64	–0.64	–0.63	–0.55	–0.55	–0.70
2008–2009	0.04	–0.08	–0.09	–0.08	–0.08	–0.03	–0.08	0.19	–0.08	–0.08	–0.09	–0.09	–0.05	–0.09
Overall	–	–0.15	–0.16	–0.15	–0.15	–0.09	–0.13	0.05	–0.15	–0.14	–0.14	–0.13	–0.11	–0.15
N° rebalances	–	50	44	48	48	46	46	50	46	50	44	48	48	48

The choice of risk measures that are more complete compared to the standard deviation affects not only the yearly ranking position of each fund but also the variability of the rankings over time. Even if the Sharpe index constructs rankings that are quite persistent over time, some more complex RAPs show a higher or at least equal persistence of the result compared to the Sharpe ratio for all the years analysed. In particular, the measures constructed on the absolute shortfall, on the distribution of losses, on asymmetry of returns or on a mean of the maximum drawdowns achieves the highest level of ranking persistence over time.

Almost all RAP measures beat a naïve diversification approach. The more complex RAPs could achieve, on the yearly and on the overall time horizon, the same performance obtained by the Sharpe investment selection criteria. Looking at the number of portfolio rebalances necessary for the portfolio investment strategy, some of the new RAP measures achieve the same performance obtained by the Sharpe index with a lower number of portfolio changes and so these portfolios could be less affected by the transaction costs.

The empirical analysis proposed has considered a small but fast-growing real estate market (like the Italian one) and, in order to define a sample sufficiently wide, it encompasses all Italian listed funds. Nevertheless, the main limit of the approach proposed is the low number of funds analysed. The small number of funds available could be significantly affected by the presence of one or more outliers in the sample and so in the next step we will include other markets in which similar funds are traded.[6] A further development of the research should consider more complex portfolio optimization rules (i.a. Lee and Stevenson, 2005) in order to test if the choice of the risk measurement approach is still relevant when complex portfolio construction rules are applied. Following the approaches adopted by other studies in the asset management industry, the investment selection could be done using an ex-ante approach instead of an ex-post approach, using the expected value of the RAP measure for each fund instead of the past value (Pastor and Stambaugh, 2002).

Notes

The authors are members of the Laboratory of Real Estate Finance instituted by the Ph.D. in Banking and Finance of University of Rome 'Tor Vergata'. This chapter is the result of the authors' common efforts and continuous exchange of ideas. The individual sections of the chapter can be acknowledged as follows: Sections 10.1 and 10.4 to Claudio Giannotti and others to Gianluca Mattarocci.

1. Our analysis does not consider RAP measures like the Treynor index, the information ratio and the Jensen α and all adjustments of these measures that remove the assumption of normality of returns. This choice is also justifiable on the basis of the problems pointed out in the literature for the correct specification of market indexes and benchmarks for the Italian real estate industry (Porzio and Sampagnaro, 2007).

2. Kappa measure could be constructed considering also higher orders but for the purpose of the analysis we select to upper limit the order to 4.
3. On the basis of a literature review, only the highest five losses are normally considered (Eling and Schuhmacher, 2007).
4. On the basis of a literature review, only the highest five losses are normally considered (Eling and Schuhmacher, 2007).
5. All measures constructed on VaR consider the minimum threshold of 95% normally used for the evaluation of hedge funds (Guizot, 2007).
6. For a deeper analysis of the problems related to identifying markets in which are traded similar financial instruments see Biasin (2003).

References

Agarwal, V. and N. Y. Naik (2004) 'Risk and portfolio decisions involving hedge funds', *Review of Financial Studies*, 17, 63–98.

Benefield, J. D., R. I. Anderson and L. V. Zumpano (2009) 'Performance differences in property-type diversified versus specialized real estate investment trusts (REITs)', *Review of Financial Economics*, 18, 70–9.

Biasin, M. (2003) 'L'esperienza di real estate investment trust statunitensi: alcune indicazioni per i fondi immobiliari italiani', *Bancaria*, 59, 70–82.

Bird, R. and D. R. Gallagher (2002) 'The evaluation of active manager returns in a not symmetrical environment', *Journal of Asset Management*, 2, 303–24.

Brueggman, W. B., A. H. Chen and T. G. Thibodeau (1984) 'Real estate investment funds: Performance and portfolio considerations', *AREUEA Journal*, 12, 333–54.

Burke, G. (1994) 'A sharper Sharpe ratio', *Futures*, 23, 56.

P. Byrne, and S. Lee (2004) 'Different risk measures: Different portfolio composition?', *Journal of Property Investment and Finance*, 22, 501–11.

Carhart, M. M. (1997) 'On persistence in mutual fund performance', *Journal of Finance*, 52, 57–82.

Carretta, A. and G. Mattarocci (2008) 'Performance evaluation of hedge funds: A comparison of different approaches', in A. Carretta, F. Fiordelisi and G. Mattarocci (eds), *New Drivers of Performance in a Changing Financial World* (Houndmills: Palgrave MacMillan).

Dowd, K. (2000), 'Adjusting for risk: an improved Sharpe ratio', *International Review of Economics and Finance*, 9, 209–22.

Eling, M. and F. Schuhmacher (2006) 'Performance measurement of hedge fund indices. Does the measure matter?', In H. D. Haasis, H. Kopfer and J. Schonberger (eds), *Operations Research Proceedings 2005* (Berlin, Springer).

——(2007) 'Does the choice of performance measure influence the evaluation of hedge funds?' *Journal of Banking and Finance*, 31, 2632–47.

Gallo, J. G., L. J. Lockwood and R. C. Rutherford (2000) 'Asset allocation and the performance of real estate mutual funds', *Real Estate Economics*, 28, 165–84.

Giannotti, C. and G. Mattarocci (2008) 'Risk diversification in a real estate portfolio: Evidence from Italian market', *Journal of European Real Estate Research*, 1, 214–34.

——(2009) 'How to evaluate risk for Italian real estate funds', *European Real Estate Research*, 2, 133–50.

Gregoriou, G. N. and J. P. Gueyie (2003) 'Risk-adjusted performance of funds of hedge funds using a modified Sharpe ratio', *Journal of Wealth Management*, 6, 77–83.

Guizot, A. (2007) *The Hedge Fund Compliance and Risk Management Guide* (Chirchester: Wiley).

Hendricks, D., J. Patel and R. Zeckhauser (1993) 'Hot hands in mutual funds: Short-run persistence of relative performance, 1974-1988', *Journal of Finance*, 48, 93–130

Hutson, L. and S. Stevenson (2008) 'Asymmetry in REIT returns', *Journal of Real Estate Portfolio Management*, 14, 105–23.

Kallberg, J. A., C. L. Liu and C. Trzcinka (2000) 'The value added from investment manager: An examination of funds of REITs', *Journal of Financial and Quantitative Analysis*, 35, 387–408.

Kaplan, P. D. and J. A. Knowles (2004) 'Kappa: A generalized downside risk-adjusted performance measure', *Journal of Performance Measurement*, 8, 42–54.

Kazemi, H., T. Schneeweis and B. Gupta (2004) 'Omega as a performance measure', *Journal of Performance Measurement*, 8, 16–25.

L. N. Kestner, (1996) 'Getting a handle on true performance', *Futures*, 25, 44–6.

Lee, S. and S. Stevenson (2005) 'Real estate portfolio construction and estimation risk', *Journal of Property Investment and Finance*, 23, 234–53.

Lin, C. Y. and K. Young (2007) 'Real estate mutual funds: A style analysis', *Financial Services Review*, 16, 261–73.

Lizieri, C. M., S. Satchell and Q. Zhang (2007) 'The underlying return-generating factors for REIT returns: an application of independent component analysis', *Real Estate Economics*, 35, 569–98.

Lizieri, C. M. and C. W. R. Ward (2000) 'Commercial real estate return distributions: A review of the literature and empirical evidence', in J. Knight and S. Satchell (eds), *Return Distributions in Finance* (Oxford: Butterworth-Heinemann).

Myer, N. F. C. and J. R. Webb (1993) "Return properties of equity REITs, common stocks, and commercial real estate: A comparison", *Journal of Real Estate Research*, 8, 87–106.

Ooi, J. T. L. and K. H. Liow (2004) 'Risk adjusted performance of real estate stocks: Evidence from developing countries', *Journal of Real Estate Research*, 26, 371–95.

Pastor, L. and R. F. Stambaugh (2002) 'Investing in equity mutual funds', *Journal of Financial Economics*, 63, 351–80.

Pedersen, C. S. and T. Rudholm-Alfvin (2003) 'Selecting a risk-adjusted shareholder performance measure', *Journal of Asset Management*, 4, 152–72.

Philpot, J. and C. A. Peterson (2006) 'Manager characteristics and real estate mutual fund returns, risk and fees', *Managerial Finance*, 32, 988–96.

Porzio, C. and G. Sampagnaro (2007) *L'investimento immobiliare* (Rome: Bancaria Editrice).

Radcliffe, R., W. Brueggman and D. Ennis (1974) 'The risk return performance of real estate investment trusts', *Journal of Financial and Quantitative Analysis*, 9, 769–70.

Rogers, D. S. and C. J. Van Dyke (2006) 'Measuring the volatility of hedge funds returns', *Journal of Wealth Management*, 9, 45–53.

Shadwick, W. and C. Keating (2002) 'A universal performance measure', *Journal of Performance Measurement*, 6, 59–84.

Shapiro, S. S. and M. B. Wilk (1965) 'An analysis of variance test for normality', *Biometrika*, 52, 591–611.

Sharpe, W. F. (1994) 'The Sharpe ratio', *Journal of Portfolio Management*, 21, 49–58.

Sortino, F. A. and H. J. Forsey (1996) 'On the use and misuse of downside risk', *Journal of Portfolio Management*, 22, 35–42.

Wu, G. and Z. Xiao (2002) 'An analysis of risk measures', *Journal of Risk*, 4, 53–75.

Young, T. (1991) 'Calmar ratio: A smoother tool', *Futures*, 20, 40.

Young, M. S. and R. A. Graff (1995) 'Real estate is not normal: A fresh look at real estate return distribution', *Journal of Real Estate Finance and Economics*, 10, 225–59.

Part III

Public Sector Issues in a Crisis Scenario

11
Economic and Financial Determinants of the Italian Local Government Ratings: An Empirical Analysis

Anna Valeria Venneri

11.1 Introduction

This research originates from some starting-points, for example the difficulty in evaluating the financial needs of local governments, that have modified their funding policies as time goes on; the lack of banking standardized systems of internal assessment of their creditworthiness (unlike corporate); an evaluation so based on ratings for the major local governments; the noted inefficiency of these external judgements for both public and private counterparts; the provisions of Authorities (Bank of Italy and Basel Committee) by which banks have to check internally ratings. While treasury services of local governments are mostly managed by even the smallest Italian banks, innovative financing services are supplied by a few operators with a heterogeneous supply, and local governments themselves use not much these instruments selecting the best supply each time. The relationship between banks and local governments has to be developed, on the one hand, researching the main partner and, on the other hand, developing the local territory. In this framework banks, especially local ones, have a strategic opportunity to take as well in order to approach SMEs.

This chapter is organized as follows: after a literature review about the quantitative estimation of ratings and an investigation on similarities and differences of the agencies evaluation methodologies of sovereign and sub-sovereign risks, this study aims to find out economic and financial determinants of Italian local governments' ratings by an empirical analysis.

11.2 Quantitative estimation of sovereign and sub-sovereign credit ratings: a literature review

In order to adequately investigate a counterpart's creditworthiness, even if statistical models alone aren't sufficient to evaluate the total risk of a borrower, they could be useful to make banking rating systems: more reliable on the one hand, they are able to highlight the indicators which are most statistically significant to explain rating; on the other hand, they allow one to obtain information about the creditworthiness of unrated counterparts.

Among the main research themes on ratings, quantitative ones play a central role especially in the US market. So these papers use agencies rating as a dependent variable and try to search for a significant relationship with a specific set of explicative variables (generally, balance-sheet indicators). These studies could be classified in three macro areas according to the counterpart they analyse: sovereign, banks, corporate. The following literature review concerns only the first category, empirical papers are distinguished according to the sovereign or sub-sovereign credit ratings they study.

11.2.1 Sovereign credit ratings

Feder and Uy (1985) first utilize a multiple logit model to replicate ratings assigned by *Institutional Investor* to a sample of 55 developing countries between 1979 and 1983 in order to identify the determinants of sovereign ratings.

Cosset and Roy (1991) use a logistic regression for ratings given in 1987 by *Institutional Investor* and *Euromoney* to 71 countries with different levels of economic development and obtain the main determinants as follows: per capita income, propensity to invest, and degree of indebtedness of the country.

Oral et al. (1992) analyse 70 countries through a generalized logistic model and find most of the ratings published by *Institutional Investor* could be explained by some simple macroeconomic indicators (GDP per capita, growth rate of exports, inflation).

Lee (1993) applies *Institutional Investor* data on a sample of 29 developing countries by a linear regression and proves that economic variables, instead of political ones, modify country ratings.

Using rating assignments by *Institutional Investor, Euromoney* and *The Economist Intelligence Unit* for the period 1980 to 1993, Haque et al. (1996) examine the correlation between ratings of over 60 developing countries and various social, political and economic factors; their results show that especially macroeconomic variables modify ratings of emerging countries.

Cantor and Packer (1996) analyse the determinants of Moody's and S&P's rating assignments to a sample of 49 countries and their impact on bond spreads. The linear regression model adopted by them explains more than 90 per cent of ratings variations and good explanatory variables are: per capita income, inflation, GDP growth, external debt, level of economic development; on the contrary, a significant negative effect is represented by a country's default history.

Following the Cantor and Packer (1996) methodology, Ferri et al. (1999) believe rating is a function of macroeconomic variables: comparing actual ratings assigned by Moody's to 17 countries in the period from 1989 to 1998 and those predicted by their model, the authors highlight differences they attribute to the agencies' qualitative judgements.

Using both a linear regression and an ordered probit model to country ratings assigned by Moody's and S&P's between 1989 and 2001, Mora (2006) is more careful than Ferri et al. in his conclusions: analysing the hypothesis that agencies aggravated the East Asian crisis by excessively downgrading those countries, the author doubts credit ratings can exacerbate the boom-bust economic cycle: assigned ratings exceeded predicted ratings before the crisis, mostly matched predicted ratings during the crisis period, and did not increase as much as predictions in the period after the crisis. So ratings are, if anything, sticky rather than procyclical (Mora, 2006), because they simply react to news, whether macroeconomic or market (for example, a country's default history).

Mulder and Perrelli (2001) find rating changes for emerging market economies have been dominated by variables other than those suggested by the empirical literature (that is, the seminal paper by Cantor and Packer). Criticizing the work by Ferri et al., they propose a more accurate estimation model: using two linear regressions, the authors analyse a homogenous sample of 25 emerging countries and their ratings assigned by Moody's and S&P's between 1992 and 1999. The results confirm significant overshooting of the credit ratings during the crisis period for the main Asian emerging markets, although part of the deterioration in the ratings was warranted *ex-post* by worsening in the economic fundamentals, mainly the reduction in investment over GDP that accompanied the crises.

Using a logit model, Oetzel et al. (2001) examine the performance of 11 risk indicators in a sample of 17 countries in the period 1980 to 1998 and find no indicator is effective to predict a significant instability of a country's risk.

Through a logistic regression applied to changes in ratings assigned by Moody's, S&P's and Fitch to 16 developing countries in the period from 1990 to 2000, Kaminsky and Schmukler (2002) show that ratings intensify the boom-bust cycle, but downgrades occur after market downturns.

Extending the methodology by Cantor and Packer (1996), Hu et al. (2002) apply an ordinated probit model instead of the linear models commonly used in literature in order to estimate sovereign transition matrices combining the relatively small amount of transition data available for sovereigns with information on sovereign defaults for a broader set of countries and over a longer period of time.

Reinhart (2002) estimates the correlation between currency crises and default through a probit model and finds in emerging market economies about 84 per cent of defaults are linked with currency crises, but only slightly less than half the currency crises in such economies are associated to default, and for developed economies there is no evidence of any connection between currency crises and default.

By using linear, logistic, and exponential transformations of the rating scales, Afonso (2003) analyses the economic determinants of sovereign credit ratings assigned by Moody's and S&P's in June 2001 to 81 countries (29 developed and 52 developing ones). The logistic transformation seems to be better for the overall sample: its absolute percentage average error of the selected model is around 23 per cent, while around 30 and 45 per cent when using respectively the linear and the exponential transformation. Six variables appear to be the most relevant to determining a country's rating: GDP per capita, external debt as a percentage of exports, level of economic development, default history, real growth rate, and inflation rate.

Comparing three different methodologies (ordered probit, ordered logit, and random effects ordered probit approaches), Afonso et al. (2009) study the determinants of sovereign ratings assigned by Moody's and S&P's to 66 countries between 1996 and 2005, finding the latter procedure is the best for panel data as it considers the existence of an additional normally distributed cross-section error. The authors identify the following relevant determinants of sovereign ratings: GDP per capita, real GDP growth, inflation, unemployment, government debt, fiscal balance, government effectiveness, external debt, foreign reserves, current account balance, default history, regional dummies and a dummy for the European Union.

Bissoondoyal-Bheenick et al. (2006) compare two alternative procedures to estimate the quantitative determinants of sovereign ratings: ordered probit and case-based reasoning. Despite the differences in approach, they produce similar results in terms of which variables are significant and forecast accuracy. The authors use six different categories of sovereign ratings at 31 December 2001: in particular, foreign and local currency ratings assigned by S&P's and Fitch, respectively, to 94 and 78 countries; bonds and notes ratings and bank deposits ratings assigned by Moody's to 94 countries. As regards significant variables, both models find that a proxy for technological development (specifically, mobile phone use) is the most important variable, apart from a range of conventional macroeconomic variables (in particular, GDP and inflation).

Mellios and Paget-Blanc (2006) compare the linear regression and ordered logistic approaches in order to identify the determinants of sovereign credit ratings assigned by Moody's, S&P's and Fitch to 86 countries at 31 December 2003. By using a principal component analysis, the authors find 13 explanatory variables and examine their effects on ratings: by the above-mentioned two techniques, they identify six determinants of sovereign credit ratings.

The evidence, consistent with other similar studies, suggests that per capita income, government income, real exchange rate, inflation rate and default history are the variables which have the most significant impact on sovereign ratings. In contrast to the findings of previous studies, corruption index, which reflects the development level, as well as the quality of governance of a country, has a strong influence on ratings. Although the two models exhibit high predictive power, the logistic model provides better results than the regression model.

Finally, following the study by Erb et al. (1995) about the predictive power of country credit ratings in discriminating between high-expected and low-expected returns countries, through a logistic regression Cruces (2006) analyses the statistical properties of all the sovereign credit ratings assigned by *Institutional Investor* to 173 countries between 1979 and 2004. Modelling ratings as a function of expected repayment capacity, the author finds that ratings effectively display volatility clustering and asymmetric adjustments, their revisions are serially correlated during most of the sample, and region and other characteristics capture common persistence in the ratings.

11.2.2 Sub-sovereign credit ratings

From the second half of the nineties, ratings assigned by international agencies to local and regional governments (LRG), especially in Western Europe, have exponentially increased: as presented in Liu and Tan (2009), this is an increase of 250 per cent from 1996 to 2005, with S&P's market leader since 2000.

Although several authors have studied the determinants of sovereign credit ratings starting from the agencies' assessments, there are not many papers about sub-sovereign ratings.

Cheung (1996) applies an ordered probit model to the nine Canadian provinces in order to estimate the relationship between provincial credit ratings, as assessed by S&P's from 1970 to 1995, and some economic variables that all result as significant: debt-to-GDP ratio, employment ratio, provincial GDP, federal transfers, provincial revenues.

Gaillard (2006, 2009) analyses more than a hundred non-US LRG ratings, as assessed by Moody's and S&P's for the period from 1996 to 2005, and demonstrates that sub-sovereign ratings are essentially correlated with their respective sovereign rating: 41 per cent of outlook revisions/rating changes on a sovereign resulted in subsequent revisions/changes on LRG ratings. The framework of relationships between central governments and their LRG explains why, on average, the latter are rated 1.85 notches lower than their sovereign. Moreover, using an ordered probit model, the author finds that three of the nineteen economic and financial variables examined (default history of the sovereign entity, GDP per capita and net direct debt to operating revenue ratio) explain 80 per cent of sub-sovereign credit ratings.

Finally, even with no empirical analysis unlike Cheung (1996) and Gaillard (2006), Liu and Tan (2009) carried out a review to compare the estimation methodologies used for LRG creditworthiness by the three main international agencies (Moody's, S&P's, Fitch).

11.3 External evaluation of sovereign and sub-sovereign risks

Before examining the evaluation criteria for sub-sovereign and sovereign risks used by agencies, it's necessary to exactly define them. In fact, one of the main problems we come across in the literature review concerns the confusion generated by the lack of a clear distinction between country and sovereign credit ratings as well as their associated risks. Therefore, the paragraph initially clarifies this definition and then analyses the methodologies for assessing sovereign and sub-sovereign risks by agencies, identifying their similarities and differences.

11.3.1 Definition of sovereign and sub-sovereign risks

Both in literature and practice, country risk and sovereign risk are sometimes improperly used as synonyms, but they are two different types of risks, related though. In general, Bouchet et al. (2003) attribute country risk to three main areas: risk of natural disasters and geo-climatic events, socio-political risk, economic risk in the strict sense. The latter, also known as country-specific economic risk, may be attributed to additional elements that, according to Meldrum (2000), are the following: economic risk, political risk, transfer risk, exchange risk, proximity or contagion risk, sovereign risk.

Country risk is the risk we are exposed to in a commercial or financial cross-border activity, as a result of political, social, and economic events occurring in a foreign country and depending on its authorities, which could affect the capability and/or willingness of a (sovereign or not) borrower to meet its obligations to a foreign lender. Otherwise, sovereign risk is the risk we are exposed to in a commercial or financial activity whose exclusive counterparty is a sovereign debtor: the central government or other agencies, institutions, and public businesses of a foreign country. So there is a different assessment methodology too: while for country risk we ask what's the probability that authorities are not able to control the political, social, and economic conditions of the country enough to affect the capability and/or willingness of a (sovereign or not) borrower to meet its obligations to a foreign lender, instead for sovereign risk we ask what's the probability that a sovereign debtor (state, government, public business) may not be able to meet its obligations to a foreign lender; in the latter case, what is important is not only the actual availability of resources to meet the debt burden, but also reputation and track record of payments (for example, the presence of previous debt restructuring) of the borrower.

After this necessary distinction between country risk and sovereign risk, we can further split the sovereign risk into sovereign risk in the strict sense if it concerns a central government and sub-sovereign risk if it concerns another sovereign debtor (local authorities, institutions, public businesses) as identified by El Daher (1999).

11.3.2 Evaluation of sovereign risk

As above mentioned, sovereign credit rating measures the possibility that a sovereign government is unable or unavailable to repay, in whole or in part and in time, its own debts and financial obligations, generating a situation of sovereign default if so. The three main international rating agencies carry out the so-called Issuer Default Ratings (IDR), general reliability's measures of the sovereign issue apart from of the specific bond's characteristics. In turn, Fitch (2006b) associated IDR equal to or less than B with their recovery ratings, assessments about the share capital that could be recovered if default occurs and, consequently, the loss given default. Fitch (2008c) and Moody's (2001, 2005c, 2006a) also provide the so-called country ceiling, that is the best credit worthiness assigned to an issue; since 2001 country ceiling may exceed its sovereign rating up to 3 notches: Fitch and Moody's assign to the Euro-area countries a single country ceiling (equivalent to AAA), regardless of the sovereign risk of their particular country.

Rather than change their opinion when any new information occurs, all three agencies use the short-term economic scenario (so-called *outlook* and declined each in its own way) to report a positive or negative rating action in the short and medium period, while awaiting new information confirming or not their risk assumption. Generally, this rating action consists of a modification of a credit rating notch, equivalent to the transition to a higher (*upgrading*) or lower (*downgrading*) level in the IDR scale.

Moreover the measure of sovereign risk, like others, can be shown point-in-time or through-the-cycle: in particular, the first risk measure is based on the issuer situation at a certain time, while the second takes into account the possible and probable developments of the current situation. Agencies explicitly affirm they follow a forward-looking perspective, so the creditworthiness of a sovereign issue is assessed by the interaction between the current situation and expected developments according to the analysts' forecasts.[1]

Having to do with entities of different countries (which have their own history and international connotation), as well as providing economic and statistical data at low frequency (often lacking or unreliable), means that the definition of a sovereign rating consists of both quantitative and qualitative elements, and through the analysts' experience also non-measurable factors (including political risk) are considered. The three major agencies recognize the need and the key role of this judgemental component: so for sovereign risks the central role of the 'willingness' to repay the debt, beyond the actual capability, makes this qualitative part very important for the creditworthiness assessment.

As regards the quantitative part of the rating process, there are different approaches and models to estimate the probability of default (PD); among the most popular ones, scoring (based on the discriminant analysis) and econometric models (probit and logit) for the PD's evaluation. In the former, used by Moody's and S&P's, each variable receives a *score* on the basis of its proximity to or distance from a risk threshold considered to be critical. By contrast, the latter directly estimate the PD despite suffering from the lack of ratings and the shortness of available time series. Scoring models have a greater flexibility and, usually, critical thresholds and scoring are calculated by calibrating the model in continuous *ex-post* audits (so-called *backtesting*). In scoring models it is also possible to include a subjective concern, through the assignment of scores on the data validity or issue credibility.

So the resulting sovereign rating is not static but dynamic, representing the evolution of both endogenous and exogenous factors. Among these, the main elements underlying the agencies' assessments include: political and administrative organization, economic-demographic and income situation, financial results and financial structure (Bhatia, 2002; Liu and Tan, 2009). Despite a different algorithm being used to estimate the sovereign rating, the items analysed by the three agencies are the same, summarized in debt, administrative, financial and economic factors (Cluff and Farnham, 1984), all valid signals of default risk and solvency of a sovereign borrower.

11.3.3 Evaluation of sub-sovereign risk

In order to assess the creditworthiness of a sub-sovereign borrower, rating agencies' approach is similar to the sovereign risk one, by defining a set of indicators and listing the evaluation criteria (Moody's, 2006b, 2008a, 2008e; Fitch, 2005, 2008a). So risk analysis for local governments is an interdisciplinary activity in which the quantitative skills of analysts are associated with attention to historical, institutional, political, and cultural factors.

The methodological framework of sub-sovereign ratings, developed similarly to the sovereign ratings one, identifies five main areas of investigation as follows:

- *operational context*, specifically national situations that may affect the risk of an economic, political or financial market crisis (so, the sovereign risk factors), *and institutional framework*, which determines the powers and responsibilities of local governments;
- *intergovernmental support*, that is the assessment both of the probability of an extraordinary involvement by central government or a third higher-level entity in order to prevent a sub-sovereign default, and of the amount and nature of intergovernmental transfers, *and administrative management* (for example, governance factors and quality of management);

- *demographic-economic structure and growth prospects*, whose analysis concerns for example: population, local GDP per capita, employment and unemployment levels, growth rates of exports and investment-to-GDP;
- *financial performance and fiscal flexibility*, namely the existence of legal, political, competitive or other limits towards fiscal flexibility;
- *financial position*, in particular debt and cash flow management, debt profile, and off-balance sheet liabilities.

Approaches in assessing LRG by the three main agencies are almost identical to each other, both as regards the rating assignment process and with reference to the criteria adopted (Liu and Tan, 2009). Differences among agencies are represented, instead, by the following elements: the relative weight assigned to each variable determining ratings, the importance attributed to qualitative variables, the changes in weights assigned to different variables over time.

Even sovereign risk factors strongly influence sub-sovereign ratings; in fact, all the three agencies analyse the creditworthiness of sub-national governments within the so-called *sovereign framework*: Standard & Poor's (2009a) and Fitch (2008b) explicitly affirm that sovereign rating is one of the determinants of sub-sovereign rating and, similarly, Moody's (2005a, 2006c, 2008g) has applied the so-called *joint default analysis* to sub-sovereign entities since 2005.

In addition, although agencies have disused the maximum forecast by the equivalence between country ceiling and sovereign rating since 2001, it remains *de facto* because they have so far assigned not many sub-sovereign ratings higher than their corresponding sovereign rating, according to certain criteria, such as strength and institutional stability, independence from government transfers, and financial flexibility of sub-sovereign governments (Fitch, 2009c).

A study by Moody's (2008d) shows how, even on the basis of the limited experience of non-US sub-sovereign defaults, essentially as a result of sovereign defaults in Russia (1998) and Argentina (2001), the sub-sovereign default rates are, on average, lower than sovereign and corporate ones. Moreover, despite the low number of observations, non-US sub-sovereign ratings assigned by Moody's between 1983 and 2007 are essentially investment grade: their changes, on average, are lower than corporate but more frequent than sovereign ratings. Instead, speculative grade sub-sovereign ratings are less stable than both corporate and sovereign ratings.[2]

Finally, the current global financial crisis is putting a strain on the credit standing of sub-national governments. For example, in December 2009 Fitch has undertaken some negative rating actions for European sub-sovereign entities, shorter than other sectors, specifying that it considers highly likely a downgrades increase in 2010 and 2011, partly as a result of the deterioration in their relevant sovereign ratings. The current financial crisis has also strengthened the focus on cash and debt management of sub-sovereign entities under the agencies criteria. Fitch (2006c, 2008b) has changed its macrocategory of *debt and indirect risk* to *debt, liquidity and indirect risk*, and in the methodology update published in July 2008 has included two new indicators compared with the previous guidelines published in October 2006, that are: debt to current revenues and direct risk to current revenues. Moody's (2005b, 2007, 2008b, 2008f, 2009) has updated the sub-sovereign ratings methodology by introducing new debt weightings that take into account public–private partnerships or securitization transactions. Standard & Poor's (2007a, 2007b, 2008, 2009a) has updated its methodology by including the evaluation of derivatives.

11.4 Determinants of the italian sub-sovereign ratings: methodology and results

Following studies by Cheung (1996) and Gaillard (2006, 2009) in order to empirically identify the main economic and financial indicators affecting sub-sovereign credit ratings, this analysis uses a multinomial ordered probit model, whose dependent variables are represented by long-term issuer ratings assigned to the Italian local governments by Moody's, S&P's and Fitch. This model has been chosen because it's the most appropriate in the case of qualitative ordinal dependent variables, such as credit ratings, which can be classified into more than two categories (Greene, 2003; Verbeek, 2006; Stock and Watson, 2007). For the purposes of this research, likewise Cantor and Packer (1996), Cheung (1996), Ferri et al. (1999), Afonso (2003), Afonso et al. (2009), Bissoondoyal-Bheenick et al. (2006) and Gaillard (2006, 2009), ratings of different agencies are first converted into numerical indicators (on a scale from 1 to 21) through a linear transformation (Table 11.1). Subsequently, a range of economic and financial explanatory variables, commonly used by rating agencies and available from their official methodologies, reports, and comments, are tested.

By expressing the probability of a rating score assigned to a sub-sovereign entity as a function of different explanatory variables, the probit model is built around a single latent variable. Therefore, the unobserved continuous measure, creditworthiness (Y), is a linear function of a set of explanatory variables or regressors (X), with a parameter vector (β) and a random disturbance term (ε). In formulas:

$$Y^*_{jt} = x_{jt}\beta + \varepsilon_{jt} \tag{11.1}$$

where Y^*_{jt} is the unobserved latent variable (i.e., the creditworthiness of each sub-sovereign entity j at time t) depending on different explanatory factors (x_{jt}). Because Y^*_{jt} is unobserved, what is observed are the credit ratings (y_{jt}) assigned to each sub-sovereign entity at 31 December of each year t, for i varying from 1 to 21.

Table 11.1 A linear transformation of ratings

	Fitch's – S&P's rating	Moody's rating	Value
Investment grade	AAA	Aaa	21
	AA+	Aa1	20
	AA	Aa2	19
	AA–	Aa3	18
	A+	A1	17
	A	A2	16
	A–	A3	15
	BBB+	Baa1	14
	BBB	Baa2	13
	BBB–	Baa3	12
Speculative grade	BB+	Ba1	11
	BB	Ba2	10
	BB–	Ba3	9
	B+	B1	8
	B	B2	7
	B–	B3	6
	CCC+	Caa1	5
	CCC	Caa2	4
	CCC–	Caa3	3
	CC, C	Ca	2
	RD*, SD**, D	C	1

Notes: * Class rating only adopted by Fitch.
** Class rating only adopted by S&P's.

Observations are so-called *panel data* (pooling of cross-section and time-series data); therefore, the sample observations are two-dimensional: they both vary as to each local government and in the time period. Literature is unanimous in arguing that the combination of both cross-section and time-series information along with a growing attention to dynamic specifications allows one to formulate and assess the best models able to explain economic events and so leads to more reliable estimates (Baltagi and Griffin, 1984; Wooldridge, 2002; Arellano, 2003; Baltagi, 2005). Therefore, the observed results are the following:

$$\begin{aligned} y_{jt} &= 21 \quad \text{if} \qquad\qquad Y^*_{jt} \le \mu_1 \\ y_{jt} &= 20 \quad \text{if} \quad \mu_1 \le Y^*_{jt} \le \mu_2 \\ &\dots \\ y_{jt} &= 1 \quad\; \text{if} \quad \mu_{20} \le Y^*_{jt} \le \mu_{21} \end{aligned} \tag{11.2}$$

where the unknown threshold parameters (μ_i or cut-off points) can be estimated jointly with the β coefficients through the maximum likelihood method. Moreover, stochastic terms (ε_{jt}) of equation (11.1) are independent and identically distributed (*i.i.d.*) across observations, and mean and variance are normalized to 0 and 1 respectively. Denoting by Φ the cumulative function of a normal distribution, the probabilities results are the following:

$$
\begin{aligned}
&Prob(y_{jt} = 21 \mid X)\Phi(\mu_1 - X\beta) \\
&Prob(y_{jt} = 20 \mid X) = \Phi(\mu_2 - X\beta) - \Phi(\mu_1 - X\beta) \\
&\dots \\
&Prob(y_{jt} = 1 \mid X) = 1 - \Phi(\mu_{20} - X\beta)
\end{aligned}
\tag{11.3}
$$

So this approach expresses the probability that each sub-sovereign entity *j* will be assigned a credit rating (from 1 to 21) at time *t*. As above mentioned, the unknown parameters to be estimated by the maximum likelihood method are the cut-off points (μ_i) and the β coefficients. The joint probability function (by convention, the log-likelihood function) can be expressed as follows:

$$
F(y \mid X) = \sum_{t=1}^{T}\sum_{j=1}^{J}\sum_{i=1}^{I-1} \ln\left[\Phi_{tj}(\mu_i - X\beta)\right] + \sum_{t=1}^{T}\sum_{j=1}^{J}\sum_{i=I} \ln\left[1 - \Phi_{tj}(\mu_{I-1} - X\beta)\right]
\tag{11.4}
$$

where $I = 21$, J = number of the rated sub-sovereign entity and *T* varies from 2004 to 2008.

11.4.1 Survey sample, explanatory variables and data sources

In this empirical analysis the sample includes all Italian provinces and provincial capitals rated between 2004 to 2008 by at least one of the three major credit rating agencies, namely 319 observations on the 31 provinces and 35 provincial capitals rated. Each rating has been transformed into a numerical indicator through the linear relationship in Table 11.1. Moreover, the numerical value of each local government rated ($i = 1, \dots, 21$) corresponds to y_{jt} in the probit model above described, where:

- t = from 2004 to 2008;
- j = from 1 to 31 provinces;
- j = from 1 to 35 cities that are the main cities of the province.

While all the 20 Italian regions have a credit rating (even if in Trentino Alto Adige rating is assigned not to the region but to the two autonomous provinces of Trento and Bolzano), only about 20–25 per cent of provinces and provincial capitals are rated from 2004 to 2008.

Furthermore, there are often substantial divergences in the evaluation (so-called *split ratings* in literature) on the same local government by agencies,

Table 11.2 Set of explanatory variables: a description

Variable	Description	Symbol	Unit of measure	Expected sign
Local GDP per capita	Local GDP/population	PILL	€*	+
Financial autonomy	Own revenues/current revenues	AFIN	%	+
Fiscal autonomy	Tax revenues/current revenues	AIMP	%	+
Current balance	Current margin/current revenues	MCOR	%	+
Expenditure on loans repayment	Debt service/current revenues	SDEB	%	–
Spending on debt	Interest payments/current revenues	SINT	%	–
Local debt per capita	Residual mortgage debt/population	INDL	€*	–
Surplus or financial needs	Net borrowing/total revenues	SALD	%	–
Southern Italy	0 = central and northern; 1 = southern	MEZ	*dummy*	–

Note: * Logarithmic transformation.

because of the differences in the relative weights assigned to each of the rating determinants (Liu and Tan, 2009; Al-Sakka and Ap Gwylim, 2010). In the survey sample smaller disparities are found between Moody's and Fitch (with 55 per cent of similar ratings and only 1 notch differences); between S&P's and Fitch divergences are not more than 1 notch (to 56.5 per cent); but between Moody's and S&P's ratings are always different, even up to 3 notches (to 10.3 per cent).

Then, among the main economic and financial indicators used by agencies to determine sub-sovereign ratings, we have properly selected (on the basis of the previous literature results) the key variables of the probit model (Table 11.2). It is expected that agencies ratings are positively depended on these indicators: local GDP per capita (PILL), financial autonomy (AFIN), fiscal autonomy (AIMP), current balance (MCOR); while adversely affected by the following variables: expenditure on loans repayment (SDEB), spending on debt (SINT), local debt per capita (INDL), net borrowing (surplus or financial needs) as a percentage of total revenues (SALD) and Southern Italy (MEZ), the latter as a dummy for the geographic location of the sampled sub-sovereign entities. Finally, before the analysis both PILL and INDL variables have been submitted to a logarithmic transformation in order to purge their unit of measure; therefore, in the following discussion we will use the two transformed variables, PILL_log and INDL_log respectively.

After that, we have analytically gathered in an *ad hoc* database both financial and demographic data by the annual reports from 2004 to 2008 of the 31 provinces and 35 provincial capitals rated in Italy. Data are published both by government sources (such as Home Office, ISTAT and Unioncamere) and by company and institutional sources. A significant problem concerned the indicator of GDP per capita for the provincial capitals, which is essential for analysis but hardly detectable. So it has been extrapolated from the provincial GDP per capita, using it as a proxy. Finally, because of the (partial and/or total) lack of data or the existence of outliers in the sample, we have eliminated 8 of the 319 observations, all related to provincial capitals, for a total of 311 observations actually considered for the empirical analysis.

11.4.2 Main results of the empirical analysis

Subsequently, the multinomial ordered probit model has been implemented by *Stata®–version 10.0*. Cut-off points are listed below with $\delta_i$rather than μ_i, since the Stata® software absorbs the intercept in them: $\delta_i = \mu_i - \beta_0$.

In addition, in the probit model the so-called *pseudo-R^2* is equivalent to the coefficient of determination (R^2) in the linear regression; it varies between 0 and 1, and measures the goodness of fit of the model, namely the variance of the dependent variable (that is, rating) explained by independent variables on the whole. There are several versions of pseudo-R^2 and the most used is McFadden's one (1974), or likelihood ratio index (LRI), expressed by default in Stata® as follows:

$$LRI = 1 - \frac{\ln L}{\ln L_0} \tag{11.5}$$

where *ln L* is the log-likelihood function of the model (and it's always negative), while *ln* L_0 it's the same function calculated with only an intercept (or constant), that is: $|\ln L| \le |\ln L_0|$.

If the estimated model has no explanatory power, the relationship between the two log-likelihood functions is equal to 1 ($LRI = 0$); on the contrary, if $\ln L = 0$, then $LRI = 1$.

The pooled results on the three samples distinguished by each agency are summarized as follows: originally, to capture the rating peculiarities for typology of local governments, we have decomposed the analysis whether it was a province or a provincial capital; then, in order to increase the number of observations so as to achieve statistically robust and more generalizable results, we have aggregated local governments rated by the same agency even for their methodologies generally reported to LRG without any distinction. Consequently, the geographical variable (MEZ) has been eliminated and an additional dummy has been included (named PROV), which is equal to 1 for

Table 11.3 Results of the ordered probit model for local governments rated by Moody

	Coeff. $\hat{\beta}$	Robust standard error
PILL_log	4.68***	0.78
AFIN	5.09*	2.01
AIMP	−6.70**	2.08
MCOR	−2.57*	1.10
SDEB	−3.50**	1.13
SINT	−19.42*	9.19
INDL_log	−0.34	0.34
SALD	0.26	3.32
PROV	−1.13	0.83
δ_1	39.17***	6.33
δ_2	40.74***	6.32
δ_3	42.21***	6.43
δ_4	45.21***	6.62
Observations	94	
Pseudo R^2	0.44	
Estimated log-likelihood function	65.34	
Wald $\chi^2(9)$	88.98	0.00

Note: * p<0.05; ** p<0.01; *** p<0.001

provinces and 0 for provincial capitals (the latter, more numerous, represent the so-called *base group*).

Including in the first pooled sub-sample the 49 provinces and 45 provincial capitals (out of 48)[3] rated by Moody's in the period 2004 to 2008, the ordered probit analysis is run on 94 observations (Table 11.3). The regression model on the whole is statistically significant: testing the hypothesis $R^2 = 0$ by the *Wald chi-square* tests, we obtain a very low *p-value* (less than 0.001) and so reject the null hypothesis. In particular, as indicated by the *pseudo-*R^2 value, 44.37 per cent of ratings assigned by Moody's to the Italian local governments are explained by the overall explanatory variables. Only six variables show statistically significant coefficients: PILL_log at 99.9 per cent, AIMP and SDEB at 99 per cent, while AFIN, MCOR and SINT at 95 per cent. But among the statistically significant variables AIMP and MCOR don't confirm their expected sign.

In the sub-sample of the Italian local governments rated by S&P's between 2004 and 2008, 23 provinces and 57 provincial capitals (out of 58)[4], for a total of 80 observations, are included (Table 11.4). The ordered probit model on the whole is statistically significant (*p-value* <0.001). However, its goodness

Table 11.4 Results of the ordered probit model for local governments rated by S&P

	Coeff. $\hat{\beta}$	Robust standard error
PILL_log	4.32***	1.02
AFIN	−0.53	2.51
AIMP	0.90	1.94
MCOR	0.81	1.11
SDEB	−0.37	0.88
SINT	−1.28	11.40
INDL_log	−0.58	0.54
SALD	−0.84	1.29
PROV	−1.72	1.25
δ_1	36.60***	7.91
δ_2	36.87***	7.92
δ_3	37.81***	8.07
δ_4	37.99***	8.11
δ_5	39.24***	8.25
δ_6	40.88***	8.28
Observations	80	
Pseudo R^2	0.18	
Estimated log-likelihood function	−87.94	
Wald $\chi^2(9)$	64.60	0.00

Note: * p<0.05; ** p<0.01; *** p<0.001

of fit (expressed by the *pseudo-R*^{2}) is limited to only 17.80 per cent, that is the percentage of ratings assigned by S&P's to the Italian local governments that all the explanatory variables can explain. In addition, only the PILL_log variable has a statistically significant explanatory power on the dependent variable (RATING) with a confidence level of 99.9 per cent and confirms its expected sign.

Despite the full availability of financial data for the Italian local governments rated by Fitch in the period from 2004 to 2008, in the estimated ordered probit model some outliers have been excluded.[5] Consequently, all the observations are 137, i.e. 64 provinces and 73 provincial capitals (out of 77) rated (Table 11.5). The ordered probit model on the whole is statistically significant (*p-value* <0.001) and, as indicated by the *pseudo-R*^{2} value, 31.35 per cent of the ratings assigned by Fitch to the Italian local governments are explained by all the explanatory variables. Four variables are statistically significant: PILL_log and SINT with a confidence level of 99.9 per cent, while MCOR and SDEB are significant at 99 per cent. But the MCOR coefficient does not confirm its expected sign.

Table 11.5 Results of the ordered probit model for local governments rated by Fitch

	Coeff. $\hat{\beta}$	Robust standard error
PILL_log	4.69***	0.70
AFIN	−1.19	1.06
AIMP	−0.87	1.01
MCOR	−2.04**	0.75
SDEB	−2.23**	0.71
SINT	−30.80***	6.84
INDL_log	0.25	0.26
SALD	3.20	1.96
PROV	−0.05	0.56
δ_1	42.35***	7.23
δ_2	42.88***	7.27
δ_3	44.42***	7.38
δ_4	45.52***	7.39
δ_5	48.23***	7.53
δ_6	48.83***	7.52
δ_7	49.79***	7.55
Observations	137	
Pseudo R^2	0.31	
Estimated log-likelihood function	122.37	
Wald $\chi^2(9)$	113.70	0.00

Note: * p<0.05; ** p<0.01; *** p<0.001

11.5 Conclusion

In conclusion, given the research limitations mentioned above, the results of empirical analysis partially confirm theoretical expectations, also highlighting differences of evaluation among agencies (so-called *split ratings*) as shown in the literature; therefore, together with the different weights assigned to quantitative indicators of the analysis, there are some doubts about the actual goodness and accuracy of agencies ratings, in this way questionable and subject to further investigations. However, the process of ratings assignment to local governments is also concerned by an essential qualitative assessment, neglected here. But even with caution in the results generalization due to the low number of observations, in agreement with theoretical expectations it's possible to outline determinants of the Italian sub-sovereign credit ratings so far.

By the pooled analyses, only the local GDP per capita is always statistically significant (at 99.9 per cent) and has the expected sign for all three agencies, while other structural and behavioural variables (for example, current balance, expenditure on loans repayment, spending on debt, financial and fiscal autonomy) are significant just for Moody's and/or Fitch, but sometimes don't have the expected sign. But contrary to theoretical expectations and empirical evidence in literature, both local debt per capita and borrowing needs are never statistically significant.

So this study contributes to improve the literature on *public finance* pointing out relevant managerial and operational implications for banks too. While many Italian banks have been implementing for a long time internal methodologies to estimate corporate ratings, that's not yet for governments. In fact, the assessment of larger institutions is often based on the agencies rating, despite the fact that the Bank of Italy has decided banks should proceed to internally verify external ratings, and recently repeated by the Basel Committee. Given the increase in banks' operations in this area as well as the risks growth, but also the absence of official rating assignments for most of the Italian local governments, it's necessary to develop methodologies and techniques for internal evaluations of their creditworthiness, both *ex-ante* and *ex-post*, in order to obtain positive socio-economic consequences (for example, the decrease of actual credit defaults.

Notes

1. Studies about transition matrix and default and recovery rates are in Moody's (2008c), Standard and Poor's (2006, 2009b), Fitch (2006a, 2007, 2009a, 2009d, 2010b).
2. Recent studies about transition matrix and default rates of sub-sovereign governments are in Fitch (2009b, 2010a) and Standard and Poor's (2009c, 2009d).
3. The city of L'Aquila was excluded for the years 2005, 2006, and 2008 because of incomplete and/or lacking data.
4. The city of Rome was excluded for anomalies due to its management by an external commissioner in 2008.
5. In particular, we have excluded the cities of Rome in 2008 and Taranto for the period 2006–8.

References

Afonso, A. (2003) 'Understanding the determinants of sovereign debt ratings: Evidence for the two leading agencies', *Journal of Economics and Finance*, 27, 56–74.

Afonso, A., P. Gomes and P. Rother (2009) 'Ordered response models for sovereign debt ratings', *Applied Economics Letters*, 16, 769–73.

Al-Sakka, R. and O. Ap Gwylim (2010) 'Split sovereign ratings and rating migrations in emerging economies', *Emerging Markets Review*, 11, 79–97.

Arellano, M. (2003) *Panel Data Econometrics* (Oxford: Oxford University Press).

Baltagi, B. H. (2005) *Econometric Analysis of Panel Data* (Chichester UK: John Wiley & Sons).

Baltagi, B. H. and J. M. Griffin (1984) 'Short and long run effects in pooled models', *International Economic Review*, 25, 631–45.
Bhatia, A. V. (2002) 'Sovereign credit ratings methodology: An evaluation', http://www.imf.org/ (homepage), date accessed 01 July 2012.
Bissoondoyal-Bheenick, E., R. Brooks and A.Y.Yip (2006) 'Determinants of sovereign ratings: A comparison of case-based reasoning and ordered probit approaches', *Global Finance Journal*, 17, 136–54.
Bouchet, M. H., E. Clark and B. Groslambert (2003) *Country Risk Assessment. A Guide to Global Investment Strategy* (New York: John Wiley & Sons).
Cantor, R. and F. Packer (1996) 'Determinants and impact of sovereign credit ratings', *Federal Reserve Bank of New York Economic Policy Review*, 2, 37–53.
Cheung, S. (1996) 'Provincial credit ratings in Canada: An ordered probit analysis', http://www.bankofcanada.ca/ (homepage), date accessed 01 July 2012.
Cluff, G. S. and P. G. Farnham (1984) 'Standard & Poor's vs. Moody's: Which city characteristics influence municipal bond ratings?' *Quarterly Review of Economics and Business*, 24, 72–94.
Cosset, J. C. and J. Roy (1991) 'The determinants of country risk ratings', *Journal of International Business Studies*, 22, 135–42.
Cruces, J. J. (2006) 'Statistical properties of country credit ratings', *Emerging Markets Review*, 7, 27–51.
El Daher, S. (1999) 'Credit ratings – an introduction (and the case of sub-sovereign ratings)', http://www.worldbank.org/ (homepage), date accessed 01 July 2012.
Erb, C. B., C.R. Harvey, T. E. Viskanta (1995) 'Country risk and global equity selection', *Journal of Portfolio Management*, 21, 74–83.
Feder, G. and L. V. Uy (1985) 'The determinants of international creditworthiness and their policy implications', *Journal of Policy Modeling*, 7, 133–57.
Ferri, G., L. G. Liu and J. E. Stiglitz (1999) 'The procyclical role of rating agencies: Evidence from the East Asian crisis', *Economic Notes*, 28, 335–55.
Fitch Ratings (2005) 'Municipalities in Europe: The impact of the institutional framework on performance', http://www.fitchratings.com/ (homepage), date accessed 01 July 2012.
——(2006a) 'Sovereign rating transition and default study', http://www.fitchratings.com/ (homepage), date accessed 01 July 2012.
——(2006b) 'Issuer default and recovery ratings: Frequently asked questions' ,http://www.fitchratings.com/ (homepage), date accessed 01 July 2012.
——(2006c) 'International rating methodology for local and regional governments', http://www.fitchratings.com/ (homepage), date accessed 01 July 2012.
——(2007) 'Sovereign rating transition and default study (1995–2006)', http://www.fitchratings.com/ (homepage), date accessed 01 July 2012.
——(2008a) 'Institutional framework of Italian subnationals', http://www.fitchratings.com/ (homepage), date accessed 01 July 2012.
——(2008b) 'International rating methodology for local and regional governments', http://www.fitchratings.com/ (homepage), date accessed 01 July 2012.
——(2008c) 'Country ceilings', http://www.fitchratings.com/ (homepage), date accessed 01 July 2012.
——(2009a) 'Sovereign 2008 transition and default study', http://www.fitchratings.com/ (homepage), date accessed 01 July 2012.
——(2009b) 'Default, transition, and recovery: 2008 default and transition study for international LRGs', http://www.fitchratings.com/ (homepage), date accessed 01 July 2012.

——(2009c) 'Rating subnationals above the sovereign in the Euro Area', http://www.fitchratings.com/ (homepage), date accessed 01 July 2012.
——(2009d) 'Sovereign rating methodology', http://www.fitchratings.com/ (homepage), date accessed 01 July 2012.
——(2010a) 'International public finance 2009 transition and default study', http://www.fitchratings.com/ (homepage), date accessed 01 July 2012.
——(2010b) 'Sovereign 2009 transition and default study', http://www.fitchratings.com/ (homepage), date accessed 01 July 2012.
Gaillard, N. (2006) 'Determinants of Moody's and S&P's subsovereign credit ratings', http://69.175.2.130/~finman/ (homepage), date accessed 01 July 2012.
——(2009) 'The determinants of Moody's sub-sovereign ratings', *International Research Journal of Finance and Economics*, 31, 194–209.
Greene, W. H. (2003) *Econometric Analysis*, (New Jersey: Prentice Hall).
Haque, N. U., M. S. Kumar, N. Mark and D. J. Mathieson (1996) 'The economic content of indicators of developing country creditworthiness', *IMF Staff Papers*, 43, 688–724.
Hu, Y. T., R. Kiesel and W. Perraudin (2002) 'The estimation of transition matrices for sovereign credit ratings', *Journal of Banking and Finance*, 26, 1383–406.
Kaminsky, G. and S. L. Schmukler (2002) 'Emerging market instability: Do sovereign ratings affect country risk and stock returns?' *World Bank Economic Review*, 16, 171–95.
Lee, S. H. (1993) 'Are the credit ratings assigned by bankers based on the willingness of LDC borrowers to repay?' *Journal of Development Economics*, 40, 349–59.
Liu, L. and K. S. Tan (2009) 'Subnational credit rating: A comparative review', http://www.worldbank.org (homepage), date accessed 01 July 2012.
McFadden, D. (1974) 'The measurement of urban travel demand', *Journal of Public Economics*, 3/4, 303–28.
Meldrum, D. H. (2000) 'Country risk and foreign direct investment', *Business Economics*, 34, 30–7.
Mellios, C. and E. Paget-Blanc (2006) 'Which factors determine sovereign credit ratings?' *European Journal of Finance*, 12, 361–77.
Moody's (2001) 'Revised country ceiling policy', http://www.moodys.com/ (homepage), date accessed 01 July 2012.
——(2005a) 'L'applicazione dell'analisi di inadempienza correlata a emittenti legati alla pubblica amministrazione', http://www.moodys.com/ (homepage), date accessed 01 July 2012.
——(2005b) 'Introduzione allo Statistical Handbook di Moody's: regioni ed enti locali non statunitensi', http://www.moodys.com/ (homepage), date accessed 01 July 2012.
——(2005c) 'Revised policy with respect to country ceilings', http://www.moodys.com/ (homepage), date accessed 01 July 2012.
——(2006a) 'The local currency deposit ceiling', http://www.moodys.com/ (homepage), date accessed 01 July 2012.
——(2006b) 'Italia: regioni ed enti locali', Moody's Rating and Analysis, http://www.moodys.com/ (homepage), date accessed 01 July 2012.
——(2006c) 'Applicazione dell'analisi di default congiunto a regioni ed enti locali', http://www.moodys.com/ (homepage), date accessed 01 July 2012.
——(2007) 'Regioni ed enti locali non statunitensi', Rating Methodology, http://www.moodys.com/ (homepage), date accessed 01 July 2012.
——(2008a) 'Italia: regioni ed enti locali. Aggiornamento' , http://www.moodys.com/ (homepage), date accessed 01 July 2012.

——(2008b) 'Regioni ed enti locali non statunitensi. Aggiornamento metodologico', http://www.moodys.com/ (homepage), date accessed 01 July 2012.

——(2008c) 'Sovereign defaults and interference: Perspectives on government risks', http://www.moodys.com/ (homepage), date accessed 01 July 2012.

——(2008d) 'Rating migration and default rates of non-U.S. sub-sovereign debt issuers (1983–2007)', http://www.moodys.com/ (homepage), date accessed 01 July 2012.

——(2008e) 'Gli enti locali italiani ed i rating Moody's', http://www.moodys.com/ (homepage), date accessed 01 July 2012.

——(2008f) 'Regional and local governments: Global crisis has widely diverging impact', http://www.moodys.com/ (homepage), date accessed 01 July 2012.

——(2008g) 'The application of joint default analysis to regional and local governments', http://www.moodys.com/ (homepage), date accessed 01 July 2012.

——(2009) 'Non-U.S. regional and local governments', http://www.moodys.com/ (homepage), date accessed 01 July 2012.

Mora, N. (2006) 'Sovereign credit ratings: Guilty beyond reasonable doubt?' *Journal of Banking and Finance*, 30, 2041–62.

Mulder, C. and R. Perrelli (2001) 'Foreign currency credit ratings for emerging markets economies', http://www.imf.org/ (homepage), date accessed 01 July 2012.

Oetzel, J. M., R.A. Bettis and M. Zenner (2001) 'Country risk measures: How risky are they?', *Journal of World Business*, 36, 128–45.

Oral, M., O. Kettani, J. C. Cosset and M. Daouas (1992) 'An estimation model for country risk rating', *International Journal of Forecasting*, 8, 583–93.

Reinhart, C. M. (2002) 'Default, currency crises, and sovereign credit ratings', *World Bank Economic Review*, 16, 151–70.

Standard & Poor's (2006) 'Sovereign credit ratings: A primer', http://www.standardandpoors.com/ (homepage), date accessed 01 July 2012.

——(2007a) 'Rating international local and regional governments: A primer', http://www.standardandpoors.com/ (homepage), date accessed 01 July 2012.

——(2007b) 'Western European local and regional government credit survey', http://www.standardandpoors.com/ (homepage), date accessed 01 July 2012.

——(2008) 'Rating liquidity assessments for municipal issuers', http://www.standardandpoors.com/ (homepage), date accessed 01 July 2012.

——(2009a) 'Rating international local and regional governments', http://www.standardandpoors.com/ (homepage), date accessed 01 July 2012.

——(2009b) 'Default, transition, and recovery: Sovereign defaults and rating transition data (2008 update)', http://www.standardandpoors.com/ (homepage), date accessed 01 July 2012.

——(2009c) 'U.S. municipal rating transitions and defaults (1986–2009)', http://www.standardandpoors.com/ (homepage) date accessed 01 July 2012.

——(2009d) 'Default, transition, and recovery: 2008 default and transition study for international LRGs', http://www.standardandpoors.com/ (homepage), date accessed 01 July 2012.

Stock, J. H. and M. W. Watson (2007) *Introduction to Econometrics* (second edition) (Boston: Pearson-Addison Wesley).

Wooldridge, J. M. (2002) *Econometric Analysis of Cross Section and Panel Data* (Cambridge: MIT Press).

Verbeek, M. (2006) *Econometria* (Bologna: Zanichelli).

12
Evolution of the Finance Function in the Italian Local Public Bodies

Fabrizio Quarta and Pasquale Stefanizzi

12.1 Introduction

In recent times several factors like financial speculation, high amount of sovereign debt in the Euro area, political and economic problems for the smaller countries and the consequent reduction of credit ratings (for example Greece, Ireland, Portugal, Belgium, and so on) as well as the increase in spreads between borrowing rates of the different actors has brought the issue of public administration funding to the fore. More specifically public finance has been over many years the focus of research by professionals and practitioners since the Government and the local authorities have experimented with new tools for collection of financial resources, due to the changed economic and financial environment. This practice has been defined by the word "Finanza Innovativa" (Matraia and Mazzillo, 2007) and it is characterized by the following characteristics:

- it is an alternative to the traditional practice,
- it includes sophisticated financial strategies and tools, compared to the usual practice in public finance,
- it is developed specifically to gather financial resources.

The use of derivatives by local authorities is a new concept in order to fit with the new context in which the local authority operates. The purpose of such operations is to ensure solvency to the local authority within the short term without compromising its strength in the longer term. The financial tools are therefore an inner part of the strategy and do not 'live' outside it (Bisconti, 2005). The combination of such financial tools is managed according to grades of responsibility by professionals from different backgrounds who must be able to interact and deal with the specific financial markets and with all the subjects institutionally involved in these markets (Trudu, 2008).

The aim of this study is to understand the innovative state of the art in public finance in Italy. The approach adopted is as follows:

- a *descriptive-deductive* introduction to the background of the cultural, social, economic and financial changes in public institutions that led to adopt new innovative financial instruments,
- an *experimental-inductive* approach to the analysis of regulatory developments and the identification of the scope of the phenomenon in Italy.

12.2 Change of setting: from derivative to self-contained finance

Since the nineties, there have been few changes in the financial setting of local authorities in Italy (Salvemini, 1998) leading to the so-called shift from derivative to self-contained finance. The areas in which the above changes have occurred can be grouped into different classes of intervention: cultural, social, financial, regulatory and institutional.

On the cultural side there has been a rapid implementation of principles of privatization from the local authorities based on efficient management (both internal and external) and the development of advanced systems of management. This has resulted in the transformation of some functions of local authorities, including the financial one, which started adopting operational tools unknown hitherto. It is not to underestimate the choice made by the law makers to separate the power to direct and control (pertaining to the policy-maker), from the management (allocated to the bureaucratic apparatus of the body).

On the social front, the general improvement of living standards of citizens has led, as in other industrialized countries, to greater interest and a more sophisticated awareness of health and the environment, better healthcare services, greater attention to recreational and cultural activities resulting in an increase of public expenditure by local authorities.

On the economic-financial side, the progressive growth of financial autonomy of local agencies determined also a reduction of funding available from the Central State. This is a result of the 1990 reforms giving more responsibility in terms of investments to the local bodies. Currently local governments are in charge of planning and managing functions. This has given them the power to develop specific policies aimed at promoting and developing the local economies as well as improving the relationship between the local community of users and the services.

12.3 Main reforms and provisions

In this complex and rapidly evolving context, a major legislative reform process has taken place that led local authorities towards the adoption of alternative means of funding able to exploit the good financial market conditions. The concessions offered by the Central Government in terms of debt and limited risks (especially that of credit) were exploited by local authorities, who have made an irresponsible and excessive use of innovative financial instruments.

12.3.1 Law of 8 June 1990 No 142

The genesis of this process is identified in the law 8 June 1990, No 142, art. 32 allowing local authorities (municipalities and provinces), to issue bonds;[1] an opportunity confirmed by subsequent laws and regulations,[2] which have widened the scope of innovation by allowing public bodies to adopt much more complex forms of direct and indirect use of the financial market.

12.3.2 Law 28 December 2001, No 448

Following Law 41 of 28 December 2001, No 448, concerning arrangements for the preparation of single and multiple annual budget, where liberalization has been provided:

- to allow access to credit by local governments,
- to enable renegotiation of mortgage contracts after 31 December 1996.

The latter activity allows opportunities for innovative finance, as it emerges from the ongoing need for public bodies to employ an active attitude towards the issue of funding and obliges them to look into more convenient alternatives as well as a different relationship between public bodies and the banking system. This has resulted in the launch of a series of activities typical of the governing body of private organizations, such as:

- comparative assessment of the cost-effectiveness of various financial instruments,
- constant verification of their efficiency.

The ongoing confrontation between the financing instruments held in the portfolio and the ongoing dynamic and competitive environment highlighted different needs of new professional skills to be included in the public authorities making up the so-called 'Finance function' within the public sector.

12.3.3 Provision 1 December 2003, n. 389

In December 2003, Regulation No 389 envisaged the opening of a dialogue between the Central State (Ministry of Economy) and the local authorities to help monitoring of financial resources and operations in derivatives markets created by them. The outcome was that:

Provinces, municipalities, unions of municipalities, metropolitan cities, Communities, consortia of local authorities and regions must notify to the Ministry of Economy and Finance all data on the use of net short-term credit from the banking system, the loans taken out by subjects outside the Government, the derivative transactions and issued bonds as well as the completed securitization transactions by the 15th of the months of February, May, August and November of each year;

the Ministry of Economy and Finance coordinates the access to capital markets by local authorities. Coordination is limited to the operations of medium-and long-term or the securitization amount equal to or greater than 100 million euro;[3]

the contracts for the management of a fund for the repayment of amortization of capital or, alternatively, of a swap for debt relief can only be concluded with intermediaries marked with appropriate credit, as certified by internationally recognized agencies of credit rating.

In the case of borrowing transactions in currencies other than the euro, you are obliged to provide for the coverage of foreign exchange risk through *exchange rate swaps*;

only in relation to due liabilities the following derivative operations are allowed – when indexed to monetary parameters of the Group of Seven most industrialized nations –:

a) *Interest rate swaps* between two people taking the commitment to regularly exchange streams of interest, linked to the main parameters of the financial market, according to contractual terms and conditions;
b) purchase of *forward rate agreement* in which two parties agree on the interest rate that the buyer of the forward agrees to pay a capital fixed at a specified future date;
c) purchase of *cap* interest rate where the buyer is guaranteed by increases in the interest payable over the preset level;
d) purchase of *collar* of interest rate where the buyer is guaranteed a level of interest rate payment, floating within a pre-fixed minimum and maximum value;
e) other derivatives containing combinations of transactions referred to above, allowing the transition from fixed to floating and to achieve a fixed threshold value, or fixed period of time;
f) other derivative transactions aimed at restructuring the debt, only if they do not provide a deadline later than that associated with the underlying liabilities. Such transactions are allowed if the flows received by the institutions are equal to those paid in the underlying liabilities and do not involve, at the time of their development, a rising profile of the present values of the individual payment flows, with the exception of any discount or prize at the conclusion of

the regular operations of not more than 1 per cent of the notional amount of the underlying liabilities;

if the total nominal amount of derivatives transactions entered into by the local authority rose to more than 100 million euros, the body will gradually strive to ensure that the total nominal amount of transactions with any single counterparty does not exceed 25 per cent of the total outstanding transactions.

12.3.4 Circular of the Ministry of Economy and Finance 27 May 2004

The Ministry of Economy is back again on the subject regarding access to capital markets by local authorities, through the explanatory circular of 27 May 2004, stating that the purpose of the provision is to ensure that access to the Public capital markets is efficient, regulated and risk averse. The types of derivative transactions allowed, in addition to the swap exchange rate (*cross currency swap*) to hedge the currency risk in the case of foreign currency debt, are those specified in points (a) to (d) in the form of '*plain vanilla*'. In particular, point (a) means excluding any form of optionality, while points (b), (c) and (d) relates only to the purchase of independent tools specifically recalled. When purchasing a collar it is possible to buy a cap and the simultaneous sale of a floor, this is only allowed to finance the protection from rising interest rates that came from the purchase of the cap. The level of the rate charged to the body, once the triggering thresholds, have been achieved must be consistent both with current market rates and with the cost of the liability prior to the termination of the derivative. With regard to 'other derivatives' under (e) and (f), it was also stated that the same shall in any event be attributable to the combination of the transactions referred to in points (a) to (d). It is believed that these types are consistent with the containment of exposure to financial risks by the Authority resulting from the rise in interest rates and thus aimed at containing the cost of borrowing. Regarding the letter (f): In addition, the prohibition of a 'rising profile of the present values' should be reported as part of the derivative to the flow of payment by the Institution. This provision is intended to prevent the local authorities from carrying out derivative transactions whose payment by the independent flows are concentrated near the end. The exception of any discount or premium, not exceeding 1 per cent of the notional amount of the underlying liabilities, was made for the restructuring of liabilities in the presence of different market conditions than at the time in which it was contracted. It was also emphasized that such discount or premium should be adjusted at the same start date (regulation) of the derivative operation and applies only to operations of the planned restructuring, in fact, from the point f). The legislation has limited to the money market or interest rates in the short term, the scope of the parameters that can be indexed as all derivative transactions described in the preceding paragraphs.

12.3.5 Law 27 December 2006, No 296

The Parliament, through paragraphs 736, 737, 738 and 739 of Article 1 of the Finance Act 2007, has further regulated the matter by inserting provisions aimed at establishing the principal use of derivatives, or to hedge against the risk of increased interest rates and, consequently, to prescribe the use of these for speculative purposes (Malizia, 2006).

12.3.6 Circular of the Ministry of Economy and Finance 31 January 2007

In order to operationalize the dictates of the Finance Act 2007, the Ministry of Economy through its circular of 31 January 2007, has clarified some aspects of interpretation. The objective of the derivative must be to give greater stability to the financial statements of entities through the control of the final cost of operations, to be evaluated in relation to exposure to market risks coming along with the same carried-out operations. In other words, the conditions of the operations must be the result of a balance between the two variables: the total cost and market risk. The Ministry of Economy and Finance has to be informed in advance of the transactions. This is valuable in both form (the census allows the operations in question) and substance (ineffectiveness of the contract in case of failure to transmit advance). The obligation to notify, prior to the signing, the Treasury Department must take place organically, i.e. through the presentation of the contract accompanied by additional documentation and detailing the underlying transactions. The information concerning the financial operations of indebtedness must be included in specific lists, and regularly updated throughout the contract period.

12.3.7 Circular of the Ministry of Economy and Finance 22 June 2007

In this circular it was stated that derivatives are instruments of debt management and not forms of debt; it follows that there should not be granted delegations of payment on these products.

12.3.8 Legislative Decree 17 September 2007, No 164

The Minister of Economy and Finance, after consulting the Bank of Italy and Consob – has defined public professional customers with a regulation as well as establishing identification criteria of public entities that – upon request – may be treated as professionals via an application process. With reference to the latter, the focus is on to the role and responsibility of local authorities (or the manager!) in signing the derivative transactions, thus defining the authority as 'qualified practitioner or professional'. This issue has important consequences when it comes to membership or not of the category of professionals since it triggers different mechanisms of control and protection of the investors. Specific to local authorities, when a manager/public servant takes responsibility by signing a contract, by also stating the category of the belonging qualified Authority he gives an objective and indisputable form of identification of the person in charge of carrying out specific financial transactions in the public sector.

12.3.9 Law 24 December 2007, No 244

Further important details about the use of derivatives by public bodies have been included in art. 1, paragraphs 381, 382, 383 and 382 of the Finance Act 2008. The objective of this legislation has been dictated to ensure greater transparency in the use of derivatives, trying to objectively and operationally involve the Ministry of Economy in the sense of the effectiveness of interest rate swap agreements. The use of derivatives must be part of a public activity, inextricably part of a conscious strategy of debt management. In order to decide clearly on the possibility of concluding a contract or not, a public administrator must have an accurate picture of the characteristics of the product they are using, the risks associated with the influence of the market parameters on the components of the product and therefore, must be aware of the effects of debt on the positions at which the product refers, more generally, on the effects that the strategy has on the budget. The same awareness needs to be, then, maintained during the life of the contract, in order to be able to verify the effectiveness of the strategy due to changes in market conditions.

12.3.10 The Legislative Decree 25 June 2008, No 112[4]

When it is turned on, a swap should come into balance with the so-called 'legs', i.e. to pay and receive equally according to the rates calculated with the structure of the time. However the up-front causes an imbalance at the start and is, in essence, a kind of financing, so it is appropriate to consider it as a debt. Article 62 of the aforementioned Legislative Decree states:

- local authorities are forbidden (for at least 12 months) to sign derivative financial instruments until the entry into force of a specific regulation;
- forced to resort to forms of debt repayment arrangements that provide for the amortization instalments, thus excluding the possibility for local governments to issue bonds with limited duration (so-called bullet);
- limited the maximum length of amortization (in terms of emissions and other debt instruments) to 30 years;
- envisaged the (paragraph 9) consideration of debt upfront, and has subsequently explained the nature of these amounts (by transposing into national law, as decided by Eurostat in a recent communication to member countries) and their inclusion in the budget among debts.

12.3.11 Law 22 December 2008, No 203

The Finance Act 2009 confirmed the blocking of transactions in derivatives, already provided with the original text of the bill, for the minimum period of one year, but allowed the restructuring of existing derivatives that due to changes in the underlying liability, are no longer effective hedges. It has dismissed the contracts of transactions in derivatives, that were concluded after its entry into force, which do not contain the information required in the contract, as well as evidence from the public to have gained a full understanding of the nature of the instrument and its effects on the budget. The nullity of the contract can only be re-valued by the Authorities. The provisions relating to the purely technical indication of the necessary information, to be described in the Italian language in the contract have been delegated to one or more subsequent regulations of the Ministry of Economy, to be adopted after consulting the Bank of Italy and Consob, likewise there should be a regulation of the types of derivative transactions allowed for the local authorities. It 'was expected to transmit monthly to the competent offices of the Court of Auditors, by the Department of the Treasury, of all documents received from 1 January 2009, and concerning the derivatives of local authorities. The review by the Court of Accounts is no longer part of the split analysis on institutions, but takes a more "focused" approach on the specific operation of the market.

12.3.12 Critical analysis of national legislation

As noted above, the Finance Act of 2002 granted to local authorities the opportunity to subscribe to derivative financial instruments in order to encourage the restructuring of debt and reduce operating costs, then this possibility has been extended to credit default swaps, CDS, but, over time, public administrators have come up with creation (in a destructive way) of speculative financial instruments without attempting any precautionary measure and with increased risk to local authorities. On top of this, the administrative teams were forced to employ a largely unknown vocabulary and to use complex software programs for the pricing of derivatives. To stem the rampant use of creative financing, the frightening increase in potential debt that would be generated at the end of the instruments in question, the high cost (determined by both the cost but also obvious from the so-called 'hidden costs') and to contain conflicts of interests within the banks (who often play the role of consultants to the local authorities, due to ignorance on the part of public administrators, and counterparties of the contracts), the Parliament (by the Finance Act 2009) made a radical choice, opposite to the previous one, forbidding to enter into new derivative contracts. A case that has attracted considerable attention and is summarized below in order to clarify the scope of operations is about the Municipality of Milan (Nicolai, 2011), which in 2005 was signed a thirty-year term swaps, tied to a bond issue of 1.68 billion euro. In four years, the town has accumulated a loss on mark to market valuation of around 300 million euro and implicit transaction costs in a range between 73 and 88 million euro. The judiciary has also shown that, already at the conclusion of the contract, the City had a loss of 51 million euro, a situation prohibited by the rules. The Milan Court charged officials of the banks (Deutsche Bank, UBS, JP Morgan, Depfa) with aggravated fraud, the leaders of the same banks are also under investigation because they would not be able to prevent crimes committed by their officials to have drawn economic benefit from their illegal conduct and have argued that the debt restructuring would rather be advantageous for the City, as prescribed by the rule. Despite the questioning of the implicit costs and the public administrator, as a qualified operator, stating in the contract to be able to determine and understand the scope of the transaction, what is not clear is the disclosure of these statements (according to the principles of fairness and transparency of the FCA). The costs involved in the price of a swap, also cause the value of the flows exchanged by the two parties to be different at the start of the contract. The lack of parity between the initial contractual positions has, for example, led the Tar in Tuscany to recognize a process of self-defence with which the Province of Pisa has annulled the decisions of a debt restructuring project with derivatives, despite allocating the decision to the competent court on the validity of the contract.[5] The copious cost issue was also the subject in mid-2009 of a hearing in the Senate of the Bank of Italy (Franco, 2009). On that occasion it was found that often derivatives are connected with implied commissions, sometimes quite expensive, which may make the contractual terms not aligned with those prevailing in the market (Vesentini, 2009).

In summary therefore the organs involved were wrong in the management of the affair:

- the Parliament, during the entire regulatory process, should have proceeded with extreme caution, weighing more practical and professional risks in the derivatives before offering the opportunity to subscribe to local authorities. In this way additional costs of justice and of bureaucratic operations could have been avoided;
- the peripheral administrators should fully understand the scope of the positive but also destructive power of the tools before assigning these, thus affecting financial stability and credibility of their budgets to public opinion;
- the Bank of Italy should have anticipated the consequences of an inappropriate usage of such financial tools;
- the State Audit Office should have acted more quickly to evaluate individual operations and alert the Parliament about the illegitimate use of the same phenomenon before it assumed huge proportions (as will be stated in the following part of the work);

- also the financial intermediaries who have created and signed operations should have been monitored. In fact they viewed the economic interests by overestimating the short term and underestimating the consequences that in the medium / long term would have created in terms of reputation to the system and increased costs of justice arising from litigation.

12.4 The size of the phenomenon

In order to understand what is the extent of the phenomenon of derivatives in local authorities it was decided to revise, through the use of some indicators of synthesis of descriptive statistical analysis, the official figures (as of 31 December 2010) regarding indebtedness of the various entities and their use of the financial instruments in question.[6]

From Table 12.1 you can conclude that the most heavily indebted local authorities were around 31 December 2010, the Regions, which are responsible, in the logic of federalism, for the highest amount of operational activities (e.g. if only to health), followed by non-capital municipalities, which absorb as much as 24.44 per cent of total debt, the capital provinces (with 23 per cent), provinces (9.01 per cent) and finally the mountain and island communities and the Unions of Boroughs (0.28 per cent).

Examining the nature of debt, the following facts emerge:

- municipalities thrive in the banking system because their base absorbs as much as 32.92 per cent of the total of this specific form of debt, followed by the regions, which account for 31.06 per cent of debt to banks;
- thanks to the high volume requirements, and thus the higher credit rating, emissions for the regions are the second most important form of

Table 12.1 Summary of outstanding debt at 31 December 2010

	Local authorities	Mortgages with banks	Public cash loans	Mortgage DD.PP. Spa	Overall issue Value	%
Regione	18,634.78	7,707.47	4,496.55	15,244.69	46,083.50	43.27%
Provincia	5,479.64	6.04	560.67	3,548.15	9,594.49	9.01%
Comune capoluogo	15,910.21	13.59	958.2	7,611.05	24,493.05	23.00%
Comune non capoluogo	19,751.59	116.08	3,658.69	2,498.07	26,024.43	24.44%
Comunità montane e isolane ed Unione dei Comuni	210.38	649.84	66.51	19.45	297	0.28%
Overall	59,986.60	7,843.83	9,740.63	28,921.40	106,492.46	100.00%

Table 12.2 Exposure with respect to derivatives for local authorities as on 31 December 2010

Local authorities	The total notional value (mln €)	N° agencies	Average notional value by agency (mln €)	N° contracts	Average notional value by contracts (mln €)
Regione	17,562.91	18	975,72	95	184.87
Provincia	3,114.03	38	81.95	119	26.17
Comune capoluogo	10,354.77	40	258.87	153	67.68
Comune non capoluogo	3,829.43	454	8.43	593	6.46
Comunità montane e isolane ed Unione dei Comuni	9.83	3	3.28	3	3.28
Overall	34,870.97	553	63.06	963	36.21

debt. Likewise the regions require funds for more than 50 per cent of total emissions;

- the less indebted public bodies are the provinces, which are the target of less than 10 per cent of all funds used by the entire system of financing of the local public spending since the less frequent appeals to the banking system, however these seem to record higher (compared to its average) deficit emissions.

As for the use of derivative financial instruments, from Table 12.2 we can see that, as of 31 December 2010, over 500 public bodies have been the recipients of these particular financial instruments, in particular: 18 regions, 38 provinces, 40 provincial capitals and 454 non-capital municipalities and 3 mountain communities or associations of municipalities, for a notional total of €36,210,764.86. The breakdown by number of entities involved has a large prevalence of Municipalities, both capital and non capital, followed by provinces and regions, with a residual component of mountain communities (0.7 per cent).

Shifting the focus to the average amounts subscribed, both in relation to the type of entity that examined the number of contracts, those made by regional and municipal capital are considered very high. Lowest average notional provincial and municipal non-capital, although the media as a tool for statistical summary, with reference to the latter case, is believed to be far too brief considering that this category of institutions may also include small countries of a few thousand inhabitants.

Table 12.3 Comparison of notional/debt

Type of debt	Regione	Provincia	Comune capoluogo	Comune non capoluogo	Overall
Total debt (mln €)	41,084.76	8,451.35	22,097.44	20,620.90	92,254.45
Total notional value (mln €)	16,554.68	3,387.45	11,558.76	3,775.58	35,276.49
Report notional / debt	40.29%	40.08%	52.31%	18.31%	38.24%

The comparison between total debt and notional swap (see Table 12.3) suggests that there is a direct proportionality (straight line ascending) between debt and notional and, therefore, with increasing debt the use of derivative instruments increases at the same speed for all public bodies (in fact it has been said in the introduction that derivatives are 'functional strategy and do not live outside of it').

The only exception to this rule is non-capital municipalities which, against a debt of 20 billion euro, have activated derivative of 3 billion euro with a relative weight of 18.31 of the seconds on the first per cent. The provincial capitals are, on the contrary, local authorities more exposed in Debt/Notional with a margin that exceeds the 50 per cent. Not very different situations are experienced by the regions and provinces for which data are respectively equal to 40.29 per cent and 40.08 per cent.

12.5 Conclusion

In short, today the system of 'financial derivative' – or that system of support and funding focused on the transfer from the state treasury – has come to an end in public finance (Vigorelli et al. 2004). This new situation has created a different attitude in the management of resources (those already available and those to be found on the capital market), forcing a reconsideration of research strategies and allocation of resources according to operational efficiency and effectiveness (Sciandra, 2008). On this assumption there has also been a transformation of 'social' tasks of public bodies, appointed to fill the role of guarantor of the conditions of developing and promoting the factors necessary to the promotion of the local territory, aimed at sustainable growth based on a model that sees economic and social forces of the territory to make a 'unique system' with the central administration. In contrast, however, the Court of Auditors[7] found that the debt is the main financial source to achieve the investment of local authorities,[8] confirming that the expansion of the tasks of local public bodies is not paid a sufficient allocation of own resources.

In this way, then the local authority has taken on the role of promoter of the development of its territory, while the State has focused on the procurement of new funding opportunities from a more structured use of capital market. In agreement with the observations by Nigro (2007), currently, the local authorities in order to respond effectively to their institutional obligations, need to develop knowledge and professionalism so far unknown, in contrast, however, the financial system (especially the banks) must function as a supportive advice on the correct identification of useful products for the purposes of the demanding public Authority, going beyond the logic of commissions from the sale of derivatives otherwise detrimental to the local community.

Notes

1. Law 142/90, art. 32: 'la contrazione dei mutui non previsti espressamente in atti fondamentali del consiglio comunale e la emissione dei prestiti obbligazionari'.
2. *Law December 23, 1994, No 724*, art. 35 and 37 containing, respectively, the issuance of bonds by local governments and local authorities' borrowing. *Legislative Decree 1, April,1996, No 239* introducing changes to the taxation of interest, premium and other gains on bonds and similar securities, issued in implementation of art. 3 of law December 28, 1995, No 549. *Legislative Decree 1, September, 1993, No 385*, art. 129, laying down provisions for securities issues. *Ministry of Economy decree 5, July, 1996, No 420,* on the regulation laying down rules for the issuance of bonds by local authorities.

   Legislative Decree 18, August, 2000, No 267, only with the text of the laws on local authorities.
3. To this end, the local government must notify the Department of the Treasury in preparation for the characteristics of the transaction. Within ten days after confirmation of receipt by the Department of the Treasury Department II of the communication, the Department itself may determine which is the most opportune moment for the effective implementation of the operation of market access. In the absence of such determination, the operation can be completed within the next 20 days after confirmation of receipt in the case of bond issues carried out on the market and within the time specified by local authorities in all other cases.
4. Converted with amendments and then merged with art. 3 of the Finance Act 2009.
5. For further information see http://www.provincia.pisa.it/interno.php?id=40025&lang=it
6. Kindly provided by Treasury Department – Directorate II, IV Office.
7. Survey included in Resolution No. 27/7/2005 6 of the Court of Auditors – Section autonomies, report to Parliament on the overall financial management of local authorities in the financial years 2003 and 2004.
8. As is known the art. 119 of the Constitution, as amended by Constitutional Law n.1/2001 has reinforced the principle, already present in ordinary legislation, the exclusive destination for investment income from debt.

References

ABI (2005) 'La gestione del rischio nelle piccole e medie imprese e negli enti locali: il ruolo dei derivati', *Bancaria,* 61, 2–10.

Bisconti, B. (2005) 'La nuova funzione finanza negli Enti locali', http://www.entilocali.provincia.le.it/ (homepage), date accessed 01 July 2012.

Fantetti, F. R. (2010) 'I contratti degli enti pubblici locali in strumenti finanziari derivati', *Responsabilità Civile,* 7, 742–52.

Franco, D. (2009) 'Indagine conoscitiva sull'utilizzo e la diffusione degli strumenti di finanza derivata e delle cartolarizzazioni nelle pubbliche amministrazioni', http://www.bancaditalia.it/ (homepage), date accessed 01 July 2012.

Lanza, M. (2009) 'Gli strumenti derivati negli Enti Locali Italiani', *Esperienze d'impresa,* 17, 83–114.

Luberti, A. (2010) 'Strumenti finanziari derivati: legittime le limitazioni all'autonomia negoziale degli enti locali', *Giurisprudenza italiana,* 10, 2022–7.

Malizia, L. (2006) 'Gli Enti territoriali nella manovra finanziaria 2006: il ruolo della finanza innovativa', *Giustizia amministrativa,* 1, 93–8.

Marotta, G. (2006) 'Aspetti giurisdizionali e responsabilità nell'utilizzo di strumenti finanziari derivati negli enti locali', *La Finanza locale,* 26, 13–41.

Matraia, C. and A. Mazzillo (2007) 'Finanza innovativa o finanza creativa? Effetti contabili e valutazioni di impatto sulle strategie finanziarie delle pubbliche amministrazioni', *Rivista italiana di ragioneria e di economia aziendale,* 107, 395–404.

Moriconi, A. M. and L. Cimbolini (2009) 'Troppa enfasi sui derivati degli enti locali' *La Finanza locale,* 6, 23–26.

Nicolai, M. (2011) *P.A.mphlet* (Sant'Arcangelo di Romagna (RM): Maggioli editore).

Nigro, M. (2007) 'Swap e mercato, un tutor per gli Enti locali', in AA.VV. *Guida agli Enti Locali - Il Sole24Ore* (Milano: Il Sole24Ore).

Romeo, G. (2006) 'Il ricorso agli strumenti finanziari derivati per la ristrutturazione del debito negli enti pubblici locali italiani', *Rivista italiana di ragioneria e di economia aziendale,* 106, 212–26.

Rossi, M. and F. Fontana (2005) 'Gli strumenti finanziari derivati nella contabilità degli Enti locali', in AA.VV. *Guida agli Enti Locali - Il Sole24Ore* (Milano: Il Sole24Ore).

Salvemini, M. T. (1998) 'Il finanziamento degli Enti Locali', http://www.cassaddpp.it/ (homepage), date accessed 01 July 2012.

Sciandra, L. (2008) 'I derivati degli Enti Locali: una rassegna delle informazioni su dimensioni e criticità', *Rivista di diritto finanziario e scienza delle finanze,* 67, 388–418.

Trudu, M. (2008) 'Problematiche connesse all'uso dei contratti su strumenti finanziari derivati da parte degli enti locali', *La Finanza locale,* 28, 26–49.

Vesentini, S. (2009) 'Il giudice civile si pronuncia sui derivati utilizzati dagli enti locali: l'up front nei contratti di Interest Rate Swap', *Responsabilità Civile,* 7, 825–35.

Vigorelli, G., P. Giarda and M.T Salvemini (2004) 'Aspetti e problemi del finanziamento degli Enti Locali, http://www.assbb.it/ (homepage), date accessed 01 July 2012.

13
Project Finance Exposures in the Supervisory Slotting Criteria Approach: Pricing and Judgemental Analysis

Pietro Marchetti and Anna Valeria Venneri

13.1 Introduction

This study fits into the research topic about the pricing and risk management models in the decisions of financial intermediaries. In particular, this work investigates the Project Finance (PF) exposures which are characterized by a specific prudential regulation in the general framework of Basel II, so called Supervisory Slotting Criteria Approach (SSCA). In the Internal Ratings-Based (IRB) approach, banks that don't meet the requirements for the estimation of probability of default (PD) under the corporate Foundation approach for their specialized lending (SL) assets (that include the sub-class of PF) are required to map their internal risk grades to five supervisory categories (strong, good, satisfactory, weak, default), each of which is associated with a specific risk weight depending on both the project's strength and the loan's maturity (M).

This research aims at investigating the impact of the SSCA on the risk-adjusted pricing of PF loans and identifying a subjective model that clarifies the specific risk weights to be considered for mapping projects to the supervisory categories, highlighting the implications on pricing.

For this purpose, we will answer the following research questions:

- In a sample of banks operating in the PF sector in Italy, what is the impact on pricing of the PF loans' classification in the five supervisory rating grades of the SSCA?
- Varying the weights assigned to each of the assessment's PF drivers in the different supervisory risk categories, what are the implications on the pricing of PF loans?

The chapter is structured as follows: Section 13.2 concerns the literature review on bank loans pricing; Section 13.3 describes the methodology and the survey sample for estimating the risk-adjusted pricing of PF loans in the SSCA; the results of this analysis are presented in Section 13.4; a subjective model of judgemental analysis that defines the specific risk weights associated with PF loans in the SSCA is proposed in Section 13.5; finally, Section 13.6 shows some conclusive evidences arising from the analysis, with the explanation of strengths and weaknesses.

13.2 Bank loans pricing: a literature review

There are many research topics about pricing, with different approaches and methodologies: on the one hand, the cost-based or profit-oriented systems (Gabor, 1977), where the price is fixed with a spread in addition (and this is the more appropriate approach for credit); on the other hand, the differential demand-based pricing (Busacca et al., 1993) or competition-based pricing approaches (Hanna and Dodge, 1995).

About the specific literature on bank loans pricing, there are two main approaches of financial intermediaries (McAllister and Mingo, 1994; Cenni, 1998):

- the comparison pricing model, according to which a financial intermediary applies a pricing on the basis of the average pricing in the market for similar loans by type, risk and maturity.
- the intrinsic value pricing approach, according to which a financial intermediary evaluates the intrinsic components of a loan that are at risk of credit exposure and other cost components, identifying the appropriate return. In this sense, the risk-adjusted return on capital (RAROC) and loan arbitrage-free pricing (LAFP) models, the second originally proposed by Dermine (1984) and adapted in the Italian context by Cenni (1998) and De Lisa et al. (2006). In the same approach also the à-la-Merton models based on the options theory (Merton, 1974; Smith, 1980), but their actual application in Italy is limited (Delzio and Maggiori, 2004).

The intrinsic value pricing approach is currently the most utilized by financial intermediaries, especially after Basel II when risk enters into the assessment of counterparties and the consequent bank loans pricing (Zazzara and Cortese, 2004); so banks, in addition to correctly measuring the risk, have to adequately define the pricing of exposures. To protect themselves from credit risk, banks apply increasing pricing to the riskier borrowers that under-represent their risk category. As banks capitalization is related to the borrowers' rating that is linked to their risk, banks adopt a rating-rate model of pricing so that a higher risk is associated with a higher pricing (Cappelletto and Toniolo, 2007). Several authors (English and Nelson, 1998; Machauer and Weber, 1998) have empirically shown that on average the loan pricing increases with the higher risk of the borrower, and vice versa.

The use of internal rating systems for credit risk, apart from reducing the minimum capital requirements and improving the management of credit risk, allows banks to take advantage of the effectiveness of pricing policies (Laviola, 2001) and evaluate the loan's performance (Pelliccioni, 2006). In fact, one of the most important and common uses of the credit risk measurement system is the determination of the 'risk-adjusted pricing' (Resti and Sironi, 2008). An adequate risk-adjusted pricing should allow the coverage of different components depending on both the well-known risk factors (PD, LGD, EAD, M) and the minimum regulatory capital required by the supervisors and 'ideally' due to the loan itself (Resti, 2007).

The main components of pricing are: expected and unexpected credit losses, operating costs and financial costs of liquidity (Zazzara and Cortese, 2004; Hasan and Zazzara, 2006). Therefore, it's possible to draw the logic scheme (in three main phases) by which a bank determines the loan pricing (Nadotti, 2002):

- identify the costs of raising funds;
- identify the costs for credit risk in the strict sense, or 'components of risk costing' (Cenni, 1998), that the bank overturns on customers by pricing;
- identify the price rises for operating risks and others specific of each transaction.

The adoption of procedures for correctly measuring credit risk at the time of lending is necessary not only for an adequate pricing policy of a price-setter bank, but also to estimate the risk-adjusted profitability of a price-taker bank (Marsella, 1997).

Hereinafter we will detail only the first of these two alternatives from a methodological point of view. Considering in the pricing estimate the specific hypothesis of PD, LGD and EL of each transaction, and measuring the economic capital absorption on the basis of the UL approach, for a price-setter and risk-adverse bank the pricing of any credit exposure is given by the following one-year Formula (13.1):

$$r_a = \frac{\left[TIT \times (1 - VaR) + (PD \times LGD) + (k_e \times VaR) + CO\right]}{[1 - (PD \times LGD)]} \tag{13.1}$$

which can also be rewritten as:

$$r_a = \frac{\left[TIT + VaR \times (k_e - TIT) + (PD \times LGD) + CO\right]}{[1 - (PD \times LGD)]} \tag{13.2}$$

where:

- r_a is the risk-adjusted pricing that includes costs not only for expected loss (EL), but also for economic capital (k_e) 'ideally' absorbed respect to unexpected loss (UL) as measured by VaR (Masera, 2005);
- TIT (internal transfer rate) represents the average cost of borrowing and approximates the risk-free rate;
- VaR (value-at-risk) indicates the percentage of bank's capital-at-risk (CaR) needed to cover unexpected losses;
- (PD x LGD) = ELR is the expected loss rate, where PD is probability of default and LGD is loss given default;
- k_e denotes the cost of economic capital held to cover unexpected losses (that is the target of return for shareholders or the return on equity for banks), measured ex-post by the actual ROE that bank pays to shareholders (Resti, 2005; Erzegovesi and Bee, 2008);
- (k_e–TIT) is the risk-premium on economic capital required by shareholders (Saita, 2000; Sironi, 2001);
- CO are the operating costs paid by banks and turned over the transaction.

One of the main limitations of this approach for determining the pricing is represented by the one-year horizon that does not capture the maturity's effects on expected and unexpected losses, and on the transaction's risk-premium, consequently. To overcome this limitation, Corbellini (2002) proposes a simple model of multi-years pricing based on balanced cash flows rather than in terms of percent, which considers the effects of maturity on different variables.

Formula (13.1) shows that TIT is paid only on the part not covered by capital-at-risk (1–VaR), and not on the 100 per cent of funding (De Laurentis and Caselli, 2006). Similarly, r_a is not calculated on the total loan, but only on its share and doesn't become expected loss [1–(PD x LGD)] (De Laurentis, 2001; Resti, 2005).

Formula (13.2) shows that among the pricing determinants there are both those 'sensitive' to the credit risk (ELR, VaR), and 'non-sensitive' ones (TIT, k_e, CO) (De Lisa et al., 2006). Furthermore, 'the remuneration for capital is not equal to the total cost of economic capital, but only to its difference from TIT' (Saita, 2000) because 'the loan is already fully funded by TIT and so it only ideally absorbs capital' (Resti and Sironi, 2008).

In addition, pricing comes from Equations (13.1) and (13.2) and represents the benchmark of a bank's credit policies (Resti, 2005) insofar as the profitability of specific business sectors and credit portfolios can be verified: therefore, pricing should not be rigidly applied but can be changed, to positive or negative, on the basis of the bank's supply policies (Comana, 2002; Pelliccioni, 2006) as well as the soft information (De Laurentis, 2001). It's necessary to determine what weight should be assigned to the risk-adjusted pricing for different counterparties, from a point of view according to which it's a mere not-binding proposal to the opposite that it interprets as a rigid and mandatory rule (Resti and Saita, 2009).

13.3 Pricing in the PF sector: methodology and sample

In order to find out the pricing in the PF sector, from a methodological point of view we consider in Formula (13.1):

- TIT is approximated by the value of Euribor-3months (Resti and Sironi, 2008) listing at 31 December every year; so it's equal to 2.21 per cent in 2004, 2.51 per cent in 2005, 3.73 per cent in 2006, 4.93 per cent in 2007;
- the values which approximate VaR and the product (PD x LGD) are taken from Tables 13.1 and 13.2 concerning the risk weights identified for SSCA by the Basel Committee on Banking Supervision, respectively, for unexpected loss (UL) and expected loss (EL) of PF transactions with maturity (M) $\geq$ 2.5 years; we underline that UL coefficients in Appendix (see Tables from 13.A1 to 13.A5) come from those in Table 13.1 multiplied by 8 per cent for supervisory purposes;
- the values of k_e and CO come from financial statements at 31 December every year as published on BankScope database for each bank belonging to the sample; so k_e is approximated by the ex-post value of ROE (return-on-equity), while CO are considered as percentage of total assets with two decimals. Furthermore, we also consider for each year four indicators available on BankScope in its Global Detailed – Standard Presentation section, that are: total assets, total equity, total operating expense, published net income.

Adding previous items in Formula (13.1), we find that for the SSCA-calculated pricing, as follows:

$$r_a = \frac{[Euribor3months \times (1 - UL) + EL + (ROE \times UL) + CO/TA]}{[1 - EL]} \tag{13.3}$$

Table 13.1 The risk weights for unexpected loss (UL) and expected loss (EL)

	Strong	Good	Satisfactory	Weak	Default
Unexpected Loss (UL)					
M <2.5 years	50%	70%	115%	250%	0%
M ≥ 2.5 years	70%	90%	115%	250%	0%
Expected Loss (EL)					
M <2.5 years	0.0%	0.4%	2.8%	8%	50%
M ≥ 2.5 years	0.4%	0.8%	2.8%	8%	50%

by which we obtain for each of the five regulatory categories (strong, good, satisfactory, weak, default) the value of risk-adjusted pricing for a sample of banks operating in the PF sector in Italy, with two decimals.

We selected our sample among the 35 banks operating in the PF sector in Italy as published in the 'Guida agli operatori del Project Finance 2007' edited by Finlombarda. Among the 24 banks operating as advisory, arranging and lending at the same time, we identified a sub-sample of 20 banks whose financial statements in euro are available on BankScope at 31 December 2004 to 2007 (see Table 13.2). We excluded The Royal Bank of Scotland and Mediobanca whose data are not comparable, respectively, as expressed in pounds and because it ended the year at 30 June instead of 31 December; we also eliminated Banca Popolare Etica and Unipol Merchant because their financial statements are not available on BankScope. Moreover, we excluded banks making a loss rather than a profit at 31 December for some years (BNL, Calyon, Interbanca, WestLB) or having anomalies in their operating costs

Table 13.2 A sample of banks operating in the PF sector in Italy

N.	Bank	Listed
1	Banca Agrileasing S.p.A. (Gruppo ICCREA)	YES
2	Banca IMI S.p.A. (Gruppo Intesa Sanpaolo)	YES
3	Banca OPI S.p.A. (Gruppo Intesa Sanpaolo)	YES
4	Banca Popolare di Sondrio S.c.p.A.	YES
5	Banca Popolare Etica S.c.p.A.	NO
6	BIIS – Banca Infrastrutture Innovazione e Sviluppo S.p.A. (Gruppo Intesa Sanpaolo)	YES
7	BNL S.p.A. (Gruppo BNP Paribas)	YES
8	Calyon S.A. (Gruppo Crédit Agricole)	YES
9	Cassa di Risparmio di Firenze – Banca CR Firenze S.p.A.	YES
10	Centrobanca – Banca di credito Finanziario e Mobiliare S.p.A. (Gruppo UBI Banca)	YES
11	Commerzbank AG (Gruppo Commerzbank)	YES
12	Depfa Bank Plc (Gruppo Hypo Real Estate)	YES
13	Dexia Crediop S.p.A. (Gruppo Dexia Crediop)	YES
14	Efibanca S.p.A. (Gruppo Banco Popolare)	YES
15	Fortis Bank (Gruppo Fortis)	YES
16	Interbanca S.p.A. (Gruppo Banca Antonveneta / ABN Amro)	YES
17	MCC – Mediocredito Centrale S.p.A. (Gruppo Capitalia / Unicredit)	YES
18	Mediobanca S.p.A. (Gruppo Mediobanca)	NO
19	MPS Capital Services Banca per le Imprese S.p.A. (Gruppo MPS)	YES
20	Natixis (Gruppo Banques Populaires / Caisses d'Epargne)	YES
21	The Royal Bank of Scotland Plc (Gruppo RBS)	NO
22	Unicredit Corporate Banking S.p.A. (Gruppo Unicredit)	YES
23	Unipol Merchant – Banca per le Imprese S.p.A. (Gruppo Unipol Banca)	NO
24	WestLB AG (Gruppo WestLB)	YES

(Banca OPI) in order not to compromise the success of the analysis. So only in 2006 we have the whole sub-sample of 20 banks.

13.4 Results

Based on the methodology and sample previously explained, we decided to assess the pricing of banks operating in the PF sector in Italy during the 2004 to 2007 period by the SSCA. The results of empirical analysis are presented in the Appendix (see Tables from 13.A1 to 13.A4), both for each year and four-years' level, where banks are indicated by the number assigned in Table 13.3. As theoretically expected, the pricing increases with the higher risk of PF exposure, with a higher raise for those projects in the 'default' category.

Table 13.3 Main indicators on pricing (2004 to 2007 period)

	2004				
	r Strong	**r Good**	**r Satisfactory**	**r Weak**	**r Default**
Max	6.28%	6.81%	9.12%	16.91%	111.06%
Min	3.25%	3.81%	6.12%	12.36%	104.62%
Mean	4.37%	4.91%	7.21%	14.11%	107.11%
Standard deviation	1.00%	1.01%	1.05%	1.59%	2.18%
	2005				
	r Strong	r Good	r Satisfactory	r Weak	r Default
Max	6.34%	6.93%	9.33%	16.66%	110.74%
Min	3.36%	3.87%	6.13%	12.82%	105.22%
Mean	4.59%	5.15%	7.50%	14.62%	107.35%
Standard deviation	0.90%	0.92%	0.95%	1.22%	1.83%
	2006				
	r Strong	r Good	r Satisfactory	r Weak	r Default
Max	7.62%	8.27%	10.78%	18.61%	112.88%
Min	4.53%	5.03%	7.30%	13.94%	107.64%
Mean	5.60%	6.16%	8.50%	15.56%	109.48%
Standard deviation	0.94%	0.97%	1.02%	1.36%	1.79%
	2007				
	r Strong	r Good	r Satisfactory	r Weak	r Default
Max	8.25%	8.79%	11.17%	18.23%	114.88%
Min	5.75%	6.26%	8.56%	15.28%	110.02%
Mean	6.68%	7.18%	9.49%	16.22%	111.99%
Standard deviation	0.82%	0.81%	0.83%	0.96%	1.72%

Table 13.4 The PF classification in a judgemental model

Range	Supervisory category
$0 \leq Y \leq 5$	Default
$5 < Y \leq 30$	Weak
$30 < Y \leq 60$	Satisfactory
$60 < Y \leq 80$	Good
$80 < Y \leq 100$	Strong

Starting from the results obtained, we developed further statistical analysis in order to determine, for all the five supervisory grades, some simple indicators (maximum, minimum, arithmetic mean, and standard deviation). Table 13.4 concerns only banks whose financial statements are available on BankScope for all the 2004 to 2007 period. So, we can observe the differences emerging by the descriptive statistics conducted on the same banks in different years (see Table 13.3).

In 2004, for the strong, good, and satisfactory categories the minimum and maximum pricing, respectively, belonged to Cassa di Risparmio di Firenze and Dexia Crediop, the former characterized by the higher CO/TA ratio, the latter by a high ROE and a low CO/TA ratio; for the weak category the maximum and minimum pricing, respectively, belonged to Depfa Bank, characterized by the highest level of ROE and the lower CO/TA ratio, and Centrobanca, with limited ROE and CO/TA; for the default category the maximum and minimum pricing, respectively, belonged to Cassa di Risparmio di Firenze and Depfa Bank.

In 2005, for all the five risk categories the maximum pricing belonged to Cassa di Risparmio di Firenze, characterized by the higher CO/TA ratio, while the minimum pricing belonged to Dexia Crediop except for the default category belonging to Depfa Bank, characterized by the highest level of ROE and the lower CO/TA ratio.

In 2006, for the strong, good, and satisfactory categories the minimum and maximum pricing, respectively, belonged to Cassa di Risparmio di Firenze and Dexia Crediop, the first characterized by a high CO/TA ratio, and the latest by a low CO/TA ratio; for the weak category the minimum pricing belonged to Dexia Crediop, while the maximum pricing belonged to Fortis Bank, characterized by the highest level of ROE and a low CO/TA ratio; for the default category the maximum and minimum pricing, respectively, belonged to BNL (with an almost zero level of ROE and the higher CO/TA ratio) and Depfa Bank.

In 2007, for all the supervisory categories the maximum pricing belonged to Cassa di Risparmio di Firenze, characterized by the higher CO/TA ratio, while the minimum pricing belonged to Dexia Crediop except for the weak category belonging to MCC, characterized by an almost zero level of ROE.

During the 2004 to 2007 period, for all the supervisory categories the maximum risk-adjusted pricing belonged to Cassa di Risparmio di Firenze, except in 2004 for the weak category belonging to Depfa Bank; instead, the minimum pricing often belonged to Dexia Crediop except for the default category belonging to Depfa Bank during the 2004 to 2006 period, while for the weak category belonging to Centrobanca in 2004 and MCC in 2007.

Our analysis confirms on average the pricing increases with the higher risk of PF exposure, and during the years it becomes stronger because of the raise in the values of Euribor-3months, ROE and CO/TA ratio, and the decrease of standard deviation. Moreover, we highlight the risk-adjusted pricing obtained is simply a benchmark for the bank's credit policies, according to which checking the actual pricing.

13.5 The subjective judgemental model: a proposal for analysis

In this section we propose a constrained judgement-based analysis for the Italian case, by which banks can assign specific risk weights in the SSCA, and we highlight its implications on pricing of PF exposures. So we use a structured mechanism for qualitative evaluation of projects by subjectively predetermined weights (De Laurentis, 2001).

In order to reduce the inevitable disadvantages of this model, we developed a 'fuzzy' analysis able to well catch information. while reducing the risk of an excessive subjective evaluation by a self-objectivity of the rules' system (if/then-type) able to correct distortions in judgements. The 'fuzzy set' theory was introduced in mathematics by Zadeh (1965) as an alternative to the traditional dichotomous view. In fact, fuzzy logic overcomes the obvious limitations of the binary approach (true/false, 1/0, and so on), for example its excessive rigidity when applied to real problems.

However, fuzzy logic is in general based on the fuzzy boundaries, which are neither clear nor defined, among set elements in and out. Each element of a fuzzy set has an associated membership value variable between 0 and 1, where 0 means it does not belong to the set, while 1 is a complete membership, and intermediate values a partial membership.

After this necessary introduction, please refer to Table 13.A5 in the Appendix, where we show the supervisory slotting criteria for PF exposures established by the Basel Committee on Banking Supervision (2004). We can interpret the proposed model in two ways:

- on the one hand, we show weights subjectively assigned to the five SSCA drivers (financial strength, political and legal environment, transaction characteristics, strength of sponsor, security package) in order to assess Italian PF exposures;

- on the other hand, we propose membership values of different risk factors for all the five supervisory categories (strong, good, satisfactory, weak, default), according to a fuzzy logic because of the membership function continuous between 0 and 1.

So we can express this as follows:

$$Y = \sum_{j=1}^{m} D_j \times \left[\sum_{i=1}^{n} \omega_i \times (x_i \times 100) \right] \tag{13.4}$$

where:

- D_j is the weight of each evaluation driver (j = 1, …, m);
- ω_i is the weight of every individual risk factor for each evaluation driver (i = 1, …, n);
- x_i is the membership value of each risk factor to each supervisory category (i = 1, …, n).

Therefore, the final judgement (Y) on the PF exposure is the result of different weights assigned to individual risk factors, the variation of which modifies the pricing of the PF loan. The project will be classified as shown in Table 13.4 according to the range in which is the final result obtained by Formula (13.4).

For example, we consider two different PF operations only on the basis of presence/absence of a semi-equity financial instrument as well as a participating loan inside the financial structure of the special purpose vehicle (SPV). The presence of the participating loan improves pricing ceteris paribus, because it affects three evaluation drivers of the SSCA, that are:

- the financial strength of the project and, specifically, its cover ratios required by lending banks;
- the strength of the sponsor, through the 'participation clause' of this particular instrument by which the sponsor has to support the project with equity injections, if necessary;
- a security package in order to support the exposure, by restrictive covenants increasing its strength.

We can assign the following weights (see Table 13.1):

- Case A (standard): $x_i = 0.6$ for all the risk drivers;
- Case B (participating loan): $x_i = 0.9$ for only the above-mentioned three advantages, ceteris paribus.

The increased weight of the above-mentioned three risk factors on the final judgement (in the previous example, from 12.6 to 18.9) allows to conclude

Table 13.5 The risk weights assigned to PF exposures in the SSCA

Driver	Case A (standard)	Case B (participating loan)
Financial strength (cover ratios)	12.0 (4.2)	14.1 (6.3)
Political and legal environment	12.0	12.0
Transaction characteristics	12.0	12.0
Strength of sponsor (sponsor support)	12.0 (6.0)	15.0 (9.0)
Security package (strength of the covenant package)	12.0 (2.4)	13.2 (3.6)
FINAL JUDGMENT (relative weight of 3 risk drivers)	60.0 (12.6)	66.3 (18.9)

the adoption of participating loans consent project to move towards the best supervisory categories with a migration effect (in the previous example, from satisfactory to good), implying also substantial advantages in terms of reducing the PF pricing, since to a higher risk corresponds a higher pricing required on the PF loan, as shown in the earlier Section.

13.6 Conclusion

This chapter aimed, on the one hand, to assess the SSCA impact on the PF pricing and, on the other hand, to identify a model of judgemental analysis in order to classify projects. The results emerging from this empirical analysis aimed at estimating the risk-adjusted pricing applied by a sample of banks operating in the PF sector in Italy confirmed theoretical expectations: on average the pricing increases with the higher risk of PF exposure (that is, from strong to default in the SSCA). Moreover, varying the risk weights assigned to each evaluation driver of every individual supervisory category also modifies pricing, increasing or reducing according to the factors the bank considers relevant to its risk exposure.

Among the strengths of this research, as well as the empirical analysis about the pricing-PF relation not much investigated so far, is the proposal of a judgement-based model to classify PF loans. In fact, international and national supervisory authorities and entities as well as banking and finance operators don't express any details, comments or criticisms about the absence of methods by which banks assign the risk weights in the SSCA up to now. This aspect is very important for a correct classification of projects since, if any, it should reduce the discretion of banks. Without a precise indication by international regulators, the same project could be differently valued based on merely subjective evaluations made by banks, but not yet confirmed by experience.

A criticism of this model comes from inevitable difficulties in subjectively assessing standard weights. In this sense, it would be useful to compare the proposed weights with those actually assigned by banks operating in the PF sector in Italy (by means of a questionnaire), identifying possible differences according to which 'calibrating' the model and then effectively apply the fuzzy logic. Similarly, the questionnaire answers should also compare the pricing actually applied by the sampling banks with that resulted by the empirical analysis, whose limit is represented by the one-year horizon, as highlighted in literature too.

Notes

1. See Diurni and Bouroche (2005), whose empirical analysis concerns the risk-based pricing in Italian bank loans.
2. See the methodological and empirical work on loans pricing by Grippa and Viviani (2001), and the review on the comparison of different international studies about the adequacy of bank loans pricing in Italy by Munari (2005).
3. These equations are uncorrected for a risk-neutral bank because in this case it has no sense to cover the eventual unexpected loss; so the VaR is zero and the pricing is cheaper.
4. This formula was used by Bocchi and Lusignani (2006) for calculating the risk-adjusted pricing in a sample of Italian firms.
5. A formula for a multi-years pricing is in Resti and Saita (2009).
6. According to Resti (2004) in the sophisticated internal transfer models, it's possible set to funding a loan with 100 per cent TIT and its relevant capital is hold to guarantee instead of funding.
7. To the compared analysis we considered only banks whose financial statements are available on *BankScope* for all the 2004 to 2007 period.
8. Further observations on fuzzy logic are in Cammarata (1997); see Cosma (2002) for a fuzzy application on credit risk; see Fanoni and Hajek (2006) and Filagrana (2007) for operating risks.

References

Basel Committee on Banking Supervision (2004) 'International convergence of capital measurement and capital standards – A revised framework', http://www.bis.org (homepage), date accessed 01 July 2012.

Bocchi, L. and G. Lusignani (2006) 'La rischiosità delle imprese italiane con Basilea 2: prime indicazioni dall'applicazione dei modelli di rating interno', *Bancaria*, 62, 14–28.

Busacca, B., M. Costabile and P. Pasini (1993) *Decidere il prezzo* (Milan: Etas Libri).

Cammarata, S. (1997) *Sistemi a logica fuzzy* (Milan: Etas Libri).

Cappelletto, R. and G. Toniolo (2007) 'Il pricing nelle banche e nei confidi alla luce dei principi di Basilea 2', *Amministrazione & Finanza*, 22, 37–44.

Cenni, S. (1998) 'Il pricing dei prestiti: modelli teorici e metodi operativi', in Corigliano R. (ed.), *Rischio di credito e pricing dei prestiti bancari* (Rome: Bancaria).

Comana, M. (2002) 'Il rating interno dei crediti: i riflessi sulla politica commerciale', *Banche e Banchieri*, 29, 603–7.

Corbellini, M. (2002) 'Un modello per il pricing del rischio di credito in base alla maturity', *Banche e Banchieri*, 29, 607–10.

Cosma, S. (2002) *Il rapporto banca-impresa: le variabili relazionali e comportamentali nella valutazione del rischio di credito* (Turin: Giappichelli).

De Laurentis, G. (2001) *Rating interni e credit risk management* (Rome: Bancaria).

De Laurentis G., and S. Caselli (2006) *Miti e verità di Basilea 2* (Milan: Egea).

De Lisa, R., F. Vallascas and M. Marchesi (2006) 'L'impatto delle garanzie sul pricing dei prestiti: un'analisi di sensitività nel quadro della direttiva che recepisce Basilea 2', *Bancaria*, 62, 44–59.

Delzio, M. F. and P. Maggiori (2004) *Rischio di credito e derivati: modelli per il pricing* (Rome: Bancaria).

Dermine, J. (1984), *Pricing Policies of Financial Intermediaries* (New York: Springer-Verlag).

Diurni, F. and J. M. Bouroche (2005) 'Credito retail e pricing del rischio: un'applicazione al mercato dei mutui in Italia', *Bancaria*, 61, 58–66.

English, W. B. and W. R. Nelson (1998) 'Bank risk rating of business loans', http://www.federalreserve.gov/ (homepage), date accessed 01 July 2012.

Erzegovesi, L. and M. Bee (2008) *I modelli di portafoglio per la gestione del rischio di credito* (Rome: Bancaria).

Fanoni, F. and S. Hajek (2006) 'L'approccio fuzzy per l'interpretazione delle stime qualitative sui rischi operativi', *Bancaria*, 62, 72–77.

Filagrana, M. (2007) 'La gestione del rischio operativo mediante fuzzy set', *Bancaria*, 63, 66–71.

Gabor, A. (1977) *Principles and Practices* (Bath: Heinemann Educational Books).

Grippa, P. and U. Viviani (2001) 'Il pricing dei prestiti bancari: un'applicazione con le nuove statistiche della Centrale dei Rischi', *Banca Impresa Società*, 20, 93–127.

Hanna, N. and H. R. Dodge (1995) *Pricing. Policies and Procedures* (London: MacMillan Business).

Hasan, I. and C. Zazzara (2006) 'Pricing risky bank loans in the new Basel 2 environment', *Journal of Banking Regulation*, 7, 243–67.

Laviola, S. (2001) 'La riforma dell'Accordo sul Capitale: il funzionamento del metodo dei rating interni', *Bancaria*, 57, 24–38.

Machauer, A. and M. Weber (1998) 'Bank behavior based on internal credit ratings of borrowers', *Journal of Banking & Finance*, 22, 1355–83.

Marsella, M. (1997) 'Credit risk management: approccio di portafoglio e ruolo del rating', *Bancaria*, 53, 58–61.

Masera, R. (2005) *Rischio, banche, imprese* (Milan: Il Sole 24 Ore Libri).

McAllister, P. H. and J. J. Mingo (1994) 'Commercial loan risk management, credit-scoring, and pricing: the need for a new shared database', *Journal of Commercial Lending*, 76, 6–22.

Merton, R. C. (1974) 'On the pricing of corporate debt: the risk structure of interest rates', *Journal of Finance*, 29, 449–71.

Munari, L. (2005) 'Il pricing dei servizi bancari in Italia: evidenze dai confronti internazionali', *Bancaria*, 61, 22–36.

Nadotti, L. M. (2002) *Rischio di credito e rating interno* (Milan: Egea).

Pelliccioni, G. (2006) 'Le opportunità e i vincoli per le banche regionali nei servizi di corporate banking', in R. Corigliano (ed.), *Corporate banking, credito e finanza delle imprese* (Rome: Bancaria).

Resti, A. (2004) 'Rating e operatività delle filiali: strumenti e prassi per mettere a profitto il sistema', in G. De Laurentis, F. Saita and A. Sironi (eds), *Rating interni e controllo del rischio di credito* (Rome: Bancaria).

——(2005) 'Il nuovo accordo di Basilea sul capitale: genesi, contenuti, impatti', www.carefin.unibocconi.eu (homepage), date accessed 01 July 2012.

——(2007) 'L'implementazione di Basilea 2: le nuove regole cambiano il gioco', *Bancaria*, 63, 30–9.

Resti, A. and F. Saita (2009) 'Prestiti bancari, rating interni e modelli VaR: quale autonomia di pricing per le unità operative?' *Bancaria*, 65, 19–31.

Resti, A. and A. Sironi (2008) *Rischio e valore nelle banche* (Milan: Egea).

Saita, F. (2000) *Il risk management in banca* (Milan: Egea).

Smith, C. W. (1980) 'On the theory of financial contracting: the personal loan market', *Journal of Monetary Economics*, 6, 333–57.

Zadeh, L. A. (1965) 'Fuzzy sets', *Information and Control*, 8, 338–53.

Zazzara, C. and A. Cortese (2004) 'Il pricing risk-adjusted dei prestiti nel nuovo contesto di Basilea 2', *Finanza Marketing e Produzione*, 22, 83–115.

Appendix

Table 13.A1 Pricing of PF exposures (2004)

n.	ROE	CO/TA	UL					EL					r	r	r	r	r
			Strong	Good	Satisf.	Weak	Default	Strong	Good	Satisf.	Weak	Default	Strong	Good	Satisf.	Weak	Default
2	5.84%	0.61%	5.60%	7.20%	9.20%	20.00%	0.00%	0.40%	0.80%	2.80%	8.00%	50.00%	3.44%	3.91%	6.13%	12.55%	105.64%
4	7.27%	2.46%	5.60%	7.20%	9.20%	20.00%	0.00%	0.40%	0.80%	2.80%	8.00%	50.00%	5.37%	5.88%	8.16%	14.87%	109.34%
8	5.61%	0.73%	5.60%	7.20%	9.20%	20.00%	0.00%	0.40%	0.80%	2.80%	8.00%	50.00%	3.54%	4.02%	6.23%	12.63%	105.88%
9	8.07%	3.32%	5.60%	7.20%	9.20%	20.00%	0.00%	0.40%	0.80%	2.80%	8.00%	50.00%	6.28%	6.81%	9.12%	15.98%	111.06%
10	2.28%	1.15%	5.60%	7.20%	9.20%	20.00%	0.00%	0.40%	0.80%	2.80%	8.00%	50.00%	3.78%	4.20%	6.34%	12.36%	106.72%
11	4.02%	1.33%	5.60%	7.20%	9.20%	20.00%	0.00%	0.40%	0.80%	2.80%	8.00%	50.00%	4.06%	4.51%	6.69%	12.94%	107.08%
12	28.45%	0.10%	5.60%	7.20%	9.20%	20.00%	0.00%	0.40%	0.80%	2.80%	8.00%	50.00%	4.20%	5.04%	7.74%	16.91%	104.62%
13	11.04%	0.13%	5.60%	7.20%	9.20%	20.00%	0.00%	0.40%	0.80%	2.80%	8.00%	50.00%	3.25%	3.81%	6.12%	13.16%	104.68%
16	1.05%	2.05%	5.60%	7.20%	9.20%	20.00%	0.00%	0.40%	0.80%	2.80%	8.00%	50.00%	4.61%	5.02%	7.15%	13.07%	108.52%
17	8.09%	2.09%	5.60%	7.20%	9.20%	20.00%	0.00%	0.40%	0.80%	2.80%	8.00%	50.00%	5.05%	5.57%	7.86%	14.65%	108.60%
19	8.88%	0.90%	5.60%	7.20%	9.20%	20.00%	0.00%	0.40%	0.80%	2.80%	8.00%	50.00%	3.90%	4.43%	6.71%	13.53%	106.22%

Table 13.A2 Pricing of PF exposures (2005)

n.	ROE	CO/TA	UL					EL					r	r	r	r	r
			Strong	Good	Satisf.	Weak	Default	Strong	Good	Satisf.	Weak	Default	Strong	Good	Satisf.	Weak	Default
1	8.97%	1.22%	5.60%	7.20%	9.20%	20.00%	0.00%	0.40%	0.80%	2.80%	8.00%	50.00%	4.51%	5.04%	7.33%	14.15%	107.46%
2	8.56%	0.71%	5.60%	7.20%	9.20%	20.00%	0.00%	0.40%	0.80%	2.80%	8.00%	50.00%	3.97%	4.49%	6.77%	13.51%	106.44%
3	10.59%	0.13%	5.60%	7.20%	9.20%	20.00%	0.00%	0.40%	0.80%	2.80%	8.00%	50.00%	3.51%	4.05%	6.36%	13.32%	105.28%
4	7.62%	2.25%	5.60%	7.20%	9.20%	20.00%	0.00%	0.40%	0.80%	2.80%	8.00%	50.00%	5.47%	5.98%	8.26%	14.98%	109.52%
7	10.61%	2.47%	5.60%	7.20%	9.20%	20.00%	0.00%	0.40%	0.80%	2.80%	8.00%	50.00%	5.86%	6.41%	8.77%	15.87%	109.96%
8	14.82%	0.64%	5.60%	7.20%	9.20%	20.00%	0.00%	0.40%	0.80%	2.80%	8.00%	50.00%	4.26%	4.88%	7.29%	14.80%	106.30%
9	12.31%	2.86%	5.60%	7.20%	9.20%	20.00%	0.00%	0.40%	0.80%	2.80%	8.00%	50.00%	6.34%	6.93%	9.33%	16.66%	110.74%
10	10.58%	0.89%	5.60%	7.20%	9.20%	20.00%	0.00%	0.40%	0.80%	2.80%	8.00%	50.00%	4.27%	4.82%	7.14%	14.15%	106.80%
11	9.31%	1.24%	5.60%	7.20%	9.20%	20.00%	0.00%	0.40%	0.80%	2.80%	8.00%	50.00%	4.55%	5.08%	7.38%	14.25%	107.50%
12	20.62%	0.10%	5.60%	7.20%	9.20%	20.00%	0.00%	0.40%	0.80%	2.80%	8.00%	50.00%	4.04%	4.75%	7.28%	15.47%	105.22%
13	8.37%	0.11%	5.60%	7.20%	9.20%	20.00%	0.00%	0.40%	0.80%	2.80%	8.00%	50.00%	3.36%	3.87%	6.13%	12.82%	105.24%
15	17.67%	0.91%	5.60%	7.20%	9.20%	20.00%	0.00%	0.40%	0.80%	2.80%	8.00%	50.00%	4.69%	5.35%	7.83%	15.71%	106.84%
17	15.78%	1.42%	5.60%	7.20%	9.20%	20.00%	0.00%	0.40%	0.80%	2.80%	8.00%	50.00%	5.09%	5.73%	8.18%	15.85%	107.86%
19	9.40%	0.90%	5.60%	7.20%	9.20%	20.00%	0.00%	0.40%	0.80%	2.80%	8.00%	50.00%	4.21%	4.74%	7.04%	13.90%	106.82%
20	10.52%	0.96%	5.60%	7.20%	9.20%	20.00%	0.00%	0.40%	0.80%	2.80%	8.00%	50.00%	4.34%	4.89%	7.21%	14.21%	106.94%
22	12.45%	1.58%	5.60%	7.20%	9.20%	20.00%	0.00%	0.40%	0.80%	2.80%	8.00%	50.00%	5.07%	5.65%	8.03%	15.30%	108.18%
24	11.85%	0.70%	5.60%	7.20%	9.20%	20.00%	0.00%	0.40%	0.80%	2.80%	8.00%	50.00%	4.15%	4.72%	7.07%	14.22%	106.42%

Table 13.A3 Pricing of PF exposures (2006)

n.	ROE	CO/TA	UL					EL					r	r	r	r	r
			Strong	Good	Satisf.	Weak	Default	Strong	Good	Satisf.	Weak	Default	Strong	Good	Satisf.	Weak	Default
1	8.96%	1.14%	5.60%	7.20%	9.20%	20.00%	0.00%	0.40%	0.80%	2.80%	8.00%	50.00%	5.59%	6.10%	8.39%	15.13%	109.74%
2	9.73%	0.51%	5.60%	7.20%	9.20%	20.00%	0.00%	0.40%	0.80%	2.80%	8.00%	50.00%	5.00%	5.52%	7.81%	14.61%	108.48%
3	11.67%	0.16%	5.60%	7.20%	9.20%	20.00%	0.00%	0.40%	0.80%	2.80%	8.00%	50.00%	4.75%	5.30%	7.63%	14.65%	107.78%
4	8.73%	2.14%	5.60%	7.20%	9.20%	20.00%	0.00%	0.40%	0.80%	2.80%	8.00%	50.00%	6.58%	7.09%	9.39%	16.16%	111.74%
6	26.90%	0.20%	5.60%	7.20%	9.20%	20.00%	0.00%	0.40%	0.80%	2.80%	8.00%	50.00%	5.65%	6.45%	9.12%	18.00%	107.86%
7	0.87%	3.00%	5.60%	7.20%	9.20%	20.00%	0.00%	0.40%	0.80%	2.80%	8.00%	50.00%	7.00%	7.38%	9.53%	15.39%	113.46%
8	15.60%	0.61%	5.60%	7.20%	9.20%	20.00%	0.00%	0.40%	0.80%	2.80%	8.00%	50.00%	5.43%	6.04%	8.47%	15.99%	108.68%
9	17.14%	2.71%	5.60%	7.20%	9.20%	20.00%	0.00%	0.40%	0.80%	2.80%	8.00%	50.00%	7.62%	8.27%	10.78%	18.61%	112.88%
10	12.60%	0.44%	5.60%	7.20%	9.20%	20.00%	0.00%	0.40%	0.80%	2.80%	8.00%	50.00%	5.09%	5.65%	8.01%	15.16%	108.34%
11	11.68%	1.07%	5.60%	7.20%	9.20%	20.00%	0.00%	0.40%	0.80%	2.80%	8.00%	50.00%	5.67%	6.22%	8.57%	15.64%	109.60%
12	18.95%	0.09%	5.60%	7.20%	9.20%	20.00%	0.00%	0.40%	0.80%	2.80%	8.00%	50.00%	5.09%	5.76%	8.25%	16.16%	107.64%
13	8.64%	0.11%	5.60%	7.20%	9.20%	20.00%	0.00%	0.40%	0.80%	2.80%	8.00%	50.00%	4.53%	5.03%	7.30%	13.94%	107.68%
14	6.91%	0.92%	5.60%	7.20%	9.20%	20.00%	0.00%	0.40%	0.80%	2.80%	8.00%	50.00%	5.25%	5.72%	7.97%	14.44%	109.30%
15	28.06%	0.96%	5.60%	7.20%	9.20%	20.00%	0.00%	0.40%	0.80%	2.80%	8.00%	50.00%	6.48%	7.30%	10.01%	19.08%	109.38%
16	13.74%	0.68%	5.60%	7.20%	9.20%	20.00%	0.00%	0.40%	0.80%	2.80%	8.00%	50.00%	5.39%	5.98%	8.37%	15.67%	108.82%
17	6.53%	1.12%	5.60%	7.20%	9.20%	20.00%	0.00%	0.40%	0.80%	2.80%	8.00%	50.00%	5.43%	5.90%	8.14%	14.58%	109.70%
19	10.49%	0.90%	5.60%	7.20%	9.20%	20.00%	0.00%	0.40%	0.80%	2.80%	8.00%	50.00%	5.43%	5.96%	8.28%	15.20%	109.26%
20	12.08%	1.11%	5.60%	7.20%	9.20%	20.00%	0.00%	0.40%	0.80%	2.80%	8.00%	50.00%	5.73%	6.29%	8.65%	15.77%	109.68%
22	12.67%	1.52%	5.60%	7.20%	9.20%	20.00%	0.00%	0.40%	0.80%	2.80%	8.00%	50.00%	6.18%	6.75%	9.13%	16.35%	110.50%
24	11.83%	0.65%	5.60%	7.20%	9.20%	20.00%	0.00%	0.40%	0.80%	2.80%	8.00%	50.00%	5.25%	5.81%	8.15%	15.22%	108.76%

Table 13.A4 Pricing of PF exposures (2007)

n.	ROE	CO/TA	UL					EL					r	r	r	r	r
			Strong	Good	Satisf.	Weak	Default	Strong	Good	Satisf.	Weak	Default	Strong	Good	Satisf.	Weak	Default
1	7.65%	1.08%	5.60%	7.20%	9.20%	20.00%	0.00%	0.40%	0.80%	2.80%	8.00%	50.00%	6.59%	7.06%	9.32%	15.82%	112.02%
2	11.42%	0.60%	5.60%	7.20%	9.20%	20.00%	0.00%	0.40%	0.80%	2.80%	8.00%	50.00%	6.32%	6.85%	9.18%	16.12%	111.06%
3	11.47%	0.15%	5.60%	7.20%	9.20%	20.00%	0.00%	0.40%	0.80%	2.80%	8.00%	50.00%	5.87%	6.40%	8.73%	15.64%	110.16%
4	8.88%	1.94%	5.60%	7.20%	9.20%	20.00%	0.00%	0.40%	0.80%	2.80%	8.00%	50.00%	7.52%	8.02%	10.32%	17.02%	113.74%
6	12.57%	0.21%	5.60%	7.20%	9.20%	20.00%	0.00%	0.40%	0.80%	2.80%	8.00%	50.00%	5.99%	6.54%	8.89%	15.94%	110.28%
9	11.61%	2.51%	5.60%	7.20%	9.20%	20.00%	0.00%	0.40%	0.80%	2.80%	8.00%	50.00%	8.25%	8.79%	11.17%	18.23%	114.88%
10	10.34%	0.80%	5.60%	7.20%	9.20%	20.00%	0.00%	0.40%	0.80%	2.80%	8.00%	50.00%	6.46%	6.98%	9.29%	16.10%	111.46%
11	11.96%	1.01%	5.60%	7.20%	9.20%	20.00%	0.00%	0.40%	0.80%	2.80%	8.00%	50.00%	6.76%	7.30%	9.66%	16.68%	111.88%
12	10.47%	0.17%	5.60%	7.20%	9.20%	20.00%	0.00%	0.40%	0.80%	2.80%	8.00%	50.00%	5.83%	6.35%	8.65%	15.44%	110.20%
13	10.52%	0.08%	5.60%	7.20%	9.20%	20.00%	0.00%	0.40%	0.80%	2.80%	8.00%	50.00%	5.75%	6.26%	8.56%	15.36%	110.02%
14	11.86%	1.22%	5.60%	7.20%	9.20%	20.00%	0.00%	0.40%	0.80%	2.80%	8.00%	50.00%	6.97%	7.51%	9.86%	16.89%	112.30%
15	5.30%	1.29%	5.60%	7.20%	9.20%	20.00%	0.00%	0.40%	0.80%	2.80%	8.00%	50.00%	6.67%	7.10%	9.31%	15.54%	112.44%
17	0.90%	1.93%	5.60%	7.20%	9.20%	20.00%	0.00%	0.40%	0.80%	2.80%	8.00%	50.00%	7.06%	7.43%	9.56%	15.28%	113.72%
19	9.95%	0.54%	5.60%	7.20%	9.20%	20.00%	0.00%	0.40%	0.80%	2.80%	8.00%	50.00%	6.18%	6.68%	8.98%	15.73%	110.94%
20	6.93%	1.07%	5.60%	7.20%	9.20%	20.00%	0.00%	0.40%	0.80%	2.80%	8.00%	50.00%	6.54%	7.00%	9.24%	15.65%	112.00%
22	12.20%	1.69%	5.60%	7.20%	9.20%	20.00%	0.00%	0.40%	0.80%	2.80%	8.00%	50.00%	7.46%	8.01%	10.38%	17.47%	113.24%

Table 13.A5 Supervisory slotting criteria for PF exposures: a judgement-based model

DRIVER	**weight**	***STRONG***	**value**	***GOOD***	**value**	***SATISFACTORY***	**value**	***WEAK***	**value**
Financial strength	20%								
Market conditions	20%	Few competing suppliers or substantial and durable advantage in location, cost, or technology. Demand is strong and growing	$0.8<X\leq 1$	Few competing suppliers or better than average location, cost, or technology but this situation may not last. Demand is strong and stable	$0.5<X\leq 0.8$	Project has no advantage in location, cost, or technology. Demand is adequate and stable	$0.2<X\leq 0.5$	Project has worse than average location, cost, or technology. Demand is weak and declining	$0<X\leq 0.2$
Financial ratios (e.g. *debt service coverage ratio (DSCR), loan life coverage ratio (LLCR), project life coverage ratio (PLCR), and debt-to-equity ratio*)	35%	Strong financial ratios considering the level of project risk; very robust economic assumptions	$0.8<X\leq 1$	Strong to acceptable financial ratios considering the level of project risk; robust project economic assumptions	$0.5<X\leq 0.8$	Standard financial ratios considering the level of project risk	$0.2<X\leq 0.5$	Aggressive financial ratios considering the level of project risk	$0<X\leq 0.2$
Stress analysis	25%	The project can meet its financial obligations under sustained, severely stressed economic or sectoral conditions	$0.8<X\leq 1$	The project can meet its financial obligations under normal stressed economic or sectoral conditions. The project is only likely to default under severe economic conditions	$0.5<X\leq 0.8$	The project is vulnerable to stresses that are not uncommon through an economic cycle, and may default in a normal downturn	$0.2<X\leq 0.5$	The project is likely to default unless conditions improve soon	$0<X\leq 0.2$

Financial structure	*20% where:*								
Duration of the credit compared to the duration of the project	10%	Useful life of the project significantly exceeds tenor of the loan	$0.7<X\leq 1$	Useful life of the project exceeds tenor of the loan	$0.3<X\leq 0.7$	Useful life of the project exceeds tenor of the loan	$0.3<X\leq 0.7$	Useful life of the project may not exceed tenor of the loan	$0<X\leq 0.3$
Amortisation schedule	10%	Amortising debt	$0.6<X\leq 1$	Amortising debt	$0.6<X\leq 1$	Amortising debt repayments with limited bullet payment	$0.3<X\leq 0.6$	Bullet repayment or amortising debt repayments with high bullet repayment	$0<X\leq 0.3$
Political and legal environment	20%								
Political risk, including transfer risk, considering project type and mitigants	10%	Very low exposure; strong mitigation instruments, if needed	$0.8<X\leq 1$	Low exposure; satisfactory mitigation instruments, if needed	$0.6<X\leq 0.8$	Moderate exposure; fair mitigation instruments	$0.2<X\leq 0.6$	High exposure; no or weak mitigation instruments	$0<X\leq 0.2$
Force majeure risk (war, civil unrest, etc.)	10%	Low exposure	$0.8<X\leq 1$	Acceptable exposure	$0.5<X\leq 0.8$	Standard protection	$0.2<X\leq 0.5$	Significant risks, not fully mitigated	$0<X\leq 0.2$
Government support and project's importance for the country over the long term	15%	Project of strategic importance for the country (preferably export-oriented). Strong support from Government	$0.8<X\leq 1$	Project considered important for the country. Good level of support from Government	$0.5<X\leq 0.8$	Project may not be strategic but brings unquestionable benefits for the country. Support from Government may not be explicit	$0.2<X\leq 0.5$	Project not key to the country. No or weak support from Government	$0<X\leq 0.2$

(Continued)

Table 13.A5 (Continued)

DRIVER	weight	*STRONG*	value	*GOOD*	value	*SATISFACTORY*	value	*WEAK*	value
Stability of legal and regulatory environment (risk of change in law)	30%	Favourable and stable regulatory environment over the long term	0.8<X≤1	Favourable and stable regulatory environment over the medium term	0.5<X≤0.8	Regulatory changes can be predicted with a fair level of certainty	0.3<X≤0.5	Current or future regulatory issues may affect the project	0<X≤0.3
Acquisition of all necessary supports and approvals for such relief from local content laws	10%	Strong	0.8<X≤1	Satisfactory	0.6<X≤0.8	Fair	0.2<X≤0.6	Weak	0<X≤0.2
Enforceability of contracts, collateral and security	25%	Contracts, collateral and security are enforceable	0.6<X≤1	Contracts, collateral and security are enforceable	0.6<X≤1	Contracts, collateral and security are considered enforceable even if certain non-key issues may exist	0.2<X≤0.6	There are unresolved key issues in respect if actual enforcement of contracts, collateral and security	0<X≤0.2
Transaction characteristics	20%								
Design and technology risk	*20%*	Fully proven technology and design	0.6<X≤1	Fully proven technology and design	0.6<X≤1	Proven technology and design – start-up issues are mitigated by a strong completion package	0.2<X≤0.6	Unproven technology and design; technology issues exist and/or complex design	0<X≤0.2
Construction risk	*20% where:*								
Permitting and siting	5%	All permits have been obtained	0.8<X≤1	Some permits are still outstanding but their receipt is considered very likely	0.5<X≤0.8	Some permits are still outstanding but the permitting process is well defined and they	0.3<X≤0.5	Key permits still need to be obtained and are not considered routine. Significant	0<X≤0.3

Type of construction contract	5%	Fixed-price date-certain turnkey construction EPC (engineering and procurement contract)	$0.6<X\leq1$	Fixed-price date-certain turnkey construction EPC	$0.6<X\leq1$	Fixed-price date-certain turnkey construction contract with one or several contractors	$0.2<X\leq0.6$	No or partial fixed-price turnkey contract and/or interfacing issues with multiple contractors	$0<X\leq0.2$
Completion guarantees	5%	Substantial liquidated damages supported by financial substance and/or strong completion guarantee from sponsors with excellent financial standing	$0.8<X\leq1$	Significant liquidated damages supported by financial substance and/or completion guarantee from sponsors with good financial standing	$0.5<X\leq0.8$	Adequate liquidated damages supported by financial substance and/or completion guarantee from sponsors with good financial standing	$0.2<X\leq0.5$	Inadequate liquidated damages or not supported by financial substance or weak completion guarantees	$0<X\leq0.2$
Track record and financial strength of contractor in constructing similar projects.	5%	Strong	$0.8<X\leq1$	Good	$0.6<X\leq0.8$	Satisfactory	$0.3<X\leq0.6$	Weak	$0<X\leq0.3$
Operating risk	*20% where:*								
Scope and nature of operations and maintenance (O&M) contracts	10%	Strong long-term O&M contract, preferably with contractual performance incentives, and/or O&M reserve accounts	$0.8<X\leq1$	Long-term O&M contract, and/or O&M reserve accounts	$0.5<X\leq0.8$	Limited O&M contract or O&M reserve account	$0.2<X\leq0.5$	No O&M contract: risk of high operational cost overruns beyond mitigants	$0<X\leq0.2$

(Continued)

Table 13.A5 (Continued)

DRIVER	weight	*STRONG*	value	*GOOD*	value	*SATISFACTORY*	value	*WEAK*	value
Operator's expertise, track record, and financial strength	10%	Very strong, or committed technical assistance of the sponsors	0.8<X≤1	Strong	0.6<X≤0.8	Acceptable	0.3<X≤0.6	Limited/weak, or local operator dependent on local authorities	0<X≤0.3
Supply risk	*20% where:*								
Price, volume and transportation risk of feed-stocks; supplier's track record and financial strength	10%	Long-term supply contract with supplier of excellent financial standing	0.8<X≤1	Long-term supply contract with supplier of good financial standing	0.6<X≤0.8	Long-term supply contract with supplier of good financial standing – a degree of price risk may remains	0.3<X≤0.6	Short-term supply contract or long-term supply contract with financially weak supplier – a degree of price risk definitely remains	0<X≤0.3
Reserve risks (e.g. natural resource development)	10%	Independently audited, proven and developed reserves well in excess of requirements over lifetime of the project	0.8<X≤1	Independently audited, proven and developed reserves in excess of requirements over lifetime of the project	0.6<X≤0.8	Proven reserves can supply the project adequately through the maturity of the debt	0.3<X≤0.6	Project relies to some extent on potential and undeveloped reserves	0<X≤0.3
Off-take risk	*20% where:*								
a) If there is a take-or-pay or fixed-price off-take contract	10%	Excellent creditworthiness of off-taker; strong termination clauses; tenor of contract comfortably exceeds the maturity of the	0.8<X≤1	Good creditworthiness of off-taker; strong termination clauses; tenor of contract exceeds the maturity of the debt	0.5<X≤0.8	Acceptable financial standing of off-taker; normal termination clauses; tenor of contract generally matches the maturity of the debt	0.2<X≤0.5	Weak off-taker; weak termination clauses; tenor of contract does not exceed the maturity of the debt	0<X≤0.2

b) If there is no take-or-pay or fixed-price off-take contract	10%	Project produces essential services or a commodity sold widely on a world market; output can readily be absorbed at projected prices even at lower than historic market growth rates	$0.8<X\leq 1$	Project produces essential services or a commodity sold widely on a regional market that will absorb it at projected prices at historical growth rates	$0.5<X\leq 0.8$	Commodity is sold on a limited market that may absorb it only at lower than projected prices	$0.2<X\leq 0.5$	Project output is demanded by only one or a few buyers or is not generally sold on an organised market	$0<X\leq 0.2$
Strength of Sponsor	20%								
Sponsor's track record, financial strength, and country/sector experience	50%	Strong sponsor with excellent track record and high financial standing	$0.8<X\leq 1$	Good sponsor with satisfactory track record and good financial standing	$0.6<X\leq 0.8$	Adequate sponsor with adequate track record and good financial standing	$0.3<X\leq 0.6$	Weak sponsor with no or questionable track record and/or financial weaknesses	$0<X\leq 0.3$
Sponsor support, as evidenced by equity, ownership clause and incentive to inject additional cash if necessary	50%	Strong. Project is highly strategic for the sponsor (core business – long-term strategy)	$0.8<X\leq 1$	Good. Project is strategic for the sponsor (core business – long-term strategy)	$0.5<X\leq 0.8$	Acceptable. Project is considered important for the sponsor (core business)	$0.2<X\leq 0.5$	Limited. Project is not key to sponsor's long-term strategy or core business	$0<X\leq 0.2$
Security Package	20%								
Assignment of contracts and accounts	20%	Fully comprehensive	$0.8<X\leq 1$	Comprehensive	$0.6<X\leq 0.8$	Acceptable Acceptable security interest in all project assets, contracts, permits and accounts necessary to run the project	$0.3<X\leq 0.6$	Weak	$0<X\leq 0.3$

(*Continued*)

Table 13.A5 (*Continued*)

DRIVER	weight	*STRONG*	value	*GOOD*	value	*SATISFACTORY*	value	*WEAK*	value
Pledge of assets, taking into account quality, value and liquidity of assets	20%	First perfected security interest in all project assets, contracts, permits and accounts necessary to run the project	$0.8<X\leq 1$	Perfected security interest in all project assets, contracts, permits and accounts necessary to run the project	$0.5<X\leq 0.8$	Fair	$0.2<X\leq 0.5$	Little security or collateral for lenders; weak negative pledge clause	$0<X\leq 0.2$
Lender's control over cash flow (e.g. cash sweeps, independent escrow accounts)	20%	Strong	$0.8<X\leq 1$	Satisfactory	$0.6<X\leq 0.8$	$0.3<X\leq 0.6$	Weak	$0<X\leq 0.3$	
Strength of the covenant package (mandatory prepayments, payment deferrals, payment cascade, dividend restrictions, etc.)	20%	Covenant package is strong for this type of project. Project may issue no additional debt	$0.8<X\leq 1$	Covenant package is satisfactory for this type of project. Project may issue extremely limited additional debt	$0.5<X\leq 0.8$	Covenant package is fair for this type of project. Project may issue limited additional debt	$0.2<X\leq 0.5$	Covenant package is Insufficient for this type of project. Project may issue unlimited additional debt	$0<X\leq 0.2$
Reserve funds (debt service, O&M, renewal and replacement, unforeseen events, etc.)	20%	Longer than average coverage period, all reserve funds fully funded in cash or letters of credit from highly rated bank	$0.7<X\leq 1$	Average coverage period, all reserve funds fully funded	$0.3<X\leq 0.7$	Average coverage period, all reserve funds fully funded	$0.3<X\leq 0.7$	Shorter than average coverage period, reserve funds funded from operating cash flows	$0<X\leq 0.3$

Index